# THE COROMANDEL COAST AND ITS HINTERLAND

# The Coromandel Coast and its Hinterland

*Economy, Society and Political System (A.D. 1500–1600)*

S. JEYASEELA STEPHEN

MANOHAR
2026

First published 1997
Reprinted 2021, 2022, 2023, 2024, 2025, 2026



ISBN 978-81-7304-076-4

*Published by*
Ajay Kumar Jain *for*
Manohar Publishers & Distributors
4753/23 Ansari Road, Daryaganj
New Delhi 110 002

*Printed at*
Replika Press Pvt. Ltd.

# Contents

# List of Tables

# List of Maps

# Acknowledgements

It is impossible to acknowledge all the kindness and help I have received while writing this book. Professor K.S. Mathew initiated me into the field of Indo-Portuguese history and spent long hours in discussion and assistance. Dr. Mrs. Vasundhara Filliozat, Paris, developed my skills in epigraphy and encouraged me in research. Professor Sinnapah Arasaratnam, Professor Sundaraj Manickam, and Dr. Jean Deloche made kind and helpful comments on various parts of this book. Others who helped were Professor Luis Filipe F.R. Thomaz, Universidade Nova de Lisboã, Portugal, and Professor Pierre Sylvain Filliozat, of the Ecole pratique des hautés études (IV$^{e}$ section Sciences Historiques et Philologiques) Sorbonne. Mrs. A Padmavati and Mr. S. Rajavelu readily assisted me in epigraphy whenever I approached them. I am deeply beholden to them all.

The Pondicherry University helped me considerably in the course of my research. This work profited greatly from the vast accumulation of data offered in ample measure at the office of the Director of Epigraphy, Mysore and Centro de Estudos Historicos e Cartografia Antiga, Lisbon. I thank Dr. K.V. Ramesh, Shri M.N. Khatti, Dr. M.D. Sampath, Dra. Maria Emilia Madeira Santos and Dra. Maria Augusta da Veiga e Sousa, of these institutions. In India I worked at different times and places at various repositories and received valuable assistance. I wish to place on record my gratitude to the Historical Archives of Goa, Panjim for permission to consult manuscripts. Thanks are also due to the Directors and the staff of the National Library, Calcutta; Ratan Tata Library, Delhi; Jawaharlal Nehru University Library, New Delhi; Library cum Documentation Centre of the Indian Council of Historical Research, New Delhi; Xavier Centre for Historical Research, Goa; U.V. Swaminatha Aiyar Library, Madras; Bibliothéque de Institut français, Pondicherry; and Sarasvati Mahal Library, Thanjavur, for providing various books and journals. In Portugal I was given extensive help by the authorities at Arquivo Nacional da Torre do Tombo, Arquivo

Historico Ultramarino, Biblioteca Nacional de Lisboa, Biblioteca da Ajuda, and Biblioteca da Academia das Ciencias de Lisboa, who put up with my demands with tolerance of an exceptional order. I am profoundly grateful to all of them.

The field study was made possible largely by the financial aid extended to cover travel and stay. I am specially grateful to Professor Irfan Habib, the Chairman and members of the Governing Body of the Indian Council of Historical Research, New Delhi, for the award of a travel grant which supported my exploration and collection of research material in India. The collection of material in the archives abroad was generously assisted by a grant from the Calouste Gulbenkian Foundation, Lisboã. I do not have adequate words to express my grateful debt to Dr. Jose Blanco, Administrador, and Dona Maria Clara Farinha, Directora Adjunta, for their support in Europe.

Much effort at typing drafts of the manuscript was put in by Mrs. Joyce Elizabeth and Mrs. Sumathi, for which I am grateful. I thank Dr. P. Pichard, Dr. F. L'Hernault and Mr. M. Ganessin for offering suggestions and helping to draw the maps included in this book. My family do not expect an expression of gratitude from me. Nevertheless it needs to be stated that, but for them I probably could not have achieved my goal. Finally I owe sincere thanks to Shri Ajay Jain, Manohar Publishers & Distributors, New Delhi for the efficiency with which this book has been brought out.

S. JEYASEELA STEPHEN

# Abbreviations

| | |
|---|---|
| *AGS* | Archivo General de Simancas |
| *AHU* | Arquivo Historico Ultramarino |
| *ANTT* | Arquivo Nacional da Torre do Tombo |
| *AOR* | Annals of Oriental Research |
| *APO-BP* | Arquivo Portugues Oriental (ed.) Braganca Pereira |
| *APO-CR* | Archivo Portuguez Oriental (ed.) Cunha Rivera |
| *ARE* | Annual Report on Epigraphy |
| *ARSI* | Archivum Romanum Societatis Jesu |
| *BA* | Biblioteca da Ajuda |
| *BM* | British Museum, Manuscript room |
| *BNL* | Biblioteca Nacional de Lisboa |
| *BPADE* | Biblioteca Publica e Arquivo Distrital, Evora |
| *CAA* | Cartas de Afonso de Albuquerque |
| *CC* | Corpo Cronologico |
| *COD* | Codice/Codex |
| *CSL* | Colecao de Sao Lourenco |
| *DI* | Documenta Indica |
| *DRI* | Documentos Remetidos da India |
| *DUP* | Documentacao Ultramarina Portuguesa |
| *EI* | Epigraphia Indica |
| *EB* | Epigraphia Birmanica |
| *EC* | Epigraphia Carnatica |
| *FL* | Folio |
| *HAG* | Historical Archives of Goa |
| *IA* | Indian Antiquary |
| *IESHR* | Indian Economic and Social History Review |
| *IGJ* | Indian Geographical Journal |
| *IMP* | Inscriptions of the Madras Presidency |
| *IPS* | Inscriptions of Pudukottai State |
| *JAS* | Journal of Asian Studies |
| *JEH* | Journal of Economic History |
| *JESHO* | Journal of the Economic and Social History of the Orient |
| *JESI* | Journal of the Epigraphical Society of India |
| *JIH* | Journal of Indian History |
| *JMBRAS* | Journal of the *Malaysian* Branch of the Royal Asiatic Society |
| *JOR* | Journal of Oriental Research |

| | |
|---|---|
| *JSEAH* | Journal of South East Asian History |
| *MJLS* | The Madras Journal of Literature and Science |
| *NA* | Nucleo Antigo |
| *NDI* | Nellore District Inscriptions |
| *QJMS* | Quarterly Journal of the Mythic Society |
| *RCI* | Registo da Casa da India |
| *RES* | Reservados |
| *SII* | South Indian Inscriptions |
| *SITI* | South Indian Temple Inscriptions |
| *TTDES* | Tirumala-Tirupati Devasthanam Epigraphical Report Series |
| *TVMTI* | Tiruvannamalai Temple Inscriptions |

# Introduction

A recent trend in writing history is the increased emphasis on micro-studies, chiefly on account of a distinct set of characteristics or aspects in the process of history found in certain areas. Such regional studies enrich and advance the macro-study of history. The present monograph probes the history of the area lying between the riverine basin of Swarnamukhi and Point Calimere, called Coromandel in the Bay of Bengal.

The Tamil coast generally remained obscure in ancient historical scholarship on maritime trade; and in the medieval ages it particularly escaped the notice of historians, content as they were to focus on dynastic history. The *Tamilakam* region had an extensive coastal front for maritime activities and attracted Roman traders even as early as the first century B.C. Archaeological excavations suggest that commerce flourished at various centres on the coast such as Arikamedu[1] near modern Pondicherry, Karaikadu[2] near Cuddalore, Vasavasamudram[3] on the mouth of river Palar near Mahabalipuram, and Vellaiyan Kudiyirruppu[4] near Kaveripoompattinam. Vellallur, Karukkakurichi, Alagankulam and Soraiyapattu-Madurakottam near Tirukoyilur in the hinterland were other famed Roman trading marts.[5] Kaveripoompattinam, the dominant port of trade, stocked huge quantities of merchandise in spacious warehouses which were stamped with the tiger emblem of the Chola ruler.[6] Trade with the Romans induced Indian merchants to sail to South-East Asia to procure additional volume of spices for sale to the Romans. The anthologies of early Tamil poems, collectively known as *Sangam* literature, speak of the maritime activities of Tamil merchants with South-East Asia during the period.[7]

Roman commerce with the eastern coast of the subcontinent declined in the third century but this does not seem to have made much difference to Tamil maritime activity. Coins of the Satavahanas and Ikshvakus, which contain the motif of a two-masted ship, speak for the uninterrupted maritime activities in the north of the region.[8] The inscription of Koetei, quoting the

*Mahabharata,* mentions the first appearance of Indian settlement in Borneo in the fifth century.[9] The *Milinda Panha* and the accounts of I-tsing relate that in the sixth century seafaring merchants from Tamil country sailed from Nagapattinam to Kedah in thirty days;[10] the trade in the south continued in the later centuries as well.

The rule of Pallavas in the region substantially boosted Tamil maritime contacts with South-East Asia. Mahabalipuram, which until then was a small coastal village, came to be called *Talacayanam* and had a fortified citadel constructed on a hill overlooking the port.[11] *Periyatirumadal,* a contemporary manuscript of Tirumangai Alvar, noted that Mahabalipuram flourished initially with the arrival of trading ships laden with gems, elephants and other luxury items.[12] *Mahavamsa,* the Buddhist monastic chronicle records that Narasimha Pallava's fleets sailed from Mahabalipuram to Ceylon.[13] The existence of guilds of Tamil merchants, such as *Manigramam* at Takuapa, *Tisai Ayirattu Ainnurruvar* at Loboe Toewa, near Pansur in northern Sumatra and *Nanadesi* at Pagan suggest that regular commerce existed within South Asia and also between the Tamil coast and South-East Asia from the time of the Pallava king Nandivarman III.[14] Trade in agricultural products also flourished both in the ports and hinterland markets, the society of *Tamilakam* being mainly agrarian.

In the tenth and eleventh centuries, the coastal regions of the Chola country, which were but a small slice of the eastern coast of India, assumed considerable importance in pan-Asian trade.[15] Under Rajaraja the Great (985-1014) Mahabalipuram became a secondary port of the Chola empire, Nagapattinam becoming the official port.[16] The financing by the Srivijaya ruler of the construction of a Buddhist *vihara* at Nagapattinam is proof that merchants from South-East Asia regularly traded with that port. It is presumed that the *vihara* was used by the South-East Asian merchants mainly, and the Chola king's endowment of land for it is an indication of the reciprocal encouragement given to the South-East Asian traders visiting Nagapattinam.[17] An inscription from Chidambaram refers to gifts received by the Chola king Rajendra I (1012-44) from the Khmer king of Cambodia.[18] Kulottunga Chola's contact with Burma is clear from an epigraph.[19] The Taoist monastery temple inscription at Canton in China also names a Chola king.[20] Four ambassadorial missions were sent to China by rulers, which advertised various commodities produced and exported from Coromandel and imported there. A flourishing emporia trade existed, wherein a variety of goods were in regular supply by a host of traders.[21] The Cholas' interest in promoting trade in various luxury goods on the Coromandel coast increased on account of the quantum of revenue brought by seafaring merchants.[22]

Coromandel also became the linchpin of international commerce for the medieval Arab traders from West Asia. It is said in Arab navigational treatises that Chola charts were used in sailing.[23] The *Jeniza* letters describe how Arab merchants sailed to South-East Asia from the ports of Coromandel. Both Chinese sources and those of West Asia mention that the Coromandel coast participated in maritime trade by exporting pearls, corals, arecanuts, cardamom, silk and cotton textiles.[24]

It is a curious gap in our historical writing that no intensive study exists on the history of the Coromandel or the Chola coast from the thirteenth to the sixteenth centuries. Studies on medieval South India mention it but in passing. Nationalistic and communalistic historical writings on Vijayanagara isolated the Coromandel region from international forces in medieval period. Chinese medieval sources, such as *Chu-fan-Chi* and *T'ung-K'ao* mention Coromandel coast and its flourishing trade till A.D. 1350. Works of the fifteenth century (1416-36), such as Ma Huan's *Yingyai Shenglan,* Gong Zhen's *Xiyang Fangaozhi,* Feixin's *Xingcha Shenglan* no longer mention Coromandel ports; they wax eloquent on the Malabar trading centres of Calicut, Cochin and Quilon, which has led some scholars to believe that maritime activities had shifted from east coast.[25]

Such belief, however, seems unwarranted. Although Malabar reached its peak of commercial activities with the coming of the Arabs and the Chinese, Coromandel continued to trade with South-East Asia. The advent of Vijayanagara kingdom extending over the Tamil country stimulated maritime trade on the Coromandel coast and led to an increase in its revenues. Noboru Karashima's studies confirm that the Chinese traded with a port called Periyapattinam;[26] an ambassadorial mission sent by the Sultan of Malacca visited the court of Vijayanagar and commercial ties were established.[27] Going by such evidence, it seems conceivable that maritime trade between the Tamil coast and South-East Asia continued unimpaired for centuries together.

But did it? Did the Coromandel region, pre-eminent for maritime trade and commerce in the past, maintain its position in the sixteenth century? Most maritime historians start with the seventeenth century, when the Dutch, the English, the Danes and the French appeared on the Coromandel coast.[28] The period immediately preceding still remains unexplored.[29]

In an age marked by mercantilism and capital formation in Europe, the Portuguese were the first to draw the Coromandel into the intercontinental trade between Asia and Europe. Coromandel under the Vijayanagar kings did feel the impact of the commercial revolution taking place in Europe in the newly developed nation states. Trade relations brought together the far-flung areas of the two continents through the opening of direct trade routes, the impact of which deserves study. Studies do exist for the western influence on the west coast of India, such as by M.N. Pearson, T.R. de Souza and K.S. Mathew.[30] Even the few scholars who have undertaken research on the eastern coast of India basing themselves on Dutch and English sources tend to confirm the prejudice in favour of the western coast. Partly, this is because Portuguese commercial establishments were concentrated in the region from Diu to Quilon on the west coast.

While investigating whether the Coromandel region kept its continuity of trade and commerce, another related and interesting question also arises: were the various sectors like agriculture, crafts and exchange on the Coromandel affected by the impact of the commercial revolution of the sixteenth century? The extent to which the polity, economy and society of Coromandel were exposed to the after-effects of the commercial revolution can be meaningfully investigated in the light of contemporary documents both in the regional languages and in Portuguese. The age of Portuguese expansion during this period must have made its impact on the Coromandel. The manner in which the Dutch, the English and the French intruded into this region in the seventeenth century tends to give the impression that some new socio-economic formations had occurred in Coromandel during the preceding century.

A few eminent historians of South India such as Nilakanta Sastri, N. Venkataramanaya, T.V. Mahalingam and A. Krishnaswami Pillai have paid attention to the political, social and economic history of the Vijayanagara empire,[31] but their discussion did not possess spatial and temporal variation. L.B.

Alayev concentrated on the socio-economic history of southern India from the fourteenth to the eighteenth century covering a vast region, but his work remains inaccessible to those ignorant of Russian.[32] The lack of ideological framework found in the writings of these historians prompted Burton Stein to work on peasants and society of South India with the help of a borrowed model, namely the segmentary state theory applied by Aidan Southall for the study on Africa.[33] But while applying this concept to Indian conditions Stein overlooked the changing pattern of South Indian polity and society. Noboru Karashima and Y. Subbarayalu followed the quantitative method, long applied by D.D. Kosambi in historical investigations. They used the epigraphical data to shed light on the South Indian economy and society during the medieval period.[34] In their attempt to reconstruct the history of South India, even going beyond the biased summaries of the inscriptions, these two scholars broke new fields of investigation.

All these studies, however, deal with a large geographical area and longer period of study, which has prevented the authors from paying adequate attention to a specific region in a specific era. As against this, the present book examines the economic, social and political systems of the Coromandel region during the sixteenth century, making use of both indigenous and foreign sources.

The historiography of medieval South India in the past three decades has witnessed rapid and steady analytical progress. Many historians have begun to use the published and unpublished texts of epigraphs, raising a number of questions both of theory and empiricism in historical debate. But while analysing the inscriptions in the annual reports of epigraphy, we find a tendency among professional historians to ignore the systematic quantitative data relating to socio-economic aspects. The present work attempts to use the statistics provided by epigraphical evidence to relate the forces at work in a multi-dimensional explanation. The corpus of stone and metal inscriptions in Tamil, Telugu and Kannada is important in this regard. Texts published in original and in translation in various series are few; unpublished inscriptions seem to be predominant for the Vijayanagar period.[35]

The Vijayanagar inscriptions have, in their turn, posed a special problem. Because different *Panchankams* or almanacs were used in different regions, dates given in the Vijayanagara inscriptions cannot be verified easily with L.D. Swamikannu Pillai's tables, given in his volumes on Indian ephemeris. This has led to their neglect by modern epigraphists, who say that these inscriptions do not strictly follow any pattern, that they are often written in poor script in colloquial style, and that they are inaccurate in dates and other details.[36]

Admittedly there are deviations; but there certainly is a definite formula in the structure of these inscriptions.[37] They confirm to the norms set forth in the *Dharma Sastra* texts.[38] As to the script followed, we find the Sanskrit portion written in *Nandi-Nagari*, and the Tamil portion in Tamil script, with *Grandha* letters to mark the Sanskrit letters.[39] *Saka* dates are generally cited along with other details. Some *Saka* dates are given in chronograms composed according to the *Katapayadi* system where Sanskrit passages occur in the inscription.[40] In the present work, the common pattern of inscriptional identification by the number of the year in which an inscription was copied and acquired by the office of the Government epigraphist is followed.

The bulk of Portuguese sources, which have been inadequately studied by researchers presumably due to lack of expertise to unearth Portuguese documents are an invaluable source to enquire into the broad economic and social framework of Coromandel in the sixteenth century. After the Romans, the Portuguese were pioneers in medieval Europe in establishing commercial relations with Coromandel. They made every possible effort to collect detailed information about the places and inhabitants of this strange new land.[41] The published works of contemporary Portuguese Chroniclers like Fernão Lopes de Castanheda, João de Barros, Gaspar Correa and Diogo de Couto contain useful information. The letters of the Jesuits form an important source since they contain detailed accounts of Coromandel historical events which served as an introduction to the Jesuit religious activities of each year.[42] These letters, generally found in the published works of Antonio da Silva Rego and Joseph Wicki, have been a valuable source in the current research. The considerable amount of unpublished archival records such as letters, mandates, receipts, account books relating to the activities of the Portuguese on Coromandel, preserved in various repositories in Portugal and other parts of Europe, have also been tapped for this study. Other primary sources include the accounts of the travellers who visited the Coromandel coast in the sixteenth century. No doubt travellers' accounts tend to suffer from historical inaccuracy, since they were not writing as professional historians, but their impressions cannot on that account be totally discounted. The works of Italian travellers such as Varthema, Ceasar de Federici and Gasparo Balbi, Portuguese accounts of Duarte Barbosa, Tome Pires and the Dutch writings of Linschoten have also been used.

Literary sources of the period are another primary source material. These contain little historical information and are mainly mythical works. The *Manipravala* style peculiar to the Vaishnava cult in the south, with Tamil freely mixed with Sanskrit words, was adopted in the literature of this period.[43] Twenty-two poets of the sixteenth century composed *Puranas* on various pilgrim centres of the Coromandel region in poetic and dialogue form.[44] Chronicles of temples called Koyil Olugu also exist, which however are generally discounted by historians since several Koyil Olugus exist in many families of the same place.[45] The veracity of literary accounts needs to be checked out with epigraphical evidence.

This study attempts to adopt both inductive and deductive modes of theoretical discussion, for while theory illuminates comparison, comparison also generates theory. Some statistical details collected from the sources have been incorporated wherever felt necessary.

## NOTES AND REFERENCES

1. For details see, R.E.M. Wheeler, A. Ghosh and Krishnadeva,"Arikamedu, an Indo-Roman trading station on the east coast of India", *Ancient India*, No. 2, July 1946, pp. 17 & 124.
2. K.V. Raman, "Further evidences of Roman trade from the coastal sites in Tamil Nadu", in Vimala Begley and Richard Daniel De Puma (eds.), *Rome and India*, Wisconsin, The University of Wisconsin Press, 1991, pp. 125-33. For details see also *Indian Archaeology*—A Review, 1056-57, New Delhi, p. 21.
3. R. Nagaswamy and Abdul Majeed, *Vasavasamudram*, Madras, 1978. Excavations at Vasavasamudram show the presence of rouletted ware and amphoral denotes Roman connection; see *Indian Archaeology—A Review*, New Delhi, 1970-71, p. 33. Roman coins of the fourth century were discovered there; see K.V. Raman, p. 125.
4. R. Nagaswamy, *Kaveripumpattinam: A Guide*, Madras, 1973, p. 3.
5. In 1898 excavations of Karuvakkurichi in Alangudi taluk of Pudukottai district unearthed 501 Roman coins. Excavations at Soraiyapattu Madurakottam near Tirukoyilur unearthed Roman coins; see *Dina Malar*,

daily (ed.), Pondicherry, 5 October 1992, p. 11.

6. R. Nagaswamy, p. 3.
7. U.V. Swaminatha Aiyer (ed.), *Silapadikkaram*; N.M.V. Nattar and A.J. Pillai (eds.), *Manimekkalai*, Madras, 1951; *Pattinapalai*, I. 129 as quoted in K.V. Subramanya Aiyer, "Largest provincial organisations in ancient India", *Quarterly Journal of the Mythic Society*, 65, I, 1954-55, p. 38.
8. K.S. Mathew, "Medieval Deccan and the maritime trade of India", Presidential address to the session of Medieval Andhra History: *Andhra Pradesh History Congress*, vol. XVI, Karim Nagar, 1992, pp. 39-53.
9. For details see, H.B. Sarkar, *Trade and Commercial Activities of Southern India in the Malayo-Indonesian World* (up to A.D. 1511), vol. I, Calcutta, 1986.
10. Ibid., p. 148.
11. Kenneth R. Hall, "International trade and foreign diplomacy in early medieval South India", *Journal of the Economic and Social History of the Orient*, vol. XXI, 1978, Leiden, pp. 75-98.
12. Ibid.
13. Ibid.
14. K.A. Nilakanta Sastri, "A Tamil merchant guild in Sumatra", *Tijdschrift voor Indische Taal-landen volkenkonde*, 7, 2, 1932, pp. 314-17; idem, "Takuapa and its Tamil inscription", *Journal of the Malaysian Branch of the Royal Asiatic Society*, 22, 1949, pp. 25-30.
15. The Chola epigraphs record, "*alaikadal naduvil Pala kalam Cheluthia*" (one who has sailed many vessels in rough sea) "*Kanthalur Salai Kalamaruthu arulia*" (one who destroyed the ships at Kantalur Salai); this depicts their maritime strength; *SII*, XXVI, 1986. For details on Leiden grants, see *EI*, XXII, pp. 213-81.
16. George W. Spencer, *Royal Leadership and Imperial Conquest in Medieval South India: The Naval Expedition of Rajendra Chola I 1025 A.D.*, Ph.D. dissertation, University of California, Berkeley, 1967, pp. 191-205. The Thanjavur inscription of A.D. 1030 mentions various ports of Malay Peninsula; *SII* I(40), pp. 105-9.
17. George W. Spencer, pp. 177-80.
18. *ARE*, 119 of 1888; *EI*, V, p. 105.
19. Epigraphia Birmanica, *EB*, I, 8, p. 165.
20. Tan Yoek Seong, "The Srivijayan Inscription of Canton" (A.D. 107), *Journal of South East Asian History*, 5, 2, 1964, pp. 17-24.
21. For details see Roderich Ptak and Dietmar Rothermund, *Emporia Commodities and Entrepreneurs in Asian Maritime Trade*, Stuttgart, 1991, p. 5; Tansen Sen, "Maritime relations between China and the Cola kingdom A.D. 850-A.D. 1279" in K.S. Mathew (ed.), *Mariners, Merchants and Oceans*, New Delhi, 1995, pp. 25-42.
22. See Kenneth R. Hall, *Trade and Statecraft in the Age of the Colas*, New Delhi, 1980.
23. Fernand, *Relations de Voyages et textes Geographiques Arabes, Persans et Turks relatifs a l'extreme Orient du VIIIe au XVIIe siecles*, vol. II, Paris, 1913-14, p. 465.
24. F. Hirth and W.W. Rockhill, *Chau-Ju-Kua: His work on the Chinese and Arab trade in the twelfth and thirteenth centuries, entitled Chu-Fan-Chi*, St. Petersburg, 1911, p. 96. S.D. Goitein, "Letters and documents on the India

trade in medieval time", *Islamic Culture*, 37, 3, 1963, p. 196.

25. Roderich Ptak, "Notes on the word Shanhu and Chinese coral imports from maritime Asia c. 1250-1600", *Archipel*, no. 39, 1990, pp. 64-80.
26. N. Karashima, *Towards a New Formation: South Indian Society under Vijayanagara Rule*, Delhi, 1992. It is difficult to accept Karashima's view that an Indian port had a Chinese name: he identifies "*Dabadan*" with Periyapattinam. He perceives Chinese da as corresponding both in meaning and sound with Tamil *periya* and *badan* with *pattinam*.
27. S. Singaravelu, "The ambassadorial mission of Lakshmana Hang Tuah from the kingdom of Malacca to the kingdom of Vijayanagara in South India", *Tamil Studies*, II(1), 1982, pp. 32-3.
28. Tapan Ray Chaudhuri, *Jan Company in Coromandel 1605-1690: A Study in the Interrelations of European Commerce and Traditional Economies*, The Hague, 1962; R.N. Banerji, *Economic Progress of the East India Company on the Coromandel Coast 1707-1746*, Nagpur, 1974; J.J. Brenning, *The Textile Trade of Seventeenth Century Northern Coromandel: A Study of a Pre-Modern Asian Export Industry*, Ph.D. dissertation, University of Wisconsin, Madison, 1975; S. Arasaratnam, *Merchants, Companies, Commerce on the Coromandel Coast 1650-1740*, Oxford University Press, Delhi, 1986.
29. Sanjay Subrahmanyam, *The Political Economy of Commerce: Southern India 1500-1650*, Cambridge, 1990.
30. M.N. Pearson, Merchants and Rulers in Gujarat, *The Response to the Portuguese in the Sixteenth Century*, New Delhi, 1974; T.R. De Souza, *Medieval Goa: A Socio-Economic History*, New Delhi, 1979; K.S. Mathew, *Portuguese Trade with India in the Sixteenth Century*, New Delhi, 1983.
31. A. Robert Sewell, *A Forgotten Empire*, New Delhi, 1962; K.A. Nilakanta Sastri, *A History of South India*, Madras, 1955; N. Venkataramayya, *Studies in the History of the Third Dynasty of Vijayanagara*, Madras, 1939; T.V. Mahalingam, *Administration and Social Life Under Vijayanagara*, Madras, 1940; A. Krishnaswami, *Tamil Country under Vijayanagara*, Annamalai Nagar, 1964; Henry Heras, *The Aravidu Dynasty of Vijayanagara*, Madras, 1927.
32. L.B. Alyev, *Southern India: Social and Economic History 14th to 18th Centuries*, Moscow, 1964 (Yuzhnaya India: Sotsialno-ekonomicheskaya Istoriya XIV-XVIII vekor).
33. Burton Stein, *Peasant State and Society in Medieval South India*, Delhi, 1980.
34. Noboru Karashima, *South Indian History and Society, Studies from Inscriptions A.D. 850-1800*, Delhi, 1984; N. Karashima, Y. Subbarayalu and P. Shanmugam, *Vijayanagara Rule in Tamil Country as Revealed through a Statistical Study of Revenue Terms in Inscriptions*, Institute for the Study of Languages and Culture of Asia and Africa, Tokyo, 1988.
35. N. Karashima, "Nayaka's rule in the region of North and South Arcot districts in South India during the sixteenth century", *Acta Asiatica*, 48, Tokyo, 1985, pp. 1-26; see footnote 6.
36. R. Nagaswamy, *Kalvettiyal* (Tamil), Madras, Tamil Nadu State Department of Archaeology, 1972, p. 42.
37. Each inscription is divided into three broad sections. The first introductory and preamble part contains Svasti Sri, the auspicious Symbol, place of issue, date, donor's name and details of his ancestry. The second detailed part

consists of information about the gift, donor's name and purpose of the grant. The concluding part contains the name of the composer, and ends with an imprecatory verse for the preservation of the grant; see George Mitchell and Vasundhara Filliozat, *Splendour of the Vijayanagar Empire,* Hampi, Marg Publications, 1981, p. 125. The copper plate inscriptions of this period follow a standard form beginning with the *prasasti* (genealogy) of the ruler and new verses added with the succession of each king, while retaining the earlier portions; T.N. Subramaniam, *SITI,* vol. III, pt. 2, p. 180.

38. D.C. Sircar, *Indian Epigraphy,* Delhi, 1968, p. 242
39. T.V. Mahalingam, "Inscriptions in Tamil Nadu", J.P. De Souza and C.M. Kulkarni (eds.), *Historiography in Indian Languages* (Dr. G.M. Moraes Felicitation Volume), Delhi, 1977, p. 84.
40. Some examples of *Bhumivandye* 1532 are in *ARE* 313 of 1950-51, *Samavedye* 1535 in *ARE* 17 of 138-39, *Tatavandye* of 1544 in *ARE* 353 of 1953-54. The practice of quoting regnal years had been entirely given up in this period.
41. K.S. Mathew, "Socio-economic history of medieval South India and Portuguese historians", Purabhilekh Puratatva, 7(1), January-June 1989, pp. 1-17.
42. John Correa Affonso, *Jesuit Letters and Indian History,* Bombay, Oxford University Press, 1969, p. 38.
43. The work of Kumara Saraswati, composed on Saluva Nayaka of Villupuram contains Tamil, Telugu, Hindustani, Kannada and Sanskrit; Somasundara Dikshitar, *Tamil Pulavarkal Varalaru: Pathinaram Nuttandu* (Tamil) (History of the Tamil Poets of Sixteenth Century), Madras, 1939, p. 43.
44. Thirty-six Siva *puranas* and five Vaishnava *puranas,* that is a total of forty-one *puranas* were composed in this period. Ulaganatha Pillai, who prepared the catalogue of Tamil works of Saraswati Mahal Library, records seven works of the sixteenth century. Srinivasa *puranam* was introduced by Kathichetti during *Nityotsavam* festival in Tirupati temple during 1543, TTDES V(466); Iraivasanallur *puranam* (1510), Chidambara *puranam* (1508), Tiruvarur *puranam* (1592), Arunagiri *puranam* (1555), Tiruttani *puranam,* Tirukalukuntra *puranam,* Tiruchengattankudi *puranam* and Kachi *puranam* are some examples of *Sthala puranas* in this period.
45. *Olugu* is defined as the register of a temple giving an account of its properties and its history in the Tamil lexicon. For Srirangam there were many *koyil olugus,* see T.S. Parathasarathy, *Koyil olugu,* Tirupati, Tirumala Devasthanam, Tirupati, 1954, p. ii.

# 1

# Historical Geography and Political Economy of the Coromandel

Most scholars are agreed that the term Coromandel comes from *Chola-mandalam.*[1] The first recorded mention of the word is in an inscription of the eleventh century;[2] and the term continued to be in use even during the sixteenth century.[3] Coromandel, thus was a creation of the medieval period.

From time to time, the Coromandel region was divided into convenient administrative units. An attempt is made here to define the Coromandel region, set the geographical limits, and depth of hinterland from the coast. The question of regional boundary is a complex one, considering that a boundary evolves with historical changes and political necessities. Even ecological changes are likely to modify geographical boundaries.[4]

Among the few studies on South Indian historical geography,[5] Nilakanta Sastri made an exceptional contribution by formally expounding the influence of geographical factors on historical development.[6] T.V. Mahalingam assumed that there were no significant changes from the *Sangam* period to the middle of the seventeenth century.[7] Some recent studies have recognised the influence of ecological factors on the agrarian and human aspects of a region,[8] while others have emphasised well-defined boundaries, thus making a complete break with the conventional approach.[9]

Some epigraphs of the Coromandel region mention a single territorial unit; others mention some villages, or a number of villages in fragmented divisions.[10] The details of territorial units in the inscriptions are sometimes damaged and lost. The annual reports on epigraphy, published by the Government of India in the form of resume, never furnish the details necessary for a serious and indepth investigation. Analysis of the original texts of inscriptions therefore throws considerable light on the subject.

The observations of the Portuguese, who sought to trace the geography of the Coromandel serves as corroborating evidence.[11]

In the study of historical geography, two methods are generally employed for handling heterogeneous spatial data in a chronological context:[12] either attention is focused on specific elements of change and clear selections made around which to organise the material; or past geography at particular points in time is reconstructed with emphasis on the spatial relationship with less attention given to the processes of change. The present study selects a particular framework to emphasise both elements.

## EXTENT OF COROMANDEL COAST AND HINTERLAND

Judging from the inscriptional evidence, the northern extremity of Coromandel during the sixteenth century was at eastern Padainadu and Atturnadu of Sulurpet taluk, which embraces the Swarnamukhi river basin in the hinterland.[13] The coast extended up to Durgarajapattinam in the Bay of Bengal.[14] Towns further north, such as Gudur and Nellore, were in the Udayagiri *rajya;* they were not in *Jayankonda-cholamandalam.* Portuguese sources of the sixteenth century therefore do not seem to be very precise since they mention that the coast ended at the port of Pulicat in the north;[15] though they were right in a way, since there were no other busy ports beyond Pulicat as far north as Durgarajapattinam.[16] It is possible that the term Coromandel gained wider currency with the extension of the coastal region beyond Durgarajapattinam during the seventeenth century.

João de Barros, the Portuguese chronicler, who has given a detailed and reliable description of the Coromandel ports during the sixteenth century, records the southern limit of Coromandel as the port of Adirampattinam.[17] Inscriptions found beyond the port of Adirampattinam also corroborate this geographical boundary, since they are located and included in *Pandyamandalam.*[18] Therefore, the two sets of historians, who define Coromandel as the name applied to the eastern coast of India, with the northern limit as the Godavari and the southern limit at Point Calimere[19] or as far as the island Mannar with the starting of the fishery coast[20] seem to be incorrect.

The eastern limit of Coromandel, being bounded by the sea, poses no problem of geographical definition. The western limit of the hinterland can be studied with detailed analysis of the various divisions. The modern geographical usage which takes the littoral as extending between 75 and 150 kilometres in width to the hinterland,[21] would not apply for a critical study of the medieval period. Inscriptions record that the town of Chandragiri and its suburbs in Chittoor district of Andhra Pradesh made up the northwestern limit of Coromandel. It embraced some parts of the eastern ghats such as Vengadam hills, Horsey hills, and Nagari hills in Chittoor district.[22] The southern portion of Tiruvengada *kottam*, which was in Penugonda *rajya* during 1546, was not in the Coromandel region, as seen in epigraphs.[23] Inscriptions found in the region bear out that the Coromandel region extended to Attur taluk in Salem district, and Tirukoyilur in South Arcot district.[24] Fernão Nuniz also mentions Tirukoyilur in his account.[25] Nuniz reports the southwestern limit of Coromandel as encompassing Srirangam, including Trichy, Kulithalai and some parts of Pudukottai area; this also is corroborated by the epigraphs.[26]

A distinction therefore needs to be made between Coromandel coast and Coromandel region. During the sixteenth century, this region with its hinterland comprised Chittoor, Nagari, Puttur, Sathyavedu, Chandragiri, Kalakhasti taluks of Chittoor district, Sulurpet taluk of Nellore district, Madras, Chingleput, North Arcot, South Arcot, Thanjavur districts and Trichy, Kulithalai, Lalgudi, Udayarpalayam, Musiri taluks of Trichy district as the external boundary.

## TERRITORIAL DIVISIONS

Various divisional names such as *mandalam, rajya, simai, uchavadi, valanadu, kottam, parru, nadu, kurram and taniyur* appear in the inscriptions. Some of these divisional nomenclatures were from the period of Cholas in the tenth century; others came in during the times of the Vijayanagara power.

*Rajya* (lit. 'country' or 'kingdom') was the largest division of the Vijayanagar empire. Chandragiri, Padaividu, Tiruvadigai and Cholamandala were *rajyas*; the first two were also called *maha-rajyas*. The name Cholamandala *rajya* appears seldom in inscriptions.[27] The *rajyas* differed in size and extent. They generally seem to have been ruled by *mahamandalesvaras* appointed by the ruler of Vijayanagara.[28]

Most commonly appearing in the inscriptions is *simai* as the

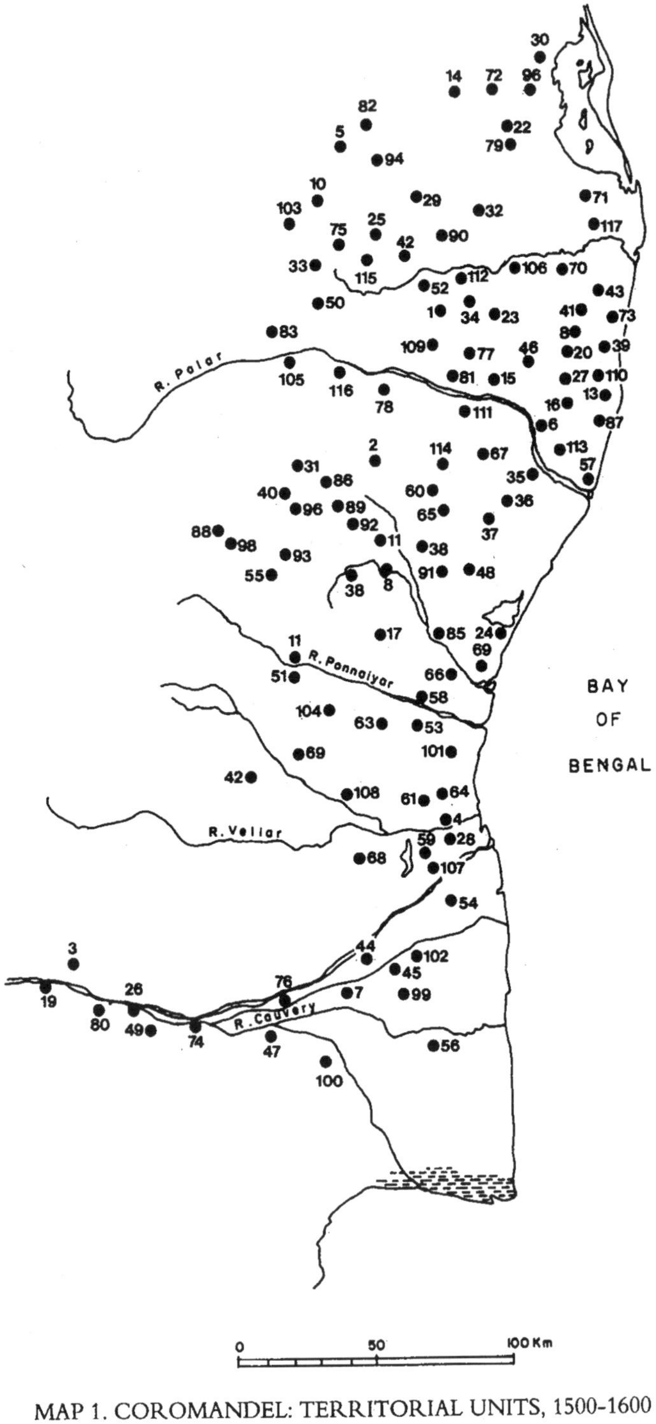


MAP 1. COROMANDEL: TERRITORIAL UNITS, 1500-1600

(For details see page 227)

core division. Each *rajya* was divided into a number of *simais*, based on some size of land. Surprisingly, Burton Stein in his study of peasant state and society in medieval South India nowhere discusses *simai* or *nayakattanasimai;* he devoted, on the other hand, fifty-one pages in his total 488 pages to the study of *nadu*. The size of a *simai* varied. *Simais* were granted to *nayakas*, which sometimes were hereditary.[29] The royal writ of taxation policy, communicated to *nayakas* of all *simais* in the Coromandel region was attested by epigraphs.[30] The existence of Bhuvanagiri *simai* and Devamandala *simai*, which were situated in different *rajyas* at different intervals of time, proves that the territorial boundaries of *simai* underwent changes. Some divisions like Irakuttanallur *simai* and Devamandala *simai* were also called by other names such as Magadai *mandalam* and Pangala *nadu*.

The boundaries of *simais* also changed frequently. Tadapalam, in Tatvavadicheri *simai* in 1521, was recorded to be in Silakonda *simai* in 1551. At the beginning of the sixteenth century, Sholingur was in Tirukkadigai *simai*; at the end of the century, it was in the newly created Paravattur *simai*. Padaividu, in Padaividu *simai*, was transferred to Nagariyil *simai*; and Poonamallee, in Poonamallee *simai*, to Palaiya *simai*. These changes occurred consequent to the transfer of the Vijayanagara capital from Penugonda to Chandragiri during the reign of Venkatapati Devaraya II.

*Kottam* as a subdivision is found in the inscriptions of Chandra-giri and Padaividu *rajyas* alone. A copper plate grant of Tiruvannamalai records twenty-four *kottams* in existence.[31] Inscriptional evidence reveals the functioning of seventeen *kottams*; the rest perhaps were assimilated into one or the other divisions. These *kottams* are referred to as administrative demarcations of the main divisions of *parru* in epigraphs[32] The interrelation between *kottam* and *valanadu* varies: a piece of evidence of 1520 equates *kottam* with *valanadu;*[33] another source mentions that *kottam* was a subdivision of *valanadu*[34] we also find that *valanadu* was a division of *kottam*.[35] It is noticed from the distribution of inscriptions in the sixteenth century that Venkunra *kottam* and its territory in Wandiwash taluk in 1513-14[36] merged with Kaliyur kottam. An inscription of 1547 mentions that it was a small area.[37] Egmore and Triplicane in present-day Madras city were in Pulal *kottam* during 1520 and were later in Puliyur *kottam* in the same Padaividu *rajya*.[38] Damal, Tiruvengada and

Tirukkadigai *kottams* were in Chandragiri *rajya*, and Palkunra, Paduvur, Amur and Kalathur *kottams* in Padaividu *rajya*. The fact that Eyir, Kunravadhana, Uttukadu, Puliyur and Sengattu *kottams* were in Padaividu and Chandragiri *rajyas* at various periods of the sixteenth century shows that the boundaries of these *kottams* frequently changed. Some *kottams*, particularly Pulal, Puliyur, Kalathur, Tirukkadigai and Sengattu were converted into respective *simai* divisions.

The *Parru* division followed the extent of cultivated area, which suggests that it was a revenue unit.[39] Inscriptions record that *parrus* (lit.: fraction) comprised many *nadus*. It may be presumed that the emergence of new social groups and population pressure brought about changes in the size of *nadus* and gave birth to *parrus*.[40] Tirubhuvanai in South Arcot was converted into three *parrus* during the sixteenth century.[41] The *parrus* of Mudiyanur, Naduvakkarai, Nemmeli and Tirubhuvanamahadevi were on the southern bank of river Pennai; Perumugai *parru* was on the banks of Kudiaru; Pullur *parru* on the southern bank of Cauvery; Irrandarru *parru* was bounded by the two rivers of Gadilam and Vellar. It is presumed that various riverine basins of Coromandel with extended cultivated areas demanded the creation of a separate revenue unit called *parru* in this period.

*Nadu* was a division of a micro locality. During the fifteenth century they began to decline without administrative functions,[42] but they continued to be units constituting a cluster of villages in the following century, becoming subdivisions of *parru*.[43] Some *nadus* like Thanigai and Thachchur were attached to *parrus* such as Narayanavanam and Murugamangalam.[44] Village Nedungundram, located in Melkundra *nadu* during 1527, was later allocated to Kulaipallur *nadu* in 1544, which shows that the geographical boundary of *nadu* changed from time to time.[45] Larger units such as Thanigai *nadu* also changed boundaries with higher units in this case, particularly between Chandragiri *rajya* and Padaividu *rajya*. Thachchur *nadu* is mentioned as being in Gandagopalan *parru* and Murugamangala *parru*; implying that *nadu* boundaries overlapped those of *parrus*.[46] Some *nadus* were raised to the status of *simai* divisions, such as Adinadu *simai*, and Ninraiyurnattu *simai*.[47] An increasing number of conversions of *nadu*, such as Mugandur, Idaiyur, Malai and Kalavai into *parru* divisions is noticed in this period.

*Uchavadi* or *chavadi* was a common administrative unit of the Vijayanagar empire in the fifteenth century.[48] During the sixteenth century, only Trichy, Thanjavur and Valudilampattu survived as *uchavadis*. Padaividu, which as late as 1489 was called *uchavadi*, lost its importance in the sixteenth century and was called *rajya*.[49] The loss of importance of *uchavadi* divisions as administrative divisions thus coincided with the growth in power of *nayaka* rulers.[50]

*Valanadu* divisions also similarly lost their importance. As discussed earlier, some of them were converted into *kottams*. They were also used in conjunction with *uchavadi* divisions, implying a loss of importance. Some *valanadu* such as Meykunratha *valanadu*, Vadakarai Rajaraja *valanadu* were reduced to the rank of *nadus* and called as Naripalli *nadu* and Malai *nadu* in the sixteenth century.

The village was the basic unit of revenue. It consisted of a number of hamlets. Coromandel Inscriptions of the early sixteenth century call big villages as *perur* and smaller ones as *cirrur*.[51] These sources also give details of the total revenue derived from a particular village including the group of hamlets.[52] A piece of evidence suggests the formation of a new village by the reconstitution of two hamlets during this period in South Arcot district.[53] *Nayakas* had appointed headmen in the villages of Tirupapuliyur near Cuddalore, Kallur, and so on. Some *talayaris* were also posted to help the village headmen in local administration.[54]

A study of these various units leads to the following general conclusions: The number of *simai* and *parru* divisions had increased. The fact that the former existed as administrative unit and the latter functioned as revenue division proves that many changes were introduced in Coromandel during the rule of Vijayanagara kings. The Chola administrative units, such as *kottams* and *nadus*, were generally converted into *simai* and *parru* divisions. In the light of the above, T.V. Mahalingam's view[55] that the political boundaries and change of empires did not exercise much influence on administration during this period may be rejected. It is, however, difficult to ascertain the exact causes which led to change and emergence of some selected units; this should be of absorbing interest for further study.

## THEORIES ON STATE FORMATION

The sixteenth century marked the zenith of territorial expansion and political sway of Vijayanagara rule in Tamil country. A recurring theme on state formation in many studies of

Vijayanagara is that the state played a key role in social transition. Various theories have been applied to the medieval South Indian state and we are told of feudal structure, segmentary state, military fiscalism, etc. in pre-modern times.

Robert Sewell's pioneering work forms the foundation for many of these studies. His work, contemplating changelessness of structure as part of the Vijayanagara polity, was heavily based upon literary sources in Portuguese and Persian and gives a bare sketch of political history. A. Krishnaswami Pillai, using the inscriptions, traced the regnal dates of fifty-eight *nayakas* from A.D. 1371 to 1530; he, however, did not speak of the forces at work and the changes in the administrative structure.[56] R. Sathiyanatha Aiyar, V. Vriddhagirisan and C.S. Srinivasachari focused on the extension of Vijayanagara rule to Madurai, Thanjavur and Gingee; none of them, however, recognised the forms of authority involving different principles in state formation.[57]

Traditional historians, thus, have presented undigested facts, without examining the anatomy of the *nayaka* chiefdoms at the local level. Great scope is offered for such study by the exploration in depth of the mass of published and unpublished inscriptions in the original text and context; Portuguese sources do help to study the Coromandel chiefdoms and their characteristics.

Discussion of Coromandel polity during this period has mostly turned around two closely related problems of military and feudal characters, neglecting the study of the main stream to analyse the anatomy of polity in Coromandel. D.C. Sircar, N. Venkataramanaya and Nilakanta Sastri discussed the polity as a system based on military tenure.[58] Basing themselves on Portuguese sources like Fernao Nuniz and Domingos Paes, who compared *nayakas* to the captains in Portugal, they construed *nayakas* as warrior chieftains. Since such construction was originally made to describe the revenue of the King of Vijayanagara, this view needs reconsideration.

The emphasis on revenue is clear from Domingos Paes's writings. For example:

> Should anyone ask what revenues the King possesses, and what his treasure is that enables him to pay so many troops, since he has so many and such great Lords in his kingdom, who, the greater part of them, have themselves revenue, I answer thus: These captains whom he has

over these troops of his are the nobles of his kingdom; they are Lords and they hold the city, and the towns and villages of the kingdom; there are captains amongst them who have a revenue of a million and a million and a half *pardaos;* others a hundred thousand *pardaos*, others two hundred, three hundred or five hundred thousand *pardaos*; and each one has a revenue.[59]

In writing thus, Paes's intention was to show clearly the control the *rayas* of Vijayanagara exercised on the *nayaka* rulers. The literary source of *Agnipurana* text, which highlights the *nayakas*' position, deserves consideration here. It speaks of *nayaka* as a leader in a territory and does not place him in the higher rank of a captain in the royal army.[60] The term *nayaka* in Sanskrit means leader or chief.[61] The inscriptional texts calling *nayakas* as *kariyakartar* or *kariyathu kadavar* also imply such meaning;[62] these expressions indicate that *nayakas* were the chief of actions and executor of transactions who probably derived the independent rights from the king. The term *amaram*, which literally means command of a thousand foot soldiers,[63] has not generally formed the suffix of *nayakattanam* in the relevant epigraphs. Also, if we treat *nayakas* as warrior chieftains, it is difficult to explain how other epigraphical evidence records the persons of various communities such as *Manradis* and *chettis* in the Coromandel society as *nayakas*.[64] The epigraphs lead to the inference that these titles were given them as chiefs of their local community. It is apparent that some exaggeration crept into applying military aspects to the title of *nayakas*. The *nayakas* might have been asked to assist the Vijayanagara rulers in times of war as loyal subordinates; but military duty played only a minor role in their selection as *nayakas*.

To quote Domingos Paes:

So the king fixes for him the number of troops he must maintain in foot; horse and elephants. These troops are always ready for duty, whenever they may be called out and wherever they have to go and in this way he has this million fighting men always ready.[65]

Fernão Nuniz enumerates the revenue of some *nayakas* in Kannada-speaking areas close to the capital city of Vijayanagara and their military contribution to the King's army.[66] We have no precise details of the strength of the army maintained by the *nayakas* in Coromandel but for a few. We have only references to soldiers who were conferred with honour and privileges for their participation in war by the Vijayanagara kings—and not by *nayaka* rulers in this period.[67] Also, we find no inscriptional evidence supporting the grant of *nayakattanam* on military tenure. According to evidence, Sevappa *nayaka* was appointed as *nayaka* of Thanjavur through matrimonial alliance with the Vijayanagara ruling family: he received Thanjavur *simai* as *sridhanam*;[68] Allasani Peddana was granted Karivachi *simai* as a nobleman performing public service; Vitthala Chinna Timma was given Chingleput *simai* on account of blood relationship.[69] This suggests that *nayakattanams* were granted based on some specific principle involving identifiable extended kinship. The view of polity based on military tenure does not stand scrutiny.

There has been a lively and long debate on the feudalistic mode of production and the rise of commodity production in India. A. Krishnaswami has equated the *nayakattanam* system with the feudal organisation of medieval Europe.[70] N. Karashima, on the other hand, has conducted his epigraphical studies to understand the attitudes, ideals and basic structure of Coromandel polity. He relates the strength of state control over *nayakas* exercised by Vijayanagara rulers to the *Tokungawa* feudalism of Japan. The result of these diverse studies has been somewhat confusing.

In the epigraphs dealing with the transactions between the Vijayanagara rulers and *nayakas* a phrase frequently occurring is *punniyam undagum padiyaga,* meaning 'for the merit of'. Karashima interpreted this phrase as proof of subordination and concluded that *nayakas* were sub-feudatories of the kings.[71] This conclusion is, however, open to question. The two examples Karashima cites refer to one *nayaka's* formal request for the construction of a temple *gopuram* and repairs of other structures.[72] It is illogical to interpret these religious grants as instances of subordination. Besides, the relation of subordination between Vaiyappa *nayaka* and Bommu *nayaka* is not clear;[73] the practice of a *nayaka* subleasing part of *nayakattanam* to a subordinate is absent here.

The Vijayanagara kings made gifts for their own merit;[74] so did *nayakas* make donations for their own merit.[75] Evidence of this can by no means prove subordination. King Achyutadevaraya in 1534 made a gift of a village for Vasava *nayaka's* merit.[76] It is hardly likely that, in this case, the emperor was a *nayaka*'s subordinate! Grants were also made for the merit of father, mother,[77] brother, wife, family,[78] ancestors, and other individuals.[79] In one inscription, *the person* for whose merit the gift was made in is most respectfully called *svami*.[80] In Hinduism, a gift made for a person's merit absolves all his sins and helps him secure a coveted place in heaven.[81] Landed property and money were gifted to gods for attaining *svarga*.[82] It is not clear how feudalism comes into such religious practice.

Karashima's other arguments for feudalism include a grant of a title by the local assembly to a chief.[83] The title conferred by the *Mudalis* of Iraivasanallur *parru* in the Pattana *simai* is in no way a feudal title and did not entail feudal obligations. While suggesting the existence of a hierarchy among *nayakas*,[84] Karashima failed to adduce evidence.[85]

Feudalism has two dimensions. One is the political or lord-vassal relationship with the fief as the base. The second is the socio-economic or the landlord-peasant relationship.[86] *Nayakattanam* was synonymous of the political dimension; but it lacked the essential socio-economic feature.[87] Karashima borrowed the concept and terminology from Satoru Nakamura's writings that deal with the ancient Japanese social formation and adopted them for the Vijayanagara state to theorise political relationships.[88] Later, Karashima with his collaborators analysed the texts of inscriptions, adopting the approach of statistical frequency to examine terms like *mahamandalesvaras, atikaris, nayakattanams*, etc. Feudal and bureaucratic terms are absent in their study, which led some scholars to treat Vijayanagara penetration of Tamil country as having been of a chiefly militaristic character.[89] This is to forget that the military capabilities of the Vijayanagara empire required a greatly enlarged money revenue; and the rulers concentrated more on revenue in Tamil country than on army. This salient feature required them to introduce revenue farming.

Burton Stein took an anti-Marxist approach. Examining the features of Vijayanagara polity in detail he discussed the Vijayanagara state as an imperial structure wherein the balance of power between the central state and all other loci of power is tilted overwhelmingly in favour of the former.[90] Refuting the application of feudalism to medieval South India, he contended that feudal polity is incompatible with the high levels of exchange, monetisation, commodity production and international commerce which took place in the sixteenth century.

The main weakness of Stein's argument lies in his application of segmentary state theory to Vijayanagara polity. He contradicted himself when he described *nayakas* as creatures of the

Vijayanagara rulers; at the same time he held that *nayakattanams* were not conferred on them but had to be given or conceded to them by the state.[91] Though Stein himself long ago began to shift his stand and introduced patrimonial type to Vijayanagara state,[92] some of his followers like Venkata Raghotham still cling to his earlier theories. In another change of stand Stein recently maintained that the Vijayanagara state was a segmentary state different from the Chola; the centralising control attained in the former over the chiefdoms of the empire was so great that it enabled the kingdom to transform itself into something other than a segmentary state.[93]

Nevertheless, while explaining the concept of pyramidal segmentation, Stein failed to analyse the centre and locality relationship of Vijayanagara rulers and *nayakas*. His discussion of the political organisation of Vijayanagara state and arguments were not founded on concrete evidence.[94]

## EMERGENCE OF NAYAKAS

In their academic outlook these scholars were oblivious that the Vijayanagara state comprised Kannada, Telugu and Tamil speaking areas and each region had its own marked differences in the process of state formation. K. Jayasree, who examined the Telugu inscriptions and literary sources dealing with the Vijayanagara period in Andhra, recently pointed out that the *nayaka*'s position and situation in the Telugu district was different from that in the Tamil region. She concludes that the major areas were given as *amarams* to *nayakas* in Telugu country during the sixteenth century.[95]

In Tamil country, the Vijayanagara presence was first seen in the northern regions from middle fourteenth century; its agricultural, industrial and commercial significance were its attractions for the Vijayanagara rulers. In the fifteenth century, they appointed *mahamandalesvaras* to rule the region. The oppressive and exploitative regime of the state officers in Tamil country came to an end in the early sixteenth century.[96] Later a highly decentralised system came about in which the king granted *nayakattanams* to *nayakas*.

According to inscriptions, *nayakas* were initially, in the fourteenth century, appointed to look after the revival and conduct of regular worship and restoration of lands and property of temples in the Coromandel region.[97] Misappropriation of temple properties by protectors of the temple had become rampant. Some *Brahmanas*, who had stolen gold from the temple treasury, were deprived of rights in temple worship and management of temple lands.[98] Nambisivappaya, an officer of the temple, who misappropriated the jewels of the deity, had his house and house site confiscated.[99] The decision to place *nayakas* in temples was taken around this time to prevent corruption.

In this arrangement, *nayakas* directly shared the administration of temples at some places. Achyutappa *nayaka* of Thanjavur obtained many temple villages, protectorship of temple treasury, and also shared in the administration of Srimushnam temple.[100] Kalattisura *nayaka* of Padaividu became the secretary, supervisor and chief executive of Devikapuram temple.[101] Krishnappa *nayaka* of Gingee controlled the affairs of Chidambaram temple.[102] Tirumalai *nayaka*, ruler of Padaividu was the authority for assigning temple lands to individuals.[103] The duty of writing and maintaining local accounts was distributed to a group of four *nayakas*.[104] Later, accountants were appointed by *nayakas* for writing temple accounts of Devikapuram and Tirutani during 1533 and 1560.[105] In the *Amuktamalyada* Krishnadevaraya explains that a separate revenue administration was needed for temples and subordinate *nayaka* rulers, since incomes from the two heads could get mixed in the accounting to the detriment of the royal treasury. Even if the revenue collector indulged in misappropriation, only a smaller part of the revenue would be lost.[106]

In course of time, *nayakas* began to appoint *atikaris, rayasam, srikaryam, maniyam, samprati*, servants, dancers, enquiry officer, accountants, superintendents[107] and various others[108] in temples. The temples at Tirupati, Kalakhasti and Kanchipuram had two superintendents,[109] the one appointed by the temple and the other appointed by the *nayaka* with specific privileges, duties and responsibilities.[110] Initially, the temple *sthanattars* opposed and resented these new appointments, considering them an imposition.[111] But these new appointees, once they had firmed up their position, replaced the officials appointed by the temple *sthanattars*,[112] whose activities were considerably circumscribed by the government appointed superintendents.[113] Thus, the royal superintendent Koppuri Oparajayya was promoted from *atikari* to *srikaryam* in a temple; the ruler also appointed a committee to repair the temple under his trusted men.[114] The *nayakas'* authority reached so high that an inscription, deviating from the usual practice of invoking the deity of the temple, begins with an invocation to Ethiraju *nayaka*.[115] In this case, allocation and reallocation of temple works were cast in the form of a *nayaka* order.[116] The right to conduct *pooja* in the temples was also farmed out to priests.[117] The dispute between two priests regarding *pooja* rights farmed out was decided by the *nayaka*.[118] A *nayaka* also transferred the management of the temple from Ramayya to Lakshmi Kumara Tatacharya for a revenue contract of five hundred *pon*.[119] This supervisor appointed a number of agents at different temples[120] of the region and levied tribute from the agents, the temple treasurer and the manager.[121] This indicates that revenue farming in temple administration was introduced in this period.

## COROMANDEL LOCALITIES AND THE VIJAYANAGARA EMPIRE

Coromandel was the fifth province of Vijayanagara empire[122] under the Saluva, Tuluva and Aravidu dynasties in the sixteenth century. Under them, the practice gained currency of granting *nayakattanams* to subordinate chiefs for supervision over the territory. *Nayakattanam* was hereditary in Gingee, Thanjavur, etc. The same *nayaka* families dominated at many places like Poonamallee, Tiruvur, Sriperumbudur, Devikapuram, Cheyyar, Tiruvannamalai, Kugaiyur, Tirukkoyilur and Bhuvanagiri in Coromandel. Some other localities—Trichy, Padaividu, Tiruvadigai, Sittamur, Tindivanam, Uraiyur, Kanchipuram, Chandragiri and Chingleput—were ruled by different families. It would thus appear that there existed multiple and differential patterns of distribution of local power.

There is also the interesting aspect of the appointment of *kirtas*. The literary source of *Achyutarayabudayam* refers to *kirtas* as individuals ruling Coromandel forest regions.[123] More knowledge about these jungle rulers will particularly help us in comparing the aspects of state formation in forest zones vis-a-vis agrarian zones. In any event, the Coromandel political system was a distinct one established at a particular point of time in history by the Vijayanagara rulers; regardless of the titles, such as *raya*, *raja* and *nayaka* given to the ruler of a region, their specific raison d'etre was ensuring the revenue of a territory.

*Nayakattanam* was given as an office[124] and some of the *simai* units granted by the Vijayanagara rulers to *nayakas* were called *nayakattanam simai*. Other divisions, such as *parru* and *nadu*, granted to *nayakas* were only called *nayakattanams*.[125] Burton Stein's view, that the domain of Vijayanagara chiefs was scattered over hundreds of square miles, with no clearly defined boundaries, may, in this context, be summarily rejected in the light of epigraphical evidence.[126]

It would appear that the Vijayanagara kings never interfered with the internal politics of any area in the Tamil country and gave the *nayakas* a free hand. The *nayakas*, in their turn, seem to have accepted the Vijayanagara king as their superior. Epigraphs demonstrate that the Vijayanagara rulers directly appointed and removed the local rulers. Thus Kempadeva Annagal was deprived of Senalur *nayakattanam* which was given to Kalama *nayaka* of Vellore in 1538.[127] Also, the king ordered the surrender of Mappedu *simai*, which was the *nayakattanam* of Timmaraja.[128]

The Vijayanagara rulers also saw to it that the *nayakas* did not grow too strong to challenge the authority of the central rule. Thus, the general of the Vijayanagara ruler invaded Tamil country to suppress the tyrannical activities of Koneti *raja*.[129] Achyutadevaraya suppressed the revolt of Saluva Chellappa *nayaka* in 1531[130] and King Venkatapatidevaraya defeated Lingama *nayaka* of Perumbedu *simai*.[131] Various inscriptions generally record that local rulers in Coromandel continued to be subordinates of Vijayanagara even after the battle of Talikota in 1565 where normal transactions were recorded as if nothing had happened.[132] According to Nuniz, *nayakas* had appointed a secretary at the court of Vijayanagara who always kept the *nayakas* informed of the happenings at the capital city.[133] The native literary source, *Rayavacakamu* corroborates this.[134]

When the Vijayanagara kings made donations of revenue to temples they communicated the royal orders to the *nayakas*, emphasising that the king's orders should not be trespassed and that this amount of revenue would be adjusted or deducted against the payment due from the *nayaka*'s share.[135]

Under the *nayaka* was the *Rayasam*, who was the executive officer of the royal orders in the *nayakattanam*.[136] Below him was the *attavani*, the chief revenue officer in charge of *kanakkars*.[137] These revenue officers, who resided at places like Tirupattur in North Arcot,[138] Kalakhasti,[139] Devikapuram,[140] and Maranjiyar in South Arcot[141] saw to revenue collection and its payment into the local treasury of the *nayakattanam*. Many *nayaka* treasuries functioned at various localities in the Coromandel region, such as Chandragiri, Trichy,[142] and Nannilam in Thanjavur district.[143] The *toshikhana atikari* was the main officer of the *nayaka* treasury. The various other *atikaris* and *talayaris* appointed at the village level directly carried out the orders of *nayakas*[144] to assist in the collection of revenue indirectly. *Ayyakarans* were chiefly responsible for the collection of revenue in a locality.[145]

*Rekhai* was a well-known practice of collecting revenue, which included a variety of sources of the village, including its many hamlets.[146] This suggests the introduction of revenue farming system, which in turn necessitated the *nayakas* to adopt this pattern at the village level. This introduced a system of government wherein grant of *nayakattanam* was associated with the administration of the territory, and collection of the revenues and remission of a part of the revenue to the Vijayanagara king.

In the Vijayanagara capital, there was a revenue department, known as *attavani*, presided by the Minister for Revenue.[147] *Karanikkams* were revenue accountants representing the king's interest; they were appointed at the headquarters of *nayakattanams* to keep a check on accounts.[148] Emperor Krishnadevaraya in his *Amuktamalyada* makes it clear that funds were exclusively collected by the king to maintain the empire. *Rayavacakamu* records the summons issued by the king for production of details regarding the number of territories, amount of revenue collected, amount unpaid and balance as overdue in each *rajya*, *simai* and other *nayakattanams*.[149]

All this suggests the existence of revenue farming, the existence of *nayakas* who ruled *nayakattanams*, and payment of revenue to the Vijayanagara rulers. Corroborating this is an inscription recording the royal instruction to the local accountant, who kept the accounts for revenue dues from Surappa *nayaka*.[150] Fernão Nuniz records that the Coromandel region yielded a revenue of 1,100,000 gold *pardaos* per annum to the Vijayanagara treasury.[151] According to the law in practice, *nayakas* had to settle their revenues on or before the festival of *Mahanavami*, which was celebrated for nine days. The exact amount of revenue due from a local ruler to the king also is mentioned elsewhere.[152] It is evident that the flow of revenue from Coromandel to the Vijayanagara capital was a routine affair, and the king never interfered so long as the *nayakas* were regular in their payments.[153]

Historically, the *nayaka* system of revenue farming in medieval South India was introduced by the Kakatiya rulers of Warangal; there were seventy-five *nayaka* rulers who paid revenue in cash to the Kakatiya kings from the twelfth to the fourteenth century.[154] Due to the disturbed political conditions of their time, the Vijayanagara kings did not at first follow this time-tested system, preferring to appoint royal officials to control the region. But when these officials turned tyrants in due course of time and many revolts took place during the fifteenth century, the Vijayanagara kings appointed many *nayakas* at various places in the Tamil, Telugu and Kannada speaking regions of the empire.

The Vijayanagara empire covered a vast area of South India and administration under a heavily centralised authority would have been difficult. Much easier was a system of polity with indirect taxation. In this system, the right to rule portions of the territory of the kingdom were farmed out to individuals in return for assured collection of revenue. This relieved the central government of the problem and expense of raising revenue through personal taxation from among a heterogeneous population with its diversity of customs. In return for the share in the right to rule over a particular territory, the *nayakas* had a strong personal interest to administer the *nayakattanams* well. In turn, this shaped the nature of the Vijayanagara state. Thus, it appears reasonable to assume that revenue farming was the single most important fact of the political economy of the Coromandel in the sixteenth century.

## NOTES AND REFERENCES

1. R. Caldwell, *A Comparative Grammar of the Dravidian Languages*, (ed) Rev. J.L. Wyatt and J. Ramakrishna-pillai, Madras, 1976, p. 23; *The Madras Tercentenary Commemoration Volume*, Bombay, 1939, p. 21.
2. *Annual Report on Epigraphy* (hereafter *A.R.E.*), 22 of 1922 cited in Y. Subbarayalu, *Political Geography of the Chola Country*, Madras, 1973, p. 15.
3. *South Indian Inscriptions* (hereafter *S.I.I.*), vol. XXIII, No. 184, pp. 375 and 379; *S.I.I.*, vol. XVII, pp. 311 and 322. Coromandel is the corruption of the term *Cholamandalam*. The Geneose traveller Hieronymo di Santo Stefano in 1499 was the first European who seems to use the term Coromandel and it was continued to be used by the Portuguese in the sixteenth century as *Choromandel*; R.H. Major, *India in the Fifteenth Century, Being a Collection of Voyages to India*, Delhi, 1974, p. 5. An inscription of the sixteenth century records that *Jayankonda*

*Cholamandalam* also formed the region of Coromandel; Henry Heras, *The Aravidu Dynasty of Vijayanagara*, Madras, 1927, vol. I, pp. 307.

4. Rajan Gurukkal, "Forms of Production and Forces of Change in Ancient Tamil Society", *Studies in History*, vol. V, No. 2, 1989, p. 164. The physiographical divisions of *Kurinji, Mullai, Marudam, Neithal* and *Palai* mentioned in Tamil classics cannot be treated as geographical because they merge with one another and their exact demarcation is impossible.
5. T.B. Ranganatha Davay, "The Historical Geography of the Cauvery delta with special reference to the Tanjore District", in *Journal of Madras Geographical Association*, vol. 12, No. 2, July 1937. Many earlier scholars on Historical Geography had generally limited their study to the location of places, boundaries of empires and routes of marching armies.
6. K.A. Nilakanta Sastri, *A History of South India from Pre-Historic Times to the Fall of Vijayanagar*, Madras, 1976, p. 34. He deals with one chapter of fourteen pages.
7. T.V. Mahalingam, *South Indian Polity*, Madras, 1940.
8. Burton Stein, "Circulation and the Historical Geography of Tamil Country", in *Journal of Asian Studies*, vol. XXVII, No. 1, 1978; David Ludden, "Ecological zone and cultural economy of irrigation of Southern Tamilnadu" in *South Asia*, New Series, vol. I, pp. 1-13; Brian J. Murton, "Geography and the Study of South India" in (ed) Burton Stein, *Essays of South India*, New Delhi, 1976; B. Suresh, *Historical and Cultural Geography and Ethnography of South India from the Chola Records*, Ph.D. Dissertation, Deccan College, Poona, 1965.
9. Fernand Braudel, *Civilization and Capitalism: The Perspectives of the World*, (Trs) Sian Reynolds, London, 1981, vol. III, pp. 27-32 and 34-40; See also ibid., *The Mediterranean and the Mediterranean World in the Age of Philip II*, (Trs.) Sian Reynolds, London, 1972, vol. I, p. 20.
10. The name of the *Simai* division is lost in the inscription itself in *A.R.E.* 90 of 1945-46, 621 of 1915, 105 of 1918; Half of the name of *Parru* is damaged in *A.R.E.* 263 of 1916.
11. The Portuguese accounts may not be very accurate and possibly contain errors since they lack Indian Geographical Studies.
12. H.C. Durby, "The Problem of Geographical Description", *Transactions of the Institute of British Geographers*, No. 30, 1962; D.W. Whittlesey, *The Horizon of Geographers*, vol. 35, No. 1, 1945, pp. 1-36.
13. *A.R.E.* 177 of 1924 and 322 of 1904; *S.I.I.*, vol. IX, pt. II, No. 508; Alan Butterworth and Venugopal Chetty (ed), *A Collection of the Inscriptions on Copper Plates and Stones in the Nellore District* (hereafter *N.D.I.)*, Madras, 1905, vol. I, Gudur 108, pp. 447-48 (1530-31). It is suggested that the merchants trading with Malacca probably who came from Kalangi riverine region in Sulurpet taluk boarded at Pulicat which was the only dominant port in this area during the early sixteenth century. Therefore, it is true that these *Chetti* traders were called in Malacca as *Klings* who came from Kalangi region on the eastern coast of India and their language was Tamil.
14. *S.I.I.*, vol. XVI, No. 679.
15. Gudur region in Kandavolu *Simai* during 1540 was located in Udayagiri *rajya; A.R.E.* 105 of 1960, Nellore was in Udayagiri *rajya; N.D.I.*, vol. II,

Inscriptions Nos. 10, 46 and 104, pp. 770, 867 and 811 during 1535, 1551 and 1591. Tom Pires, *The Suma Oriental of Tome Pires and the Book of Rodrigues,* New·Delhi, 1990, vol. I, p. 64; vol. II, p. 27.

16. A Portuguese manuscript approximately dated 1580 descibes the voyages made from the Coromandel coast to other coastal areas in India, like Orissa coast and Bengal coast. The voyages to Masulipatnam and Pipli undertaken from the Coromandel coast shows that Port Masulipatnam was not included in the Coromandel coast. See Francisco Paulo Mendez da Luz (ed) "Livro das cidades e fortalezas que coroa da Portugal tem nas partes da India das Capitanias, e mais cargos que nelas na e da importancia delles", *Studia,* No. 6, Lisboa, 1960, pp. 352-53.
17. Manoel Severim da Faria, *Vida de Joao de Barros,* Lisboa, 1778, pp. 184-312.
18. Tirukalambur in Tirumayyam taluk was in *Pandyamandalam* during 1502. Karur taluk was in *Pandyamandalam*. Tiruvurangulam in Alangudi taluk was in Sundara Pandya Valanadu during 1515. Tirupattur in Ramnad during 1532 was situated in *Pandyamandalam*. For details please see chronological list of inscriptions of the Pudukottai State, 1929, Nos. 728, 748 and 772; T.N. Subramanian, *South Indian Temple Inscriptions* (hereafter *S.I.T.I.*), Madras, 1953, vol. II, p. 677.
19. Duarte Barbosa, *The Book of Duarte Barbosa,* (ed) Longworth Manuel Dames, London, 1918, vol. I, p. 227.
20. Sanjay Subrahmanyam, *The Political Economy of Commerce: Southern India 1500-1650,* Cambridge, 1990, p. 93. As early as 1524-25, Portuguese manuscripts point out existence of separate *Feitor* and Captain for Coromandel coast and pearl fishery coast and the jurisdiction of Adirampattinam comes under Captain of Coromandel while Kilakkarai under the Captain of pearl fishery coast. See MSS. Arquivo Nacional da Torre do Tombo (hereafter A.N.T.T.) *Corpo Cronologico* (hereafter *CC*), Pt. IIa, Maco 117, Doc. 170; Doc. 489; Pt. IIa, Maco 129, Doc. 749; Doc. 208.
21. S.J. Mangalam, *The Historical Geography and Toponomy of Andhra Pradesh,* New Delhi, 1986, p. 1.
22. *A.R.E.*, 60 of 1941-42; *S.I.I.*, vol. XVII, Nos. 267, 269 and 271; Sadhu Subrahmanya Sastry, *Tirumalai-Tirupati Devasthanam Epigraphical Series* (hereafter *T.T.D.E.S.)*, Madras, 1930, vol. IV, Nos. 16, 61 and 87.
23. Ibid., 55 of 1907.
24. Ibid., 403 of 1913, 423 of 1913, 262 of 1934-35 and 74 of 1903; *S.I.T.I.*, vol. III, pp. 1076-77.
25. Tirukoyilur is referred to as *Truguel* in Portuguese. Vasundhara Filliozat, *The Vijayanagar Empire: As Seen by Domingos Paes and Fernao Nuniz, Two 16th Century Porutugese Chroniclers,* New Delhi, 1980, p. 161.
26. *S.I.T.I.*, vol. II, p. 693; *ARE*, 93 of 1938; Vasundhara Filliozat, *The Vijayanagar...*, op.cit., p. 161.
27. *Epigraphia Indica* (hereafter *E.I.*), Calcutta, 1915-16, vol. XIV, p. 170; vol. XII, pp. 340-357 (1577); *A.R.E.*, 312 of 1921; S.R. Balasubramanian, "The Chidambaram Inscription of Achutadevaraya", *Journal of Oriental Research,* vol. XII, pt. II, 1938 April-June, pp. 169-78, Slokas 7-10, line 3.

28. T.A. Gopinatha Rao, *Copper Plate Inscriptions belonging to the Sri Sankaracharya of the Kamakotipeetha*, Madras, 1916, p. 18.
29. *T.T.D.E.S.*, vol. II, No. 126; vol. II, No. 87.
30. Sadhu Subrahmanya Sastry, *Report on the Inscriptions of the Devasthanam Collections with Illustrations*, Madras, 1930, pp. 251-52.
31. *S.I.T.I.*, vol. III, pp. 1076-77. A trusted minister of Krishnadevaraya was Ambi Aram Valartha *Mudaliyar* also confirms the existence of twenty-four *kottams* in this region in K.S. Venkataram, *The Andhra Case for Madras Re-examined*, Madras, 1949, pp. 34-35.
32. *Irandayira Veli Parru* cuts across the boundaries of Amur *Kottam*, Kalathur *Kottam* and Sengattu *Kottam*. See Ravi Arvind Palat, *The Agrarian System of Jayangonda Cholamandalam*, M.Phil dissertation, Jawaharlal Nehru University, New Delhi, 1981, p. 230.
33. *A.R.E.*, 624 of 1904.
34. Ibid., 740 of 1909 and 66 of 1904.
35. *E.I.*, vol. III, p. 119.
36. *S.I.T.I.*, vol. III, pp. 1077-78.
37. *A.R.E.*, 321 of 1925.
38. R. Nagasamy (ed), *Chennaimanagara Kalvettugal*, Madras, 1970, Sl. No.79 of 1967.
39. *Ayira Veli Parru, Irandayira Veli Parru and Arayira Veli Parru* suggest that this being numerals 1000, 2000 and 6000 added to the unit of land measurement called *Veli*.
40. N. Karashima, *Studies in Socio-Cultural Changes in Rural Villages in Tiruchirapalli District*, Tokyo, 1980, p. 24.
41. *A.R.E.*, 368 of 1917.
42. A. Krishnaswami, *Tamil Country under Vijayanagara*, Annamalainagar, 1964, p. 84 and 93. See also *A.R.E.* 476 of 1921.
43. *A.R.E.*, 8 of 1933 (1537).
44. *T.T.D.E.S.*, vol. III, No. 2, pp. 21-23 (1506); *A.R.E.*, 149 of 1941-42 (1560).
45. *A.R.E.*, 708 of 1904 (1527) and 704 of 1904 (1544).
46. *S.I.I.*, vol. XVII, No. 765 (1522).
47. *T.T.D.E.S.*, vol. V, pp. 123-127 (1545); vol. IV, No. 167, pp. 317-18 (1541).
48. Y. Subbarayulu, "*Chavadi*, an administrative division of the Vijayanagar empire", in *Proceedings of the South Indian History Congress*, 1987, pp. 84-87.
49. *A.R.E.*, 384 of 1938 and 13 of 1939.
50. N. Karashima, "*Nayakas* Rule in the Region of North and South Arcot Districts in South India During the Sixteenth Century", *Acta Asiatica*, No. 48, Tokyo, 1985, pp. 1-26, fn. 9.
51. *S.I.I.*, vol. XVI, No. 98; *A.R.E.*, 158 of 1924; 312 of 1944 (1491).
52. *T.T.D.E.S.*, vol. IV, No. 23; *A.R.E.*, 272 of 1913; *S.I.T.I.*, vol. I, p. 119, vol. III, pp. 1209-10.
53. *A.R.E.*, 479 of 1937-38 (1531).
54. Ibid., 21 of 1938-39 (1592). Sevandinathan is mentioned as the headman of the village; *A.R.E.*, 155 of 1938-39 (1507). The inscription records *Uliyam Talayari* (*Talayari* in service); *A.R.E.*, 294 of 1897 (1524). This

inscription is from Manimangalam village. See line three of the inscriptional text.

55. T.V. Mahalingam, *Economic Life of Vijayanagar Empire,* 1951, Preface.
56. Robert Sewell, *A Forgotten Empire,* New Delhi, 1962, p. 101. A. Krishnaswami Pillai, op. cit., pp. 181-86.
57. C.S. Srinivasachari, *A History of Gingee and its Rulers,* Annamalainagar, 1943; V. Vriddhagirisan, *The Nayakas of Tanjore,* Annamalainagar, 1942. There is a similar work on the history of the *Nayakas* of Madurai and it does not fall within the Coromandel regional study; R. Sathiyanatha Iyer, *The History of the Nayakas of Madura,* Madras, 1924.
58. D.C. Sircar, *Indian Epigraphical Glossary,* Delhi, 1966, p. 214; K.A. Nilakanta Sastri, *Sources of South Indian History with special reference to South India,* Madras, 1964, p. 79. He discusses Vijayanagara polity as a confederation of chiefdoms in which the ruler of Vijayanagara is the greatest chief of all chiefs. See his work also "A History of South India", op. cit., p. 257. N. Venkataramanayya, *Studies in the History of the Third Dynasty of Vijayanagara,* Madras, 1935, pp. 170-75.
59. Robert Sewell, op. cit., pp. 280-81.
60. B.B. Misra, *Polity in the Agnipurana,* Lucknow, 1958, Agnipurana 104, 10-11. For details see also Vishnu Dharmottara another source, Pt. II, Chapter 24.
61. R. Sathiyanatha Iyer, op. cit., p. 331.
62. *A.R.E.,* 355 of 1912, 395 of 1912, 41 of 1922 and 65 of 1922; *S.I.T.I.,* vol. I, p. 994.
63. H.H. Wilson, *Glossary of Judicial and Revenue Terms,* London, 1855, p. 21.
64. *A.R.E.,* 358 of 1912, 374 of 1912, 384 of 1912 and 65 of 1941; 69 of 1938-39 (1513).
65. Robert Sewell, op. cit., pp. 280-81.
66. Ibid., p. 379.
67. Lands were given to the soldiers who died in wars posthumously to their family and it is called *Uttirapatti.*
68. T.S. Kuppuswami Sastri, *A Short History of the Tanjore Nayaka Princes,* Tanjore, 1903, p. 3.
69. *A.R.E..,* 591 of 1919 and 592 of 1919; *A.R.E.,* 1916, p. 143.
70. A. Krishnaswami, op. cit., pp. 170-75, 181-86.
71. N. Karashima,"*Nayaka*'s rule", op. cit., p. 15.
72. Ibid., vol. XVI, 294 (1584); *A.R.E.,* 266 of 1916; *S.I.I.,* vol. XVI, No. 295 (1584); *A.R.E.,* 270 of 1916.
73. *S.I.I.,* vol. XXII, No. 127; *A.R.E.,* 127 of 1906 (1532).
74. *S.I.T.I.,* vol. I, pp. 331-32 (1530).
75. *A.R.E.,* 348 of 1913 (1582), 384 of 1919 (1530) and 334 of 1913.
76. Ibid., 271 of 1908 (1534).
77. Ibid., 118 of 1943-44 (1567) and 119 of 1933 (1570).
78. Ibid., 50 of 1935.
79. Ibid., 19 of 1943-44 (1567). Inscriptions in the Pudukottai State, Pudukottai Samasthanam, 1929, No. 897.
80. Ibid., 355 of 1912.
81. The Manu Dharmasastra, IV 229 cited in *Rêvue de l'Histoire de Pondichery,* vol. XII, 1976-80, p. 110.

82. *T.T.D.E.S.*, vol. III, p. 193. By gift one attains *Svarga* (celestial region) by giving protection to the grant one reaches *moksha* (everlasting heaven).
83. *A.R.E.*, 11A (CP) 1934-35 (1596); N. Karashima, op. cit., p. 38.
84. N. Karashima, *South Indian History and Society: Studies from Inscriptions A.D. 850-1800*, Delhi, 1984, pp. 161 and 165.
85. Burton Stein, *Vijayanagara: The New Cambridge History of India*, Cambridge, 1990 (reprint), vol. 1.2, pp. 60-63.
86. K. Jayasree, *Agrarian Economy in Andhra under Vijayanagar*, New Delhi, 1991, p. 59.
87. Burton Stein (ed.), *Essays on South India*, Delhi, 1976, pp. 64-91.
88. Noboru Karashima, *Towards a New Formation: South Indian Society under Vijayanagara Rule*, Delhi, 1992.
89. Velacheru Narayana Rao, David Shulman and Sanjay Subrahmanyam, *Symbols of Substance: Court and State in Nayaka Period Tamil Nadu*, Delhi, 1992.
90. Burton Stein, *Vijayanagara*, op. cit., p. 99.
91. R. Champakalakshmi, "Peasant State and Society in Medieval South India, Review Article", *Indian Economic and Social History Review* (hereafter *I.E.S.H.R.*), vol. XXIII, No. 3 and 4, p. 425.
92. Anna Libera Dallapicola, *Vijayanagara City and Empire*, Stuttgart, 1985, pp. 74-79.
93. J. Pouchepadass and H. Stern (eds.), *Colection Purusartha* (13) "De la royaute a l etat dans le mondie Indien" (From Kinship to State: The Political in the Anthropology and History of the Indian World), Paris, 1991, pp. 217-38.
94. Burton Stein, *Peasant State and Society in Medieval South India*, Delhi, 1980, pp. 22 and 404-05.
95. K. Jayasree, op. cit., p. 63.
96. N. Karashima, *Towards ...* , op. cit., see chapter I.
97. *A.R.E.*, 27, 28, 29 of 1888 (1364, 1364, 1369); *S.I.I.*, vol. I, p. 50, vol. I, pp. 122-125; *A.R.E.*, 34 of 1916.
98. Ibid., 115 of 1931; *A.R.E.*, 189 of 1929.
99. Sadhu Subrahmanya Sastry, op. cit., p. 167.
100. *A.R.E.*, 270 of 1916 (1584).
101. Ibid., 356 of 1912.
102. Samuel Purchas, *His Pilgrims*, Glasgow, 1905, vol. X, pp. 208-209. Fr. Nicholas Pimenta records that twenty *Brahmins* died by casting themselves from the top of the temple *Gopuram* raising objection to *Nayakas* improvement in the temple.
103. *A.R.E.*, 372 of 1912.
104. Ibid., 298 of 1912. See also, *S.I.I.*, vol. V, No. 1403.
105. Ibid., 356 of 1912 and 133 of 1942-43.
106. K.A. Nilakanta Sastri and N. Venkataramayya, *Further Sources of Vijayanagar History*, Madras, 1946, vol. III, p. 154.
107. *A.R.E.*, 127 of 1956-57, 579 of 1919, 495 of 1919 and 12 of 1905; *S.I.I.*, vol. XVI, No. 71; *T.T.D.E.S.*, vol. VI, p. 205; K.A.N. Sastri and N. Venkataramayya, Further Sources, op. cit., p. 154; T.A. Parthasarathy (Trs), *Koyil Olugu*, Tirumalai Tirupati Devasthanams, Tirupati, 1954, p. 76.

108. Ibid., 322 of 1913, 154 of 1924(b), 104 of 1911, 587 of 1919, 89 of 1906, 79 of 1967, 243 of 1903, 235 of 1903.
109. Sadhu Subrahmanya Sastry, op. cit., pp. 276-77; *A.R.E.*, 152 of 1924 and 587 of 1919.
110. *A.R.E.*, 89 of 1906.
111. V.H. Hari Rao, *Koyil Olugu*: The Chronicle of the Srirangam Temple with Historical Notes, Madras, 1961; V.H. Hari Rao, *History of Srirangam Temple*, Tirupati, 1976, pp. 183-85;
112. *A.R.E.*, 89 of 1906.
113. Ibid., 94 of 1913.
114. *T.T.D.E.S.*, vol. III, No. 167, pp. 344-45.
115. R. Nagasamy, Chennaimanagara..., Sl. No. 79 of 1967. Ibid., 81 (f) of 1967. Please see also *A.R.E.*, 243 of 1903.
116. Ibid., 81 (e) of 1967. Also see *A.R.E.*, 235 of 1903.
117. *A.R.E.*, 101 of 1918 (1524).
118. Ibid., 413 of 1913 (1504).
119. Ibid., 1920, p. 115.
120. Ibid.
121. *A.R.E.*, 1916, p. 147.
122. Duarte Barbosa, op. cit., vol. I, pp. 183-84.
123. S. Krishnaswamy Ayyengar, *Sources of Vijayanagar History*, Madras, 1924, p. 159.
124. M.D. Sampath, *Chittoor Through the Ages*, Delhi, 1979, p. 159.
125. *A.R.E.*, 110 of 1933-34, 111 of 1933-34, 48 of 1948-49, 579 of 1926 and 75 of 1934-35.
126. Burton Stein, *Vijayanagara*, op. cit., p. 73.
127. *A.R.E.*, 194 of 1921.
128. Ibid., 61 of 1947.
129. For details see, *Indian Antiquary* (hereafter *I.A.*), No. XL, p. 142.
130. Burton Stein, Vijayanagara..., op. cit., p. 99.
131. K.A. Nilakanta Sastri, op. cit., vol. III, p. 154.
132. *A.R.E.*, 430 of 1928-29. The view of Nilakanta Sastri who described the independency of *Nayaka* declaration after the battle of Talikota may be rejected in the absence of evidences. See Nilakanta Sastri, *Further Sources*, op. cit., vol. III, 1946, p. 299.
133. Vasundhara Filliozat, *The Vijayanagar*, op. cit., p. 152.
134. S. Krishnaswamy Ayyengar, *Sources*, op. cit., p. 159.
135. *S.I.I.*, vol. XXIII, p. 121; *A.R.E.*, 151 of 1907; *S.I.I.*, vol. XXIV, No. 363, p. 36; *A.R.E.*, 44 of 1938-39. The annual revenue of the villages in *Rekhai Pon* are found in many inscriptions. Ambattur 400 (1554), *T.T.D.E.S.* V, p. 406; Pichattur 210 (1583), *T.T.D.E.S.* VI, Part I, pp. 33-40; Poonamallee 320 (1592), *T.T.D.E.S.* VI, Part I, pp. 55-62; Valuthareddy alias Villupuram 250 (1534), *T.T.D.E.S.* IV, p. 63; Gummidipoondi 100 (1549), *T.T.D.E.S.* V, pp. 330-331; Nagari 440 (1553), *T.T.D.E.S.* V, pp. 370-86; Villiyanoor 400 (1551), *T.T.D.E.S.* V, pp. 347- 52.
136. The office of *Rayasam* during Vijayanagara period corresponds to the office of *Tirumandiraolai* of the Cholas.
137. V. Vriddagirisan, op. cit., p. 314.

138. *T.T.D.E.S.*, vol. III, pp. 213 and 361; vol. IV, pp. 72-73.
139. *S.I.I.*, vol. XVI, No. 98.
140. *A.R.E.*, 368 of 1912.
141. Ibid., 98 of 1935-36.
142. Ibid., 131 of 1942-43.
143. Ibid., 53 of 1913.
144. Ibid., 105 of 1937; *S.I.I.*, vol. V, No. 652; *A.R.E.*, 98 of 1936 (1523) and 294 of 1897 (1524).
145. *T.V.M.T.I.*, Nos. 403, 406 and 407.
146. *S.I.I.*, vol. XVI, No. 98; *A.R.E.*, 158 of 1924; *T.T.D.E.S.*, vol. IV, No. 23; *A.R.E.*, 272 of 1913.
147. R. Sewell, *Forgotten Empire*, op.cit., p. 340.
148. *A.R.E.*, 13 of 1922.
149. K.A. Nilakanta Sastri and N. Venkataramayya, *Further Sources*, op. cit., p. 144.
150. *S.I.I.*, vol. XXIII, p. 121; *A.R.E.*, 151 of 1907.
151. Vasundhara Filliozat, *The Vijayanagar*, op. cit., p. 161.
152. *A.R.E.*, 493 of 1907.
153. Chellappa Saluva *Nayaka* stopped sending revenue, therefore he was suppressed by king Achutadevaraya in 1531. Burton Stein, Vijayanagara, op. cit., p. 99.
154. M. Somasekhara Sarma and N. Venkataramanayya, "The Kakatiyas of Warangal" in G. Yazdani (ed.), *The Early History of Deccan*, London, 1960, p. 670. See also, S. Jeyaseela Stephen, "The state, decentralization and revenue farming: some aspects of Vijayanagara rule in the Coromandel region during the sixteenth century", *Journal of the Institute of Asian Studies*, XI (1), September, 1993, pp. 1-16.

2

# Agrarian Relations and Agricultural Production

Historical research on sixteenth century Coromandel agrarian economy grew along with the general survey of the Vijayanagara empire. T.V. Mahalingam's pioneering work for the first time introduced discussion on the eleemosynary tenures of land such as *brahmadeyas, devadanas* and *mathapuras.*[1] Burton Stein presented a new interpretation of peasant society and culture vis-a-vis land, although heavily based on secondary sources.[2] Ravi Arvind Palat questioned his use of segmentary state theory on account of his heavy reliance on the economic unit *nadu* since new divisions other than *nadu* emerged in Coromandel during the Vijayanagara period.[3] Karashima also spoke of a new type of land holders of Coromandel, but he did not directly participate in the debates on the social and economic issues although providing vast scope for historical interpretations by scholars.[4] Peter A. Granda studied property rights and land control in Tamil Nadu from A.D. 1350 to 1600. Another researcher recently traced the economic implications of temples as the power centre of agrarian integration in Tamil country and believed that the *nayakas*' claim as protectors of temples was an ideological one which enabled them to determine the structure of land relations involving temples and other peasant groups.[5] All these works, covering such a long span of time of the Vijayanagara era do not highlight the specific changes in the agrarian sector from time to time within the broad framework of continuity. The vast area of Tamil country with various micro regional peculiarities at the local level in the system of landholding, revenue assessment and collection besides a variety of other aspects still remains unexplored. We shall therefore discuss these factors with reference to localities of Coromandel in the expansion of agriculture to understand the economic system.

Scholarly views on pre-modern Coromandel agrarian

economy fall into three groups. The dominant one, that of the nationalist historians, related it to privileged landholding based on a sort of communal private property with the caste principle. The second view of the Marxist historians discussed feudal tenure based on alienation, the primary form of subinfeudation. Thirdly, practising historians viewed the state functioning with localised system of peasant production with extensive commodity production in various places.

It is proposed here to study Coromandel agriculture with the nuclear area of *nayakattanams,* with villages in the locality controlled by *nayakas.* This is because the various appointments of *nayakas* made by Vijayanagara kings resulted in a more direct management of agrarian resources by producing changes in the system of agriculture in Coromandel. This crucial development began as late as the fifteenth century, and the emergence of *nayakas* replacing the *periyanattars* and their activities, by controlling agrarian surplus in the locality. We shall discuss various types of tenures, agricultural products and expansion of agriculture which took place in the sixteenth century.

Lands were owned by kings.[6] These they donated to religious institutions like *Mutts*[7] and temples,[8] which became landowners, having alienated land rights to individuals. A. Krishnaswami and N. Venkataramanaya's view, that all lands were owned by Vijayanagara kings, may not pass muster.[9] Various temples appear to have been major landowners in Coromandel, with many rulers donating increasing amount of lands in the villages for the needs of temples.[10] Many of these temple lands were situated far away and therefore could not be directly managed by temples. The Tirupati temple had lands even in the distant Tirukadaiyur in Thanjavur region.[11] The Tiruvannamalai temple held lands as far as Tiruvidaimarudur near Kumbakonam, which the temple officials decided to sell during 1534-35.[12] The authorities of the Takkolam temple were short of funds to construct *gopuram* and other structures, so they sold the lands.[13] Many lands in villages granted to temples remaining uncultivated, their possession was restored from the temples, and peasants were encouraged to use them with the promise of tax-free provision. Village Velanandal in Polur taluk, for example, was restored from the possession of Varadaraja Swami temple at Kanchipuram.[14]

Temples also transferred land rights to individuals in payment of services.[15] An order issued by temple officials shows that *kaikolars* were granted certain concessions in the land rights of temple lands.[16] Individuals holding temple lands in general and caste bound communities in particular emerged as landowners and occupants of land in sixteenth century Coromandel. The tillers, however, were distinct from them.[17] Thus landowners, holders and cultivators emerged as three separate groups. The number of landholding *Brahmanas* seems to have decreased.[18] *Kaikolars* made over their share of lands to their own community so that lands did not pass into the hands of other communities.[19] Gift of purchased land particularly emerged in Coromandel as a system of adding value with a view to establishing clear title over the property since the lands began to pass into the hands of a number of people.[20]

Noboru Karashima examined the term *kaniyatchi* and related it to land rights. Inscriptions of the sixteenth century mention *ulavu kaniyatchi, kaniparru kaniyatchi, palatalai kaniyatchi* and *kudiruppu kaniyatchi*, in common with notices of sale and transfer of land rights.[21] These land rights were sold; and a similar precedent transaction was cited for the deal.[22] The sale deed, called *kanivilaipramanam,* was granted not for proprietorship but only for the right to cultivate the land.[23] In the Tirukoyilur region there are three pieces of evidence about the perpetuity of this transaction, which bound the descendants of the vendee to the obligations made in the grant.[24] Transfer by way of *kaniyatchi* was hereditary[25] with the right also to sell, donate and mortgage the land.[26] Some epigraphical details show that the cultivating peasants of wet and dry lands fixed the price of land.[27] In granting lands, temples insisted that the peasants cultivating the land should not be evicted in any transfer of cultivating rights.[28]

There is evidence that temple lands lying within the reach of temple management were directly cultivated by temples[29] through appointed agents who supervised the work. Thus Araindu Nirappan was the agent of Varadaraja Swami temple at Kanchipuram.[30] He paid the agricultural labourers daily wages in cash or kind, and the entire proceeds went to the temple granary.[31] Lands belonging to Kamatchiamman temple at Kanchipuram were also directly cultivated and the agricultural labourers of the temple were dedicated to the service of Goddess Kamatchi during 1563.[32] This is indicative of serfdom. These peasants could not work in fields other than those of the temple since they were owned by the temple for life. Other evidence in the areas of Tindivanam[33] and Tirupati[34] mentions a system called *strotriya*. In this system, the temple earned a fixed revenue income and had no other rights over the land nor power to interfere with the occupants. Possibly, therefore, peasants consisted of various groups such as bonded labour, free labour, owner cultivators, and landless cultivators.

## TYPES OF LAND TENURES

Coromandel epigraphs record wet lands given out for share-cropping, under a system called *varam*. Evidence from Kanchipuram records that temple lands were leased out to local cultivators alone.[35] The share of the temple, called *melvaram,* in one case was three-fourths of the yield.[36] In another case, this share was one-third of the produce.[37] *Kudivaram* was the cultivator's share. The share of *melvaram* was reduced in times of drought and failed crops.[38] Generally, in normal times *melvaram* ranged between 33 and 75 per cent.

Vijayaragavacharya has opined that the cultivators of the lands of Tirupati temple took half of the produce as their share.[39] Burton Stein points out that this was the share government used to collect before it granted the land to the temple; that the rate of revenue increased when the land was granted to the temple and the share of *melvaram* varied between 51 and 75 per cent.[40] Since the share of *melvaram* for lands of the Kanchipuram temple also ranged between one-third and three-fourths, Stein's view seems probable.

*Kuttagai* was another system of lease for wet lands, with a fixed annual share of produce, no concession being allowed even in the case of failed crops. This system of allowing no concession whatever directly encouraged intensive agricultural production since the cultivators could not countenance failed crops. During 1540, 200 *kalam* of paddy was collected according to four *padikallu* in the Thanjavur locality.[41] Service tenures called *kodage* were also held by individuals for specific services to the state.

Under *kattu kuttagai* system, lands were leased out generally to one particular section of the community, particularly to weavers, for a fixed sum of money. Thus, the weavers at Tellar paid thirty-two *panams* annually as *kattukuttagai*[42] and the weavers of Panatalai also paid a fixed annual amount.[43] This suggests that the temples considered it fit to lease the lands to raise capital.

Under *malaiyan kattu kuttagai* (or *manaiyan kattu kutagai*)[44] lands were leased out generally to *nayakas*. The expression stands for unchanging (*malaiyan*) gross (*kattu*) lease (*kuttagai*).[45] It appears that both wet and dry lands were given under this lease system. Tirumalai *nayaka* was given lands under this system by the *sthanattar* and other authorities of Attuvampadi temple in return for an annual payment of twenty *panams* and forty *kalams* of paddy.[46] He also acquired land from the temple authorities of Devikapuram against an annual payment of fifty *panam* and fifty *kalam* of paddy.[47] Both inscriptions record that the lease holder was allowed to bring in cultivators of his own choice.[48] It is evident that the lease payment under this system was generally fixed between a half and a quarter of the produce. But Uthi *nayaka* of Arcot, another lease holder under this system, had to pay a fixed quantity of paddy to the Tiruvannamalai temple.[49] Considering the general emphasis on payment in kind and cash annually by the lease holder, it is probable that, in the larger interests of expansion of agriculture, many temples promoted the *malaiyan kattu kuttagai* system.

## VARIETIES OF CROPS

Paddy was the most commonly grown crop under wet cultivation.[50] Ativirarama, the Tamil poet of the sixteenth century, has described the process of harvesting paddy where the paddy sheaves were brought to the threshing floor, and the grains separated either by beating the ears of grain on a hard surface or by making bullocks tread on them. The heap of stacked up paddy was compared to a mountain, signifying abundant rice production.[51] Gaspar Correa's account in Portuguese corroborates Ativirarama's description.[52] Varthema, the Italian traveller, also records that the eastern parts of Pulicat produced plenty of paddy.[53] Indigenous sources mention the types of rice grown such as *samba*,[54] *rajana*,[55] *kuruvai*[56] and *pancavarai*,[57] *rajana* being of superior quality. Portuguese sources record varieties such as *girasal, meio, amateur cultoras, arroz pachay*[58] and *arroz jobacal*. *Arroz pachay* is probably the modern-day Tamil equivalent of *pacharisi*, meaning raw rice; *arroz jobacal* perhaps being *kuttarisi* in present-day Tamil, meaning hand pounded rice; *girasal* was rice of high quality; and *meio* and *amateurcultoras* were rice varieties of ordinary quality.[59] Apparently, multiple varieties of paddy were cultivated in the Coromandel region.

Cotton was another popular crop. The climate of Papanasam taluk in Thanjavur district was highly conducive for the cultivation of cotton.[60] Cotton was mainly cultivated on black soil called *karisal* land. The Tamil proverb suggesting the sale of wet land in exchange of *karisal* land indicates the wisdom of growing cotton.[61] Cotton was also cultivated on alluvial soil in the Srirangam region.[62] *Nellu parutti* (paddy cotton), *varaku parutti* (millet cotton) and *tani parutti* (single or special cotton) are mentioned in the Tiruvaigavur region as the three varieties grown in Coromandel.[63] The rate of taxation on the first two varieties having been more, we infer that these were superior to *tani parutti.*

Sugarcane was grown in areas where regular and longer duration of water supply was available. Tamil proverbs indicate that sugarcane was raised in the alkaline soil of Coromandel and it was cultivated at two feet distance in the field. Epigraphs inform us that sugarcane cultivation flourished on the southern banks of Pennai river,[64] upper valley of Vellar river[65] and Palar riverine basin of Kanchipuram region.[66]

Oil seeds such as gingelly, castor and linseed were cultivated at Tirukalambur,[67] Ponnarur,[68] Thirumayam,[69] Aragalur[70] and Kanchipuram.[71] A Tamil proverb describes that seven ploughings for gingelly and sowing of seed by seven castes ruined the cultivators.[72] This suggests the lengthy process involved in growing oil seeds. It is also corroborated by the Portuguese accounts[73] that oil seeds were sown and reaped in the Coromandel region.

## CLASSIFICATION AND RECLAMATION OF LANDS

There were five categories of cultivable lands in the Coromandel region, their distinguishing feature being the relative availability of water. They were *nanjey*,[74] *punjey*,[75] *thottam*,[76] *nattam*[77] and *padugai*.[78] *Nanjey* were wet lands easily irrigated by river waters. They were also called by various indigenous names such as *nirnilam*, *vilainilam* and *payirnilam*, meaning irrigated lands, productive lands and crop lands. *Nanjey* lands were further classified into *oru poo* (single crop), *iru poo* (double crop) and *kadai poo* (final crop yielding) lands.[79] Kuruvai lands referred to monsoon paddy and *pasanam* to winter paddy lands.[80] The above classification of land proves the existence of close correspondence between land, the range of cropping pattern, and the season too.

Dry lands, known as *punjey*, were entirely dependent upon the monsoons. The inscriptions of Coromandel refer to dry lands as *kollai*,[81] usually in contrast to *nanjey*. Some inferior quality of grains, *cholam, kambu*, oilseeds, and pulses were cultivated in *kollainilam*.[82]

*Thottam* were horticultural lands dependent on well water for cultivation. They are mentioned as *patti*, *nandavanam* (flower garden) and *toppu* (fruit garden) in epigraphs. Some *nandavanam* were as large as 10,000 *kuzhi*.[83] *Manai puzhakkadai*,[84] meaning backyards of houses were generally used for raising *maruvam, davanam, tulasi* and other aromatic herbs.[85]

*Nattam* and *karambai* were wastelands, which were potentially cultivable but left uncultivated. Their nomenclature as *karandhai pill* in the inscriptional texts suggests grass grown lands.[86] This is corroborated by another piece of evidence which states that peasants used these wastelands as pastures for grazing of cattle and the *nayaka* rulers collected certain fixed amount of cash from them.[87] Some epigraphs record the purchase of uncultivated wastelands by individuals and brought under cultivation in this age of agricultural expansion.[88]

*Padugai* (also called *attrupadugai* in Tamil) were silt lands in river beds. The changing geographical conditions brought this new type of very fertile soil. Commercial and value crops such as sugarcane and betel were generally grown on *padugai* soil. In Pattiswaram near Kumbakonam nine and a half *veli* of *padugai* land were cultivated.[89]

We may conclude, therefore, that land was classified into five categories based on the mode of cultivation, nature and types of crops, irrigation and season.

Our earlier discussion on *kuttagai* system showed clear signs of intensive agricultural practice in wet lands. Epigraphical evidence relating to clearing of forest lands and cultivating virgin soil, on the other hand, points to extensive agricultural farming.[90] In *Amuktamalyada*, the king Krishnadevaraya speaks of reclaiming cultivable land from jungles for distribution among peasants, to increase the state's agricultural income. Temples contracted out their forest lands to individuals for reclamation. The transaction was called *adai-olai* and the contract fee was called *adaippukuli*,[91] which consisted of a fixed annual amount of *panam* and paddy.[92] The entire task of reclamation was done at the contractors' own expense,[93] and involved levelling, digging, and removal of stumps.[94] Land reclamation provided a means of living for the Telugu and Kannada migrants to the Coromandel region.

Epigraphs furnish some details regarding reclaimed forest lands, which were converted into new peasant settlements called *palayams.*[95] Thus Ekkappa *nayaka* cleared the forests in Thachchur *nadu*, made the lands cultivable in Narasingapuram area of North Arcot district and settled peasant cultivators there. He levied no taxes for the first three years; and from the fourth year onwards collected three *panam* per annum per family.[96] *Mahamandaleswara* Ramaraja Venkatapatidevamaharaya similarly formed a *palayam* in Arunagirimangalam and gave the reclaimed land to peasants, besides some facilities, on specific terms.[97] The boundaries of this *palayam,* which are well defined in the inscription, make it clear that it was different from the village settlement called *ur* in the neighbourhood.

It transpires that Kamakapa *nayaka* developed a new *palayam* at Manalur in 1560 as *pettai*, that is, a mart for agricultural produce.[98] At Sinandel a *palayam* and *pettai* developed together. These instances show that *palayams*, which began as peasant settlements on reclaimed forest areas, emerged later as agricultural marts in the latter half of the sixteenth century.[99] The evolution of *palayams* as territorial units under a *palayakarar* with military camps was probably the next developmental stage of *palayams*. Seventy-two *palayams* existed under Visvanatha *nayaka* with *palayakarars* in the Madurai *nayaka* territory alone.

Clearly, there was regional variation in the functioning of *palayams*. In this light, Brian Murton's view,[100] that all *palayams* in Tamil country before A.D. 1750 were a territory with military encampment may not be applicable to the region of Coromandel. Inscriptions clearly mention that the military camps were called *padai parru*; army officials were appointed and royal forces stationed here. Tepperumalnallur near Kanchipuram and Mahipala Kulakalachcheri near Uttiramerur were some such places in the Coromandel region.[101]

Several orders issued by rulers contain details of distribution of reclaimed wastelands given to peasants for cultivation.[102] *Nayakas* collected *kadamai* on these as land dues.[103] The peasants could grow on these lands crops that suited the wet or dry season, including plantain, sugarcane, turmeric, ginger, arecanut and coconut.[104] Their approximate revenue was tentatively calculated in the beginning to help peasants.[105]

A special type of hereditary land right also seems to have emerged, with people who were not cultivators in Coromandel localities being granted the right. In six epigraphs, the term *ulavu* is prefixed to *kaniyatchi. Ulavu* may be taken as the right of cultivation or ploughing. *Ulavu kaniyatchi* consisted of a permanent lease of temple wasteland[106] in return for the payment of a fixed sum of money and certain amount of paddy annually.[107] The lease-holder was authorised to reclaim the wasteland and grow the crops of his choice. Inscriptions contain verses particularly related to reclaiming pond, bank and land.[108] Phrases such as *kudiyum erri* refer to colonising the land, with cultivators residing near the land and ploughing it. This indicates that the recipients of the lease rights were not cultivators themselves.[109] The temples did not benefit very much from this arrangement,[110] in which the non-cultivating class dominated and introduced absentee landlordism. The temple authorities granted this right to Sadasiva *nayaka*, Namasivaya *nayaka*, Tirumalai *nayaka*, and other recent Kannada migrants to Padaividu.[111] Other individual recipients of these land rights included officers such as Kuntavanayinar, Ambalatadi, Gangu Reddi and Tiruvikkai Velalagiyar, the headman of Tirupapuliyur.[112]

## WATER MANAGEMENT

The *nayakas* focused on providing irrigational facilities and invested funds in the creation of minor irrigational systems, which brought about agricultural expansion.[113] Nayinappa *nayaka* made lands cultivable by digging wells at various places in South Arcot district,[114] and at Devikapuram in North Arcot district.[115] Ramappa *nayaka*, Tirumalai *nayaka*, Ellappa *nayaka*, Bhaiyappa *nayaka* and Sriranga *nayaka* improved certain tracts of land in Tirukkadaiyur,[116] Tirupati,[117] Chandragiri[118] and Padaividu[119] by excavating new tanks and channels.

Whoever financed or executed the construction of such irrigation works, got for his pains a small share of the produce,[120] the major share of the enhanced produce going to the cultivators. The right of the former, called *dasavanda*, was personal, heritable and transferable.[121] Stône records mention that a piece of rent free land was granted for building or repairing a tank on condition of paying one-tenth of the produce.[122] The *nayakas*' motivation for constructing irrigation works came partly from the material gains accruing to themselves, and partly from the spiritual merit this was supposed to bring, since such an act was among the seven *satantaka* acts which brought *punya* and ensured one's happiness in the next world.

For maintaining existing irrigational works *nayakas* raised funds through various sources. One source was state funds and incomes of fish lease from tanks. Thus Sevappa *nayaka* allocated the income from the lease of fishery in the tank at Kodungalur for deepening the tank in Nedungunram locality.[123] Pottu *nayaka* gave the money from fish lease of Senalur tank in South Arcot district to be spent on the tank itself.[124] Damal Kama *nayaka* ordered that money realised by the sale of fish from Sripurushamangalam tank in Cheyyar region should be spent on repairs of the tank.[125]

The *nayakas* also invested their personal funds in improving tank irrigation. There was a system of donor's share at the temples called *vittavan vilukadu*. In this, one-fourth of the sacred foodstuffs offered at the temple were given to the person investing in the improvement of the irrigational resources of the temple.[126] A Tamil inscription speaks of a deed called *silasasanam* with this provision made by *sthanattar* of the temple in favour of Mallappa *nayaka* of Nedungunram. This assignment was valid for all generations, as long as the sun and moon existed.[127] This probably resulted in the regular trade in *prasadam*, in one instance such sale reaching 4600 *panam*.[128]

During the Chola period there was an irrigational dam, a grand *anaicut*, called *kaveri kalanai* on river Cauvery. A tax called *kallanai*, levied by the *nayaka* of Thanjavur, was presumably collected for maintaining the dam.[129] The tax was applicable at Tiruvenkadu in Shiyali taluk, Kunur in Kumbakonam taluk, Kundalur in Nannilam taluk and Thanjavur taluk, which shows that it was imposed on all the areas of the Cauvery delta.[130] When this dam breached in 1596 the *nayaka* of Thanjavur repaired it, probably with the taxes collected on maintaining the dam.[131]

The rate of *nirkuli* or irrigation tax levied on the lands in Kodangi, Nellikuppam, Timmanankuppam, Vengalakuppam and Palaveri was fixed by Lingamayya *nayaka* in Chingleput district.[132] *Nirkuli* was also levied on wet lands, dry lands, garden lands and groves in Tiruppunduritti area by Achutappa *nayaka* of

Thanjavur.[133] References to the levy and collection of *nirkuli* by *nayakas* in Chandragiri and Chittoor,[134] and removal of water cess by *nayaka* in Sittamur and Gingee by royal proclamation,[135] are indicative of the control exercised by *nayakas*. Some of these water taxes were gifted to temples.[136] Two epigraphs suggest that officers designated as *jala-sutrada*, Singayya Bhatta[137] and Tiruvenkata Chirukkan[138] by name, supervised the digging and maintenance of canals and channels in the department of *varigripakarana* or water works. This contradicts the traditional views of N. Venkataramanaya and Burton Stein that there was no department of irrigation or public works in the Vijayanagara domain.[139] Irrigation was, however, a local subject included in the *nayakattanam* administration; the centre was not much concerned with it.

Where more than one village depended on the same source of irrigation the management of the irrigational system was collective. This probably led to water disputes. A dispute arose between temple authorities and the residents of the locality when one irrigational channel was dug in Tirupati, which was settled by an officer named Yagnarasar appointed by *nayaka*. This officer inspected the site and found the objections raised to be legitimate.[140] Another irrigation dispute between the Srirangam and Jambukeswaram temples was decided by the officer Mallar Ayyangar appointed by *nayaka*, who directed that the irrigation tank in Sembiyanallur should be used by the Srirangam temple.[141] Similar evidence also describes an irrigation agreement made between the trustees and treasurers of the Siva and Vishnu temples of Perumbakkam, which permitted the former to dig a channel within the limits of Perumbakkam to carry water to the tank of Tiruvamattur in exchange for 300 *kuzhi* of wet lands as compensation in Vedampattu village. This deed was drawn in the presence of Bommu Reddi, an officer appointed by Achutappa *nayaka*, who settled the dispute.[142] In another instance, an order of *nayaka* gave the benefit of irrigational canal flowing through Akkalimangalam and Pudupalayam when the people of Iraiyur village declined to use it.[143]

## LAND REVENUE ASSESSMENT AND COLLECTION

Agricultural revenue being *nayakas*' main source of income it was necessary to ascertain the exact extent of cultivated land before assessing land revenue. Trinetranatha Kachchiraya, *nayaka* of

Srimushnam, ordered annual land measurement.[144] Land survey officers in the various localities maintained detailed survey account of agricultural landholdings.[145] The length of measuring rods varied considerably, between fourteen feet and fifty-four, and there were nine such variations. An effort was made to evolve a standard rod to suit local convenience.[146] At some places the old units of rods were replaced; at others, new units were used alongside the old one, in keeping with the established practice of the region.[147] Cultivated wet lands and uncultivated dry lands were measured with different rod lengths to fix the rate of land revenue.[148] The absence of a uniform measure probably caused certain difficulty to the people, but it increased the effective rate of surplus extraction.

*Nayakas* introduced and adopted rods of land measurement of their own choice. Specified land measuring rods by various rulers like Vangara *nayaka*, Pattu *nayaka*, Mummidi *nayaka*, and Nagama *nayaka* are found only in Tiruttani during the sixteenth century.[149] In Tiruvallur, a land measuring rod introduced by Chennamarajan *nayaka* at Kuvam coexisted with another rod length fixed by Kondamarajan during the sixteenth century.[150] The existence of several rod measurements suggests that *nayakas*' agrarian approach was arbitrary in their *nayakattanams*. It is therefore construed that the Vijayanagara rulers exercised no control over the land measurement rods of Coromandel and *nayakas* of the region alone had the right of remeasurement and altering measuring rods. This non-interference of Vijayanagara rulers is indicative of the extent of local autonomy enjoyed by *nayakas*.

Land was measured in terms of *veli, ma, kuzhi* and *kunta*. On one *ma* of land the agricultural tax was twenty *panam* and on one *veli,* 400 *panam*. Apparently, therefore, *veli* was the highest unit of land measurement and *ma* was its sub-unit.[151] *Veli* as a unit was particularly used in the Thanjavur region.[152] *Kuzhi,* frequently mentioned in the stone records of North and South Arcot districts, is a sub-unit of *ma*; it was used only in Tamil-speaking areas of Coromandel.[153] *Kunta,* a land unit adopted at Nagalapuram and Chittoor, was peculiar only to the Telugu-speaking region.[154] In the absence of detailed study on the Coromandel agrarian system in the fifteenth century, it is difficult to spell out the changes and continuities that occurred during the sixteenth century. The only conclusion possible is that the agrarian system in Coromandel had its own diverse elements in each locality.

In some epigraphs, portions dealing with the aspect of land revenue have been damaged.[155] But judging from the evidence that Trinetranatha Kachichiraya ordered collection of revenue of fifteen *panam* on one *ma* of dry land and twenty *panam* on one *ma* of wet land,[156] a differential land revenue assessment existed on the basis of soil classification in Srimushnam.

There was differential taxation also on land newly brought under cultivation. Thus *kadamai* tax was waived on the reclaimed land for the first year, and *ponvari* was waived the next year; but a *nali* of paddy was collected during the third year as was prevalent in the neighbouring Ataiyur *nadu*.[157] Some information on *kar* and *pasanam* crops with *ponvari* has unfortunately been damaged in this inscription.

Similarly, in some wastelands newly brought under cultivation revenue charges were waived for certain years by the government.[158] Additional incentives were offered for bringing more wastelands under cultivation through exemption of *jodi* tax by an arrangement made between the temple authorities and the officers of *nayakas*. While fixing revenue rates on reclaimed waste lands certain important facts were taken into account. This is borne out by the fact that the cultivator was asked to pay ten *panam* and ten *kalam* of paddy in the first year but fifty *panam* and fifty *kalam* in the fifth year.[159] Graded assessment was done with the object of encouraging cultivation.

Land revenue was assessed and collected according to the type of crop. Thus Appar *nayaka* collected two *panam* on *pasanam* or first crop and seven *panam* for *kuruvai* or second crop from each cultivating peasant in the Devikapuram region.[160] Revenue on cash crops such as sugarcane and perishables like fruits and vegetables was collected in cash. Revenue rates for mustard, greengram and sugarcane were fixed on par with those prevailing in adjacent villages. Similarly, other agricultural products such as betel, plantain, areca and coconuts were assessed for three-fourths of the old rates in Kanchipuram locality.[161] Blighted crops (*savi*), and crops otherwise damaged (*alivu*) were excluded in revenue assessment.[162] It may therefore be concluded that the revenue was assessed on the actual yield received from the lands.

The rate of taxation also differentiated between the type of cultivators. Thus, Chinnappa *nayaka* fixed three categories of assessment. The residents of the seventeen *parru* divisions of Srimushnam *nayakattanam* had to pay twenty-eight *panam* on wet lands and twenty *panam* on dry lands; cultivators who were moving in and out of the *parru* had to pay, respectively, twenty *panam* and fifteen *panam*; and cultivators who lived outside the jurisdiction of the seventeen *parru* divisions but undertook cultivation in the Srimushnam locality paid fifteen *panam* and ten *panam* respectively.[163] The criterion for assessment in this instance was the cultivators' stability and mobility of residence. In all instances, however, the main criterion for assessment of land revenue was the net yield from the land.[164] This inscriptional evidence goes against the view mentioned in the literary source *Krishnaraja Vijayam*, where the land revenue assessment and collection made from the gross yield of land are described.[165] Going by our evidence, a multiple system of land revenue assessment and collection existed, and the Vijayanagara centre exercised no control in the Coromandel localities.

Tamil inscriptions record land tax called *kadamai* and *kudimai* collected by *nayakas*.[166] Revenue terms such as *ponvargam* and *ponvari, nelvargam* and *dhanyavargam*[167] indicate that revenue was collected both in kind and cash.[168] A Telugu inscription provides details of the levy of agricultural tax by Bangaru *nayaka* in the form of grain from the harvested lands of Tiruttani *simai*.[169] Another inscription details Immadi Ramayappa *nayaka's* order, according to which the measure of *marakkal* ought to be the unit followed for collecting taxes in the form of available commodity in Magadai *mandalam*.[170] Sriram Ragava *nayaka's* order said that one *kuruni* of paddy should be collected from each threshing floor of all tenants of the temple lands in Sriperumbudur *nayakattanam*, and the paddy was realised in cash (*pon*).[171] It is further believed that there was sufficient quantity of coins in circulation and the government collected taxes in cash. A variety of duties and exactions were also collected from local controllers of land.

The variation in the amount of revenue, both in cash and kind, besides the variations in the methods followed in tax collection, indicate that many taxes were local in character. Some *Brahmin* assemblies such as *mahajanas* of Palaiyar, Tirumakkottai and Siruvayal that collected revenue during the fifteenth century had declined and they lost their independence to collect revenues in the sixteenth century.[172] Other *Brahmin* assemblies like *mahajanas* of Kanchipuram came under the influence of *nayaka* who controlled them.[173] A drive for collection of revenue by *nayakas* in their *nayakattanam* by appointing tax collectors is found in epigraphs.[174] The *nayakas* thus emerged as the chiefs of the locality who collected revenues.

With more and more forest and wastelands reclaimed and brought under cultivation, the extent of agricultural land began to be marked with boundary stones,[175] called *yelle kallu* in the Tamil inscriptions. The texts record the precise location of the boundary stones and the reasons for such placement.[176] The emblems used by Saivites on their boundary stones were called *tiruchulakkal*,[177] those of Vaishnavites *tiruvazhikal*,[178] and those of Jains *srimukkodaikkal*.[179] We have no references to the emblems used by Buddhists and Muslims on their boundary stones. Possibly, encroachment and also shifting boundaries due to floods and natural calamities necessitated the planting of boundary stones.

Disputes arose from removal and shifting of boundary stones. In some cases, where details of the removal of boundary stones could not be traced, the *nayaka* solved the dispute by buying the land.[180]At Nagalapuram in Chittoor district three persons who had removed the boundary stone were ordered arrested, and the dispute ended when the stipulated amount of fine was ordered to be paid into the temple treasury.[181] Illegal possession of lands at the villages of Avaram and Sittadi was settled by verifying the existence of boundary stones containing the Siva emblem.[182] Lands misappropriated earlier in the village of Uttamasili were restored by producing an original grant of copper plate possessed by Singarachar.[183]

Two epigraphical texts throw light on the procedure followed in settling land disputes. On receipt of the petition, an enquiry was ordered; the officials concerned conducted the enquiry and submitted a report to the ruler; the ruler then registered the order;[184] and both parties to the dispute deposited a sum of money as arbitration fees in advance into the treasury.[185] In one case in 1553, when disputes over the legal status of land arose, recourse was made to the records of the provincial treasury.[186] The restoration of several illegal possessions of land from the individuals by the state through the system of civil procedure points to the fact that landed interests were zealously protected in the period of agricultural expansion during the sixteenth century.[187]

To explain agrarian stagnation, some scholars have blamed the capitalistic world system as preventing economic development in the periphery. Their dependence theory partly opposes and also complements the theory of Asiatic mode of production.[188] We have argued here that agricultural expansion was possible in the Coromandel region through revenue farming. Irfan Habib has suggested in his Study of the Mughal Economy that revenue farming led to the collapse of the agrarian system and the corrupt nature of the State necessitated the introduction of this form of fiscal control.[189] In the light of our evidence and foregoing discussion we may say that revenue farming did not always characterise short-run maximisation and expanding revenue burden.[190] It was an organisational means of agrarian expansion, which partly depended, on the one hand, on the degree of control and supervision exercised by the Vijayanagara rulers in Coromandel localities, and on the other on the tenure period of *nayakattanam* that was left undisturbed so long as the revenue farmer paid regular revenues. Thus revenue demand presupposed the stimulation rather than neglect of cultivation. It may therefore be concluded that *nayaka* revenue farming had a constructive effect upon agriculture in the Coromandel localities ensuring agricultural expansion.

## NOTES AND REFERENCES

1. T.V. Mahalingam, *Economic Life in Vijayanagar Empire,* Madras, 1951, pp. 86-91.
2. Burton Stein, *Peasant State and Society in Medieval South India,* Delhi, 1980, p. 416.
3. Ravi Arvind Palat, *The Agrarian System of Jayankonda Cholamandalam, 1335-1565,* M.Phil dissertation, Jawaharlal Nehru University, New Delhi, 1980.
4. Noboru Karashima, "Nayak's Rule in the Regions of North and South Arcot districts in South India during the Sixteenth Century", in *Acta Asiatica,* 48, Tokyo, 1985, pp. 1-26.
5. Peter Granda, *Property Rights and Land Control in Tamil Nadu 1350-1600,* Ph.D. dissertation, Michigan University, 1984. Venkata Raghotham, *Temples, Kings, Warriors: Role of Warrior Chieftains in the Political Structure of Late Medieval South India AD 1350-1565,* Graduate division of the University of Hawaii, 1987.
6. *Epigraphia Indica* (hereafter *E.I.*), vol. XVI, No. 22, pp. 310-23.
7. Robert Sewell, *List of Inscriptions and Sketch of the Dynasties of Southern India,* Madras, 1884, Madras Museum Copper Plate 146, Plate No. 8.

8. T.N. Subramaniam, *South Indian Temple Inscriptions* (hereafter *S.I.T.I.),* Madras, 1955, vol. III, pp. 1138-39 (AD 1544 ); *A.R.E.* of 1937-38 (1520).
9. A. Krishnaswami, *Tamil Country Under Vijayanagara,* Annamalai Nagar, 1964, pp. 179-80; N. Venkataramanayya, *Studies in the History of the Third Dynasty of Vijayanagara,* Madras, 1935. He argued on the basis of Nuniz and Paes account and failed to notice inscriptions which contradicted his view. The notion of Asiatic mode of production with its basis on the idea of property in land being absent is set aside with the findings of emergence of private property in land. At the same time absolute property existed in land will have to ignore the various shades of right that different sets of people enjoyed on the same piece of land, a situation of what social anthropologists called multiplicity of rights. See Dharma Kumar, "Private Property in Asia? The case of Medieval South India", *Comparative Studies in History and Society,* vol. 27, No.1, April 1985, pp. 340-66; See Arivilimangalam copper plate inscriptions of Srirangaraya dated AD 1577 in *E.I.,* XII, pp. 340-58; Karashima traced the emergence of private property in the river Cauvery valley of Coromandel between eleventh and thirteenth centuries, N. Karashima, *Socio-cultural changes in village in Tiruchirapalli district,* Institute of the School of Languages and Culture of Asia and Africa, Tokyo, 1983.
10. Krishnadevaraya donated eighty-two villages to Chidambaram temple. *A.R.E.* 2 of 1935-36. Achyutadevaraya donated sixty-four villages to the same temple. See Balasubramanyam, "Chidambaram Inscription of Achyutadevaraya", *Journal of Oriental Research,* vol. XII, pp. 169-78. Sadasivaraya donated thirty-one villages to Sriperumbudur temple, *E.I.,* vol. IV, pp. 5-6. Achyutadevaraya donated fourteen villages to Varadarajaswamy temple of Kanchipuram, *A.R.E.,* 384 of 1919. Further Srirangam temple had 292 villages, Tirupati temple had 187 villages. See V. Harirao, *History of Srirangam Temple,* Tirupati, 1976; Burton Stein, *Vijayanagara,* Cambridge, 1990, p. 90.
11. Sadhu Subrahmanya Sastry, *Tirumala-Tirupati Devasthanam Epigraphical Report Series,* vol. III, No. 142, Madras, 1935, pp. 299-301. The extent of land was 1600 *kuzhi* in extent.
12. *South Indian Inscriptions* (hereafter *S.I.I.*), vol. XXIII, p. 184; *Annual Report on Epigraphy*, 271 of 1907.
13. *A.R.E.,* 269 of 1921.
14. Ibid., 88 of 1942-43 (1552).
15. Ibid., 386 of 1916 (1578). This reference deals with a land grant to a shepherd.
16. Ibid., 99 of 1932.
17. Ibid., 346 of 1923-24 (1563). See also *A.R.E.* 356 of 1911.
18. *S.I.T.I.,* vol. I, pp. 317-18.
19. *A.R.E.,* 285 of 1928-29.
20. Peter Granda, "Gift after Purchase in Vijayanagar period", in *Journal of the Epigraphical Society of India,* VI, 1976, pp. 25-31; on Srirangam, *A.R.E.,* 58 of 1937, 97 of 1937, 35 of 1939, 92 of 1939, 36 of 1938-39 (1534) 97 of 1939, 155 of 1939, 288 of 1951, 321 of 1951 (1508) and 342 of 1951; on Kanchipuram, see *A.R.E.,* 657 of 1919 (1555), 158 of 1919 (1516),

668 of 1919 (1517), *S.I.T.I.*, vol. I, 346 (1521); on Tirupati *T.T.D.E.S.*, vol. IV, 161, V, 66; on isolated villages, *A.R.E.*, 211 of 1942.

21. *A.R.E.*, 354 of 1912 line two of the transcript runs as follows *"Ulavu kaniyatchi silasanam Pannikuduthapadi"*; *A.R.E.*, 67 of 1935, *S.I.I.*, vol. VIII, No. 113, 352 of 1912 (1519); Srinivasan, *Tiruvannamalai Temple Inscriptions* (hereafter *TVMTI*), Nos. 379 and 402, Pondicherry, 1990. Kudiyiruppu refers to residence and Palatalai probably suggests multiple rights in land existed in the Coromandel region. The inscriptions of Pandya *mandalam* in this period refer to *Ilanginai Kaniyatchi, Tiruvali Kaniyatchi, Tirupattu Kaniyatchi, Kankani Kaniyatchi and Kanakku Kaniyatchi.* Terms such as *Ilanginai* refers to royal seal, *Tiruvali* means *pooja* and festival, *Kankani* relates to supervision. *A.R.E.*, 617 of 1918 (1561), 597 of 1918 (1572), 598 of 1918 (1572); Gopinatha Rao, *Travancore Archaeological Series* (hereafter *T.A.S.)*, vol. I, Madras, 1910, p. 277; Transcript lines 11-12, 494 of 1918 (1567) and 497 of 1918 (1567).
22. Ibid., 269 of 1921 and 354 of 1912; *T.T.D.E.S.*, vol. V, Nos. 84, 98, 139 and 352.
23. Ibid., 356 of 1912. Transcript line 5. The text runs as follows: *"Tirumalai Nayakar Kumarar Ayyan Kumarar Kalatiswara Nayakar Ayyanukku Kaniyatchi Pannikuduthapadi Nanjai Kuzhi Ayiram Inda Vagaippadi Sudandiram Undanathellam Kaniyatchiyaga Pannikuduthom"*.
24. Ibid., 321 of 1921 (1521), 325 and 333 of 1921 (1522).
25. Ibid., 31 of 1921.
26. *TVMTI*, No. 429; *S.I.I.*, VIII, No. 113; *A.R.E.*, 71 of 1945-46.
27. *A.R.E.*, 70 of 1938-39 (1534).
28. Ibid., 67 of 1934-35 (1548); *S.I.I.*, XVII 263, VII 398 and 750; *A.R.E.*, 321 of 1922, 305 of 1928-29 and 235 of 1934-35.
29. Ibid., 512 of 1912 (1540), 10 of 1913 (1586) and 191 of 1938-39 (1592).
30. Ibid., 441 of 1919.
31. Ibid.
32. *A.R.E.*, 334 of 1954-55.
33. Ibid., 306 of 1910 (1527); Burton Stein, *Peasant State and Society in Medieval South India*, p. 83.
34. *T.T.D.E.S.*, vol. III, No. 91 (1514).
35. *A.R.E.*, 226 of 1913.
36. Heitzman suggests that the *melvaram* denoted the share of the State in the produce of land in Vijayanagara inscriptions; *A.R.E.*, 655 of 1909-10, *S.I.T.I.*, vol. I, No. 389, pp. 372-73.
37. Ibid., 66 of 1915.
38. Ibid., 655 of 1909-10.
39. T.K.T. Viraragavacharya, *History of Tirupati*, Tirupati, 1953, p. 21.
40. Burton Stein, *All the Kings Mana, Papers in Medieval South Indian History*, Madras, 1984, pp. 68-69.
41. *A.R.E.*, 274 of 1901.
42. Ibid., 62 of 1934-35 (1507).
43. Ibid., 403 of 1914.
44. Ibid., 92 of 1940-41 (1513)
45. N. Karashima, "Nayaka Rule", fn. 24.
46. *A.R.E.*, 92 of 1940-41 (1513).

47. Ibid., 352 of 1912 (1519).
48. Ibid., 92 of 1940-41 and 352 of 1912.
49. *S.I.I.,* vol. VIII, No. 113.
50. *Ner Payir Vilai, Nelluyara Kudiuyarum.*
51. *Kunirumbineer Kuraithari Kurmayir Kodupoya Menivanduyar Karaiyenappon Pala Veindu Neerina Karuppa kattinarrelittuvai Neetha Tuniratha Ner Pandiyir Parpala thoguppar.*
52. Gasper Correa, *Lendas da India* (4 vols.), vol. V, Lisboa, 1858-64, pp. 593-97.
53. Ludovico di Varthema, *The Itinerary of Ludovico di Varthema of Bologna from 1502 to 1508,* London, 1928, p. 195.
54. *T.T.D.E.S.,* III, No. 119 (1517).
55. Ibid.
56. *A.R.E.*, 587 of 1915.
57. *S.I.I.,* vol. III, No. 151.
58. Duarte Barbosa, *The Book of Duarte Barbosa,* New Delhi, 1989, vol. I, p. 192; ANTT, MSS. *Corpo Cronologico* (hereafter *C.C.),* Maco 15, Document 129 (6 November 1508) and Maco 41, Document 144 (7 September 1513).
59. A.B. de Braganca Pereira, *Arquivo Portugues Oriental* (hereafter *A.P.O.* - BP), Tomo IV, vol. II, Pt. I, Bastora, 1937, p. 317.
60. *A.R.E.*, 78 of 1931-32 (1429).
61. *Kaniyai Vitru Karisalai Vangu.*
62. *S.I.I.,* vol. XXIV; *A.R.E.,* 15 of 1936-37.
63. *A.R.E.,* 59 of 1914. It is possible that cotton plants were raised mixed along with cultivation of rice and millet in the field which proves the mention of *Nellu Parutti,* and *Varaku Parutti* in the epigraphs. The term *Tani Parutti* shows that cotton was also cultivated separately in the fields.
64. Ibid., 103 of 1918 (1404).
65. Ibid.
66. *A.R.E.,* 655 of 1919.
67. K.R. Srinivasan, *Inscriptions in the Pudukottai State* (hereafter *I.P.S.)*, No. 722, Pudukottai, 1941 and 1946.
68. *T.V.M.T.I.,* No. 440.
69. *I.P.S.,* No. 722.
70. *A.R.E.*, 420 of 1913 (1505)
71. Ibid., 607 of 1919.
72. *Yellukku Yelu ulavu uludum Kettan, Yelu Vidichu Visiyum Kettan.*
73. Vasundhara Filliozat, *The Vijayanagar Empire,* New Delhi, 1980, p. 20.
74. *A.R.E.,* 375 of 1953-54, 354 of 1953-54, 98 of 1939-40, 107 of 1947-48, 189 of 1904 and 355 of 1912; *S.I.I.,* vol. XXIV, pp. 325 and 359; *S.I.T.I.,* vol. I, pp. 40-41 and 76-77.
75. Ibid., 354 of 1953-54 and 98 of 139-40; *S.I.I.,* XXIV, p. 359 and vol. XVI, No. 131; *S.I.T.I.,* vol. I, pp. 40-41, 76-77 and 113.
76. Ibid., 288 of 1978-79, 237 of 1903, 192 of 1951-52, 334 of 1954-55; *T.T.D.E.S.,* vol. III, pp. 103-108 and 213; *S.I.T.I.,* vol. I, pp. 34-35; *S.I.I.,* XVI, pp. 178-79.
77. *S.I.T.I.,* vol. I, pp. 40-41 and vol. II, p. 749.
78. *A.R.E.,* 354 of 1953-54, 375 of 1953-54 and 107 of 1947-48.

79. Ibid., 8 of 1921-22.
80. Ibid., 199 of 1940-41 (1512).
81. *S.I.T.I.*, vol. I, pp. 40-41.
82. *S.I.I.*, XVII, pp. 325-326; *A.R.E.*, 354 of 1912.
83. *T.T.D.E.S.*, vol. IV, No. 107 and vol. V, No. 85-A.
84. *A.R.E.*, 216 of 1917, 78 of 1931-32 and 51 of 1914.
85. Sadhu Subrahmanya Sastry, *Report on the Inscriptions of Tirumala Tirupati Devasthanam*, No. 56-A, Tirupati, 1930, p. 32.
86. *A.R.E.*, 448 of 1922 and 563 of 1912 (1511).
87. Ibid., 199 of 1940-41 (1512). This reference mentions that the amount fixed was four *panams*.
88. Ibid., 516 of 1912.
89. Ibid., 259 of 1927; *S.I.T.I.*, vol. II, p. 570. This inscription has the word *Bhagyesaya* at the beginning. It is a chronogram in the *Katapayadhi* system of giving date in Saka 1514 which corresponds to A.D. 1592
90. *T.V.M.T.I.*, No. 379.
91. *T.T.D.E.S.*, vol. III, No. 103, p. 211; Vadamalai annagal, a resident of Nagalapuram paid money for reclamation of land at Mudiyur village in 1515.
92. *A.R.E.*, 367 of 1912.
93. Ibid., 177 of 1903, line 15, 563 of 1902 (1511) line five of the text runs as follows: "*Viruppadervarudaya Kaniparru ana Virasingadevar Karandapil Punjai Nilathil Ayiram Kuzhi Thammudaya Kaiyil diraviyam ittu Tiruttikondu* Anupavikka".
94. *T.T.D.E.S.*, vol. III, pp. 16-18, No. 611, pp. 246-56, No. 276, pp. 11-14.
95. Ibid., 45 of 1935 (1518) and 168 of 1930.
96. *A.R.E.*, 149 of 1941-42 (1560).
97. Ibid., 52 of 1934 (1553).
98. Ibid., 470 of 1938.
99. Ibid., 81 of 1943.
100. Brian Murton, "Some propositions on the spread of village settlement in interior Tamil Nadu before A.D. 1750 " in *Indian Geographical Journal*, vol. XLVIII, Dec. 1973, No. 2, p. 58.
101. *I.P.S.*, No. 727 (1526), 731 (1514), 736 (1522), 743 (1519) and 745 (1530); *T.T.D.E.S.*, vol. I, p. 202, vol. V, p. 37, 1514, vol. III, pp. 17, 30, 52, 90 and 118; *A.R.E.*, 658 of 1919 and 613 of 1919.
102. *A.R.E.*, 46 of 1921, 312 of 1922 and 270 of 1916; *S.I.I.*, vol. XVI, p. 295; *A.R.E.*, 416 of 1920 and 433 of 1920.
103. *S.I.I.*, vol. XVII, p. 263.
104. *A.R.E.*, 353 of 1912 (1514).
105. Ibid., 307 of 1921.
106. Ibid., 56 of 1913 (Krishnadevaraya period).
107. Ibid., 367 of 1921 (1530) and 389 of 1912 (1514).
108. Ibid., 353 of 1912.
109. Ibid., 354 of 1912 and 368 of 1912; N. Karashima, *South Indian History and Society: Studies from Inscriptions AD 850-1800*, Delhi, 1984, pp. 162-63.
110. N. Karashima, *South Indian History*, p. 164.

111. *A.R.E.*, 353 of 1912 (1519), 354 of 1912 (1505), 383 of 1912; *T.T.D.E.S.*, vol. II, p. 24, vol. VI, p. 139 & vol. V, p. 183 (1546), Line five of the epigraphical text runs *"Sandhadhiyadi varai Ulavadi Kaniyatchiyaga Anupavittu Kondu"*; Sadhu Subrahmanya Sastry, op. cit., pp. 245-74; *A.R.E.*, 368 of 1912.
112. *T.V.M.T.I.*, No. 381 (1509); *A.R.E.*, 367 of 1912 (1530).
113. *A.R.E.*, 394 of 1912. Transcript lines four and five runs as follows: *"Kinarum vetti Kalaniym Tiruti Payir Seidu Kollakkadavaragavum"*. The word *Kinaru, Kinarru Nir Piratti* is found very frequently in the Tiruvannamalai region. See *T.V.M.T.I.*, No. 375 (1506), 379 (1508), 392 (1519), 395 (1532).
114. Ibid., 388 of 1912.
115. Ibid., 387 of 1912.
116. *T.T.D.E.S.*, vol. III, pp. 1-3.
117. Ibid., vol. IV, pp. 74 and 105-6.
118. Ibid., vol. III, pp. 103-8.
119. Ibid., vol. IV, pp. 150-51.
120. M. Rama Rao, *Telugu inscriptions of Andhra Desa*, Tirupati, 1969, vol. I, Pt. I, No. 891 (1592); *A.R.E.*, 388 of 1916 (B).
121. Burton Stein, *Peasant State*, p. 426.
122. *A.R.E.*, 179 of 1913 (1533), 94 of 1913 and 388 of 1916(b).
123. Ibid., 145 of 1924.
124. Ibid., 194 of 1921 and 64 of 1942.
125. Ibid., 183 of 1921-22.
126. *S.I.T.I.*, vol. I, p. 342 (1549) and p. 339 (1541). The Kanchipuram inscriptional text runs *"Vittavan Vilukkadu Nalil Onrukku"*.
127. *T.T.D.E.S.*, vol. IV, pp. 264-65.
128. Ibid., No. 72, 74 and 93, V, No. 88, III, No. 157 and 159.
129. *A.R.E.*, 39 of 1897 (1580).
130. The Inscriptions are found during the years of 1514, 1519 and 1533 A.D.
131. *E.I.*, vol. XII, p. 343; *A.R.E.*, 426 of 1924.
132. *A.R.E.*, 54 of 1934-35 (1507).
133. Ibid., 119 of 1931 (1588).
134. Ibid., 251 of 1904.
135. *S.I.T.I.*, vol. I, pp. 43-44.
136. *A.R.E.*, 177 of 1941-42.
137. *Epigraphia Carnatica* (hereafter E.C.), vol. X, Bangalore, 1905, Gb. 6.
138. *T.T.D.E.S.*, vol. II, pp. 329-32 (1504).
139. N. Venkataramanaya, op. cit., p. 187.
140. *T.T.D.E.S.*, vol. I, No. 224.
141. *A.R.E.*, 16 of 1938-39 (1533).
142. Ibid., 9 of 1922.
143. Ibid., 265 of 1936-37 (1532).
144. Ibid., 247 of 1916 (1504-1505), line eight of the transcript of the inscription runs, *"Varusham varusham thorum Nilam Alanthu"*.
145. Ibid., 10 of 1922-23 (Krishnadevaraya period).
146. Ibid., 247 of 1916 (C).
147. Sadhu Subrahmanya Sastry, op. cit., pp. 248-49.
148. *A.R.E.*, 291 of 1940; *T.T.D.E.S.*, vol. III, No. 142, pp. 299-301 (1520).

149. Ibid., 181 of 1942-43 and 184 of 1942-43.
150. Ibid., 58 of 1947-48.
151. Ibid., 247 of 1916 (1504) and 266 of 1939-40.
152. *S.I.I.*, vol. XIII, p. 379 (1573). Some references also point out that *veli* was used in other regions. Please see V. Rangachari, *A Topographical List of Inscriptions of the Madras Presidency* (hereafter *I.M.P.)*, vol. I, Madras, 1917, p. 523.
153. *A.R.E.*, 259 of 1930, 199 of 1940-41, 355 of 1912 and 395 of 1912.
154. *S.I.I.*, vol. XVI, No. 8.
155. *A.R.E.*, 31 of 1933-34 (1540).
156. Ibid., 247 of 1916 (C).
157. *T.V.M.T.I.*, No. S. 28, pp. 611-12.
158. *A.R.E.*, 352 of 1912, 353 of 1912, 358 of 1912, 312 of 1922 (1552), 48 of 1916 and 49 of 1916 (1537).
159. Ibid., 389 of 1912.
160. Ibid., 199 of 1940-41 (1512).
161. *S.I.T.I.*, vol. I, pp. 372-73; *A.R.E.*, 54 of 1914 and 655 of 1910. An epigraph of Krishnadevaraya period at Koyilanur mentions *Tenna-marathu vari* called tax on coconut trees in Villupuram region; *S.I.I.*, vol. VI, No. 72, p. 39.
162. *A.R.E.*, 54 of 1914 and 1915, para 44, fn. I.
163. Ibid., 246 of 1916.
164. *I.P.S.*, No. 711.
165. S. Krishnaswami Aiyangar, *Sources of Vijayanagar History*, Madras, 1919, p. 130.
166. *E.I.*, XXI, No. 19, p. 119; *A.R.E.*, 335 of 1921 and 452 of 1921.
167. *T.T.D.E.S.*, vol. I, 200, II 18, III 66-68; vol. II 18, III 66-68, 70, 75, 91 and 217.
168. Inscriptional texts mention *Palavakaiyilakira Mutal*. See *T.V.M.T.I.*, No. 379 (1508). *Palanelvarkattilakira Mutalum, Pala Tanniyavarkattilakira Mutal*, see *T.V.M.T.I.*, No. 408 (1539-40); No. 416 (1551), No. 417 (1551).
169. *A.R.E.*, 112 of 1942-43 (1575).
170. Ibid., 96 of 1918.
171. Ibid., 189 of 1922 (C) (1590).
172. Ibid., 259 of 1917 and 178 of 1926.
173. *E.I.*, XXIII, p. 199 (1531).
174. *T.V.M.T.I.*, 403, 406 and 407.
175. *S.I.I.*, vol. IV, No. 245 and vol. IX, Pt. II, No. 583.
176. Ibid., vol. XVII, p. 326 (1524).
177. *S.I.T.I.*, vol. II, p. 927.
178. Ibid., vol. I, p. 355. The text of the Kanchipuram inscription runs *"Nangellai Kalilum Tiruvalikal natti"*. On Srirangam please see, *S.I.I.*, vol. XXIV, No. 326, p. 359; *S.I.I.*, vol. IX, Pt. II, No. 440.
179. See C.T. Kotraiah, "Land Boundary Stones", *Journal of the Epigraphical Society of India* (hereafter *J.E.S.I.)*. Also see *Chronological List of Inscriptions of Pudukottai State*, 1929, p. 101.
180. *A.R.E.*, 129 of 1914.
181. *S.I.I.*, vol. IX, Pt. II, No. 526 (1529). The author thanks Dr. Vasundhara

Filliozat for the original Kannada Inscriptional translation. See also *A.R.E.*, 619 of 1904.

182. Ibid., vol. V, No. 704, (1544); *S.I.T.I.*, vol. III, pp. 1138-39; *A.R.E.*, 140 of 1895; see also *Tiruvidaimarudur Kalvettugal*, Tiruvidaimarudur, 1960. The text informs that *Koildevakanmi Tiruchitrambala-bhattar* reported the matter to the Vijayanagara emperor regarding misappropriation of temple lands.
183. *A.R.E.*, 264 of 1930 (1540).
184. *S.I.T.I.*, vol. III, pp. 1138-39 (1544).
185. Ibid., vol. III, Pt. II, pp. 191-92 (Sadasivaraya period).
186. *A.R.E.*, 403 of 1925-29 and 294 of 1910 (Ponnur, Wandiwash taluk).
187. Ibid., 412 of 1913.
188. Immanuel Wallerstein, *The Modern World System: Capitalist Agriculture and the Origins of European World Economy in the Sixteenth Century*, New York, 1974. Andre Gunder Frank, *Capitalism and Underdevelopment in Latin America*, New York, 1969.
189. Irfan Habib, *The Agrarian System of Mughal India, 1556-1707*, Bombay, 1963.
190. For detailed arguments on constructive effects on agriculture through revenue farming, see Andre Wink, *Land and Sovereignty in India: Agrarian Society and Politics under the Eighteenth Century Maratha Svarajya*, Cambridge, 1986, pp. 341-42 and "Maratha Revenue Farming" in *Modern Asian Studies* (hereafter *M.A.S.*), vol. XVII (4), 1983, pp. 591-628.

# 3

# Craft Economy of the Hinterland and the Coast

It has been generally pointed out that craft production in India expanded during the sixteenth century.[1] But a recent study of Tamil country under Vijayanagara, on the ground that less number of inscriptional terms related to craft economy were found at Thanjavur and Trichy *uchavadis* than in the Padaividu *rajya* and Valudilampattu *uchavadi* of Coromandel,[2] suggests that an uneven presence of terms related to industry is indicative of uneven growth of manufacturing. This is difficult to accept.

It also seems incorrect that increased agrarian concentration affected crafts. In fact inscriptions of Cauvery delta mention that crafts like weaving flourished at Tirupullanam, Tillaisthanam, Konerirajapuram, Tiruvidaimarudur, Achutamangalam, Tripattavellur, Nathamangudi, Kandiraditham, Kamarasavalli, Gangaikondacholapuram, Tiruvaigavur, Tiruvalanjuli, Tiruvenkadu, Tirunaithanam, Tirukannapuram, Thanjavur, Kapisthalam and Vedaranyam.[3] An analysis of the inscriptions regarding centres of manufacture, types of products, taxation, availability of raw materials for growth of crafts, patronage provided by rulers and temples for survival of crafts will show that an increase in internal and external demand brought about an expansion in production and enhanced the status and position of weavers.

## TEXTILE VARIETIES AND WEAVING CENTRES

Coromandel was major textile producing area, the others being Cambay and Bengal. Yarn of different materials was used, generally distinguished as cotton or silk. A Tamil literary source describes the process of ginning. The ginned cotton was further scutched with a stick. The possibility of the breaking of fibres due to scutching was averted with the use of the carder's bow.[4] The yarn was spun around spindles and the cloth woven in the

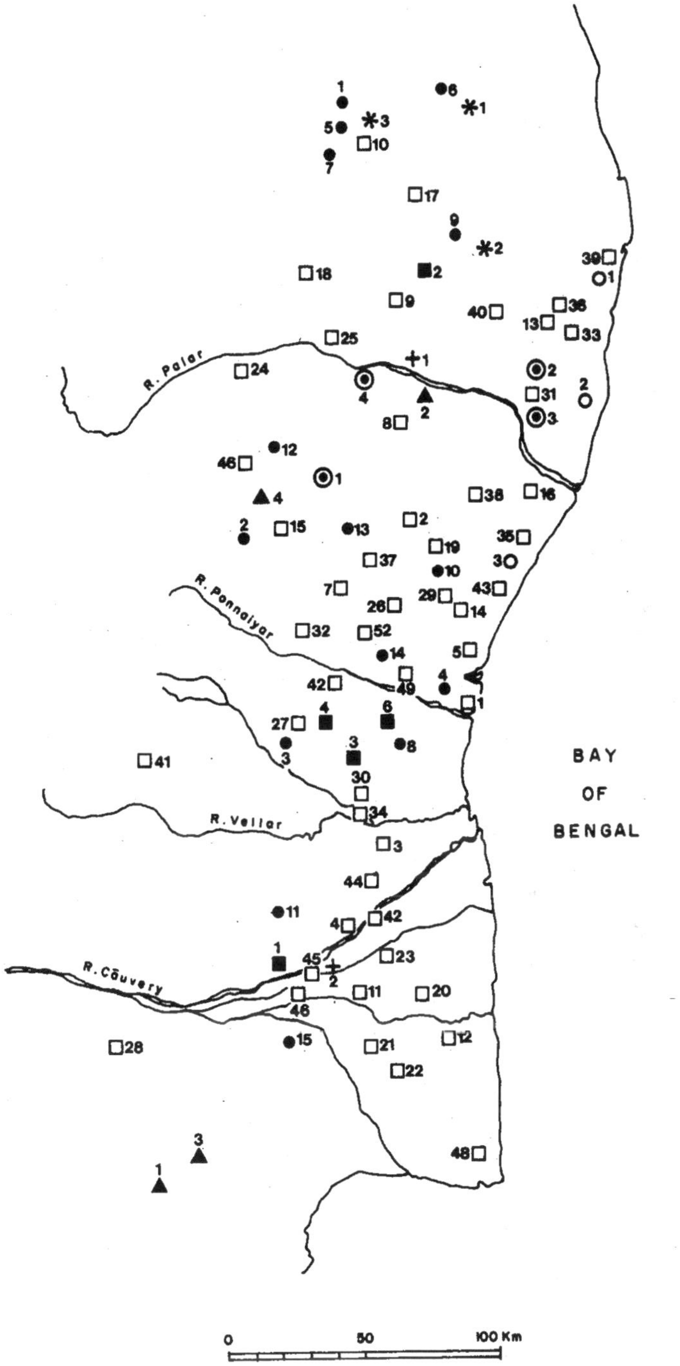


MAP 2. COROMANDEL: CRAFT PRODUCTION CENTRES, 1500-1600

(For details see page 228)

looms. The woven cloth was bleached and washed.

Cloth of various designs was manufactured. A Tamil literary source describes some delicate designs resembling the slough of a snake.[5] Cloth varieties were specialised depending on the place of manufacture and were often named after the place of production and the cloth used in weaving. The Portuguese used the word *panos* (lit.: a piece of cloth with the breadth and length of a petticoat) for medium quality cloth of linen or cotton. There were various sizes with differing yarn counts and types such as printed, stripped, plain and spotted.

Patterned cloth (*pintados* in Portuguese) was the best known, trade in it having been standardised long before the Portuguese came to Coromandel.[6] Patterned cloth could be printed or painted. The patterning was done during the dyeing after weaving,[7] with blocks having a design on a cut or raised relief. An outline pricked through with a fine point was laid on the cloth, which was then treated with a small charcoal filled bag to register the design. The cloth was next painted. More painted cloths were probably produced by block printing.

Chintz was the best known patterned textile of Coromandel, the word chintz itself being a derivative of the vernacular *chitta* or spotted cloth famous in the area. Chintzes produced in the neighbourhood of Masulipatnam and Petapoli were brought to the ports of Pulicat and Santhome on the Coromandel coast for trade with South-East Asia during the first half of the sixteenth century. Printed chintzes of Pulicat were in great demand in Malacca, Achin and Bantam.[8] The patterned cloth of Santhome also fetched a good market in the Malay archipelago.[9]

Coromandel plain cloth was either calico or muslin. Calico of various grades was produced, the best being the smaller fabrics, described as densely woven cotton patches. Some of them were set with mirror work. Ordinary calico came next, of the same size as long cloth, some of the varieties being a fine type with a higher yarn count.[10] Blue calico, called *morin* in the Portuguese sources (*nilakachchai* in Tamil)[11] came third. Indigo was commonly used in dyeing. Most calicoes were merely washed and bleached, though a few were painted.[12] Pulicat was the entrepot for wax-resistant calicoes of Coromandel.[13] *Putavai* was a common and coarse calico, generally thirty-five yards long.[14] The coarsest was *permudichchilai,* generally twelve yards long, probably a stout cloth used for sail making and packing.[15]

Among the muslins of Coromandel were white muslins used for turbans, called *tapis* in Portuguese, veil cloth called *beatilha* in Portuguese, and red muslins.[16]

There are also references to silk in epigraphs. *Pattu,* the Tamil word for silk, indicates mulberry silk produced by silkworms. Late twelfth century Chinese sources mention that mulberry trees were grown in the Chola kingdom and coloured silk threads were woven into cloth and exported from the ports.[17] Caesar de Federici, the Italian traveller during 1560, also observed that silkworm was grown in Coromandel and the tussah hung from the plant.[18] The silk yarn was dyed in different colours, woven into cloth that displayed patterns of flowers, and cut into pieces measuring about five feet by thirteen feet, which were very expensive.[19] Linschoten, another traveller of the sixteenth century to the Coromandel region, records that sarees called *sarasas* or *sarangs* were made of cloth interwoven with gold and silver thread.[20] Kanchipuram, Devikapuram and Nerumbur were some of the leading manufacturing centres of silk textiles. The fame of Kanchipuram is further established from the Madras Museum copper plates.[21] *Pattu selai, manchetti selai, ponneluthu selai, pattavalipattu* and *sallapattu* were manufactured at Kanchipuram during 1532 and 1586,[22] which have an affinity to the inscriptional term *pattu vargam* referring to silk saree or silk cloth.[23] These rich ornamental silk varieties, called *patolas,* had no reverse side.

In a pioneering study on the history of weaving, Vijaya Ramaswamy had identified and catalogued seventy-four medieval textile centres in Tamil Nadu between the eleventh and fifteenth centuries.[24] As in previous times, textile industry continued to flourish in many weaving villages during the sixteenth century as well. Tiruvennainallur, Srimushnam, Kanchipuram, Anniyur, Tiruchengattankudi, Omalur, Tiruppangadu, Tiruchengodu and Iraivasanallur were leading centres of textile manufacture.[25]

A cluster of new weaving centres sprang up in Coromandel,[26] possibly on account of the heavy demand for exports to South and South-East Asia by the Portuguese. *Nayakas* reclaimed forest lands and encouraged the formation of new settlements of weavers. Colonisation of *kaikolars* was duly encouraged by tax-free provision for periods ranging between one and six years, where we find references to weaving.[27] Tirubhuvanai, Naduvak-karai and Nenmalai were some of the new settlements of weavers which emerged in the hinterland of the port of Kunimedu during the sixteenth century.[28]

There was a tendency of weavers of a particular category to concentrate at some centres on account of sponsorship by various temples. *Kaikola* weavers were one such category attracted with privileges to settle down in sites owned by the temples.[29] Lands were assigned by Perumukil *nayaka* for raising *tirumadaivilagam* at Mangadu village during Achyutadevaraya's reign.[30] The term *tirumadaivilagam* literally meant temple square but in the wider sense it referred to the sites owned by the temples, where weavers had settled in the streets around temples.[31] Various such streets, generally called *perunderuvu* which meant large streets where many looms functioned are mentioned in epigraphs. These settlements of weavers, besides enhancing temple revenue, connected the temple neighbourhood with the main centre. Weavers' settlements in the *madaivilagam* of the temples at Pennadam, Marakkanam, Nerkunram, Devanur, Edaiyanur, Pulliparakoyil, Tiruvadigai, Tiruvottiyur, Anniyur, Tellar, Sriperumbudur, Srimushnam and Attur are mentioned in epigraphs.[32]

The privileges offered by temples to the weavers to settle on temple lands were diverse. Some obtained the rights to manage the lands in the temple villages.[33] Others received land from the temples for building their houses on condition that they supplied textiles.[34] We find the practice of some offerings made by these *madaivilagam* weavers to temples. An order of Tirumalainambi describes the agent of Tirumalai Khumbati Tatacharya, the temple supervisor, who requested *padinda kanikkai*, literally known as registered offerings payable to the temple treasury from the weavers of Manampadi village.[35] Similarly, the *sthanattar* of Tiruvannamalai temple asked the weavers to donate a portion of the income from one handloom to god Anandapillaiyar, and from two handlooms for maintaining flower gardens of the temple during 1574.[36] It would appear from these epigraphs that the temple income substantially increased through weavers' settlements.

## TAXATION AND TEXTILE TECHNOLOGY

Taxes on looms are generally called *tarikadamai* in the inscriptions.[37] They were levied only on working looms, dormant ones being exempt.[38] Whenever rulers attempted to increase the loom tax, weavers deserted in large groups, and the rulers had to backtrack.[39]

During the fifteenth century, temple authorities collected loom taxes at places such as Tiruppanangadu, Kanchipuram, etc.[40] But inscriptions of the sixteenth century mention collection of loom taxes by *nayakas* alone. This change meant that the rulers were superior to the temples and government had the exclusive right to collect taxes. The Tirchengattankudi inscription records that the *nayaka* fixed the taxes on looms in Nannilam area during the sixteenth century.[41] Manampadi records also state that the tax rates on weavers were fixed by officials appointed by *nayaka* in consultation with the local people.[42] Vinaitirtarpillai, the local ruler, regulated loom taxes at Valangaiman in Thanjavur region.[43] Muthuraja Isuvappayan, another ruler, donated the loom taxes collected from village Kilapalayam, a hamlet of Iraivasanallur, to the local temple.[44] Vengappayan, the *pradhani* of Surappa *nayaka* appointed Gangarayan, a *kaikkolamudali*, as the *pidaram* of the village; he was allowed to run looms free of tax at Iraivasanallur during 1535.[45] In 1574, *nayakas* deprived the weavers of South Arcot district of their privileges as regards handloom tax.[46] From the above, it is concluded that *nayakas* above all controlled weaving in Coromandel.

Loom taxes, originally assigned to the temples, were in many cases transferred by rulers to the state during the sixteenth century. *Nayakas* directly collected loom taxes and few of them gifted the collection to the temples. The resulting reduction in revenue[47] prompted the temples to request the *madaivilagam* weavers for payment of offerings.

The levy of loom tax in the region consisted of a minimum of one and a quarter *panam* and a maximum of six *panam*. The average standard rate was three *panam* per annum. The towns of Vrinchipuram and Kanchipuram emerged as centres of large-scale textile manufacture; the highest rates of loom taxes, six and five and a half *panam* respectively, were collected here. In the fifteenth century, the loom tax ranged between a minimum of quarter *panam*[48] and a maximum of one and a half *panam*.[49] Also, monthly collection of loom tax, which was prevalent in the Tirukachiyur and Tiruvâkkarai regions during the fifteenth century,[50] seems to have been given up in favour of an annual collection. The change probably came about with the advent of annual payment of revenue by *nayakas* to Vijayanagara rulers.[51] Therefore, we may surmise that *nayakas* increased the rate of loom tax and thoroughly changed the mode of collection.

Textile-dyeing centres existed at Devikapuram, Tiruppanangadu, Kulathur and Manimangalam.[52] The word *pattadai* occurring in the inscriptional texts literally means workshop.[53] We find mention of *ur pattadai* (village workshop), *chillarai pattadai* (retail workshop),[54] *chekku pattadai* (oil workshop) and *cakkili pattadai* (leather workshop).[55] *Pattadai* used as a prefix to *nulayam* shows that revenue tax on yarn was levied from *pattadai*. Taxes on textile dyeing units were collected from *vyaparis* and *chetti* merchants who owned the dyeing centres.[56] *Pattadai nulayam* taxes were collected from dyeing centres by order of *nayakas* in Coromandel.[57] *Nulayam* was a common levy, particularly referring to tax on thread. These taxes could be possibly related to the flourishing weaving controlled by *nayakas*. *Padinda kanikai* was offering by weavers to the temples, generally made from *madaivilagam* looms. Thus taxes other than *tarikadamai* were levied on weavers.

According to the Tamil literary source *Senguntar Kummi*, in the fifteenth century, patterned horizontal loom was used for figured weaving called *pukkatu* in Tamil country.[58] Although references to *kombu tari*[59] and *chattit tari*[60] are found in epigraphs, it is difficult to suggest the nature of these looms. In the sixteenth century there was a technological change from the patterned loom to a draw loom.[61] The terms *sadirasakkudam* and *achukattu* literally mean a four-cornered frame and bunch of cords used in this particular type of weaving; in other words, a draw loom. It is also mentioned that this particular type of weaving with specific number of *pujams* and threads ranging from 60 to 120 was a monopoly of Muslim weavers.[62] Possibly, the growing demand for textiles necessitated the invention of the drawloom, which is associated with the Islamic culture newly introduced during the sixteenth century.

Huge brick vats were used for dyeing cloth. Various colours were used in dyeing. Portuguese sources record that lac from Pegu was used as a red dye.[63] Scarlet in-grain dye was imported from West Asia to Pulicat.[64] The root of the chang plant, which yielded a fine red dye, was much used. Sapan wood and Brazil wood were also used in dyeing textiles at Santhome and Chandragiri regions.[65]

ORGANISATIONAL CHANGES

Some organisational changes with capitalistic elements may also be noted.[66] Ten looms were kept under a master weaver during 1525. The suffix *mudali* (lit.: chief of the community) found in the inscriptions is a title associated with *kaikolars*, indicating the social predominance they gained by handling *mutal* (capital).[67] Weavers who emerged as merchants attained the suffix *chetti* or *nayakar* in the inscriptions of Kanchipuram and Chidambaram.[68] *Kaikola* weavers as merchants have been suggested in the inscriptional texts, which use the term *kasaya vargatar*.[69] These developments suggest capitalistic relations of production in Coromandel weaving during the sixteenth century.

The dyeing centres in Coromandel were generally owned by many *kaikolars*.[70] Another epigraphic evidence from Kulathur in Chingleput region refers to *kaikola* weavers as *pala pattadaiyar*, which literally implies the owners of many workshops or dyeing centres.[71] Looms were owned by different types of weavers like *saliyar*,[72] *parayar*[73] and *seniyar*.[74] Merchants too owned looms.[75] P. Shanmugam's suggestion that temples possibly owned a few looms during the Vijayanagara period in Tamil country is not borne out by any direct references in epigraphs.[76]

There is a suggestion in the inscriptions to small-scale and large-scale textile production in Coromandel. In an inscription of 1538 from Tirupati there is mention of the greater potential for the emergence of large-scale merchant capital in putting out work to weavers.[77] The inscription suggests that the merchant paid off the worker for his work and sold the work if finished, or put it out for further finishing. The cloth merchants of Tirupati and Kanchipuram had to produce goods to certain specifications,[78] which the weavers could not individually ensure since the operation called for an investment of large capital in such export varieties. The lack of market information with the weavers may have been another factor why they did not venture into independent manufacture for export. In the circumstances the merchants gained control over production through their capacity to control capital by supplying raw materials, and cash advances.[79] This intervention by the merchants to control production and labourers was a significant development in the sixteenth century, which was reversed in the succeeding centuries.

There is an inscription imposing control over weavers, which suggests the strict observance and application of the putting out system, with widespread control exercised by merchants. The inscription contains an injunction to all villages in Tirupati and Kanchipuram regions that the weavers who violated the rule of the monopolistic privilege of weaving of cloth were charged a fine of twelve gold *varahans*.[80] Available evidence on the organisation of textile production is scanty. Therefore, we may agree with Tapan Ray Chaudhuri's view that the organisation of weaving in the Coromandel region during the sixteenth century had not developed into a full-fledged putting out system.[81] The fine mentioned in the inscription is a clear indication that merchants controlled production. A piece of Portuguese evidence corroborates this. It explains that twelve houses of weavers at Pulicat supplied textiles to a Portuguese trader, Luis Mendes de Vasconcellos; and the viceroy permitted him to lay claim to these twelve families when preparing for his voyage from Coromandel to Malacca for trade in textiles in 1547.[82] This sway of merchant capital over production in Coromandel was what Karl Marx called exploitation through trade.[83] The Coromandel merchants' putting out system turned to be an appropriate form for controlling the production of textiles. Their role was not merely to organise production and exchange of goods at interregional and international levels but to engage in capital formation. This local merchant capitalism in a limited way paved the way for societal and commercial changes at an international level.[84]

## MANUFACTURE OF SUGAR, OIL AND SALT

Essential consumer products such as sugar, oil and salt were manufactured in Coromandel. Sugarcane juice was boiled and evaporated to manufacture jaggery. Jaggery (*karuppukatti*) was also made from palmyrah juice and generally formed part of temple offerings.[85] The Portuguese term for sugar, *jagara*, was a derivative of the South Indian *chakkarai,* which meant any unrefined sugar.[86] Duarte Barbosa's account has it that sugar was available as powder and solid chunks.[87] Sugar manufacture flourished on the southern banks of Pennai river,[88] upper valley of river Vellar[89] and Palar basin of Kanchipuram.[90] The compulsory cultivation of sugarcane imposed by Vijayanagara rulers in the upper valley of Vellar river[91] suggests a scarcity of sugar; the imposition was probably made to meet the sugar demand in Coromandel. It is confirmed by Portuguese manuscripts that sugar was imported from Bengal into Coromandel.[92] Sugarcane cultivators were prohibited from carrying sugarcane outside their village. But when people opposed this restriction and threatened to migrate, the rulers relaxed their control. The heavy taxes levied in the manufacture of sugar indicated its demand and scarcity.[93] Chikkaparvata *nayaka* relaxed some of the conditions, removed the excess taxes, and allowed the people to follow their own practice of sugar production.[94] Apparently, as Fernand Braudel says, the commodity market for sugar expanded in India[95] but Coromandel sugar production could not meet the local demand.

Oil was extracted from the seeds of gingelly, castor and linseed cultivated in Coromandel for varied uses, as an item of food, as a cooking medium, and lighting at home and temple.[96] Traditional oil mills, called *chekku* [97] in Tamil, were worked with a pair of bullocks. Oil manufacture flourished at Tiruvannamalai,[98] Tirukalambur,[99] Ponnarur,[100] Tirumayam[101] and Kanchipuram[102] and it was taxed by *nayakas*. An order of a *nayaka* describing the taxes levied on the producers of oil at Kanchipuram mentions villages exempted from the tax.[103] Narasa *nayaka* remitted the tax on oil mills to the local people.[104] Some *nayakas* ordered the supply of oil to the local temples; the unit of measurement was *kurumban marakkal*, which was equal to four *nali*.[105] Hence it is surmised that *nayakas* controlled the agro-crafts of sugar and oil production in the hinterland.

Salt was manufactured on the Coromandel coast. Tamil literary evidence suggests that salt was manufactured by allowing the sea water to run into salt pans which was then evaporated by sunlight.[106] The salt crystals thus formed were scraped with a plank and collected into large heaps, covered with straw.[107] The site of salt manufacture was known as *uppalam*. Salt pans existed at various coastal villages of Coromandel such as Tiruvottiyur[108] near Madras, Taiyur[109] near Kovalam in addition to Mahabalipuram[110] in Chingleput district and Marakkanam[111] in South Arcot district. Temples and *mutts* of the coastal villages owned salt producing lands endowed on them by *nayakas* and villagers.[112] These were leased out, with salt producers holding *kudivaram* of salt production and the temples and *mutts* retaining *melvaram*.[113] We have not come across lease deeds specifying various conditions for maintaining the salt pans, but some traces of rules and regulations introduced by *nayakas* to exercise control over salt production exist. An inscriptional text mentions a salt pan called *padampakka nayaka peralam.*[114] The suffix *peralam* denotes a large salt producing centre at the hamlet of Padampakkam near modern Manali, controlled by the *nayaka*. Taxes were collected also on the salt beds by *nayakas* of Coromandel[115] and Namasivaya *nayaka* exempted the salt pans owned by Sivaloganatha *mutt* from tax.[116] Also, Sellappa *nayaka* separated a hamlet from Araiyanseri near modern Kelambakkam in Chingleput district and gave it to Taiyur temple for worship and repair with the proceeds of ten salt pans.[117] One may expect that on account of the overarching control of *nayakas*, the development of crafts suffered.

## METAL, STONE AND WOOD WORKS

Portuguese sources record that iron was available in the hinterland of port of Kunimedu.[118] One may surmise that iron from the mines in the Salem region reached Kunimedu port. Iron was used for manufacturing cannons and cannon balls. It would appear that Ambur and Gudiyattam region had gun foundries famous for manufacture of cannons in Coromandel and individual manufacturers of cannon paid tax on them.[119] An inscription records the remission of cannon tax on an individual belonging to the *anjujati panchalattar* of Kaliyettam *simai* by Akkappa *nayaka*, the *dalavay* of Vijayanagara. The manufacture of cannon in Coromandel is corroborated by three Portuguese manuscripts which mention that the factor and captain of Coromandel coast purchased locally manufactured cannon balls in the hinterland of the port of Pulicat and sent them to Cochin.[120] On 16 August 1524 the Portuguese captain of Coromandel exported 250 cannon balls. The ambassadors from the *Sultan* of Malacca, who visited Coromandel were received by the *shahbhandar* at Nagapattinam with gun salutes, which indicates that Coromandel had developed artillery as well.[121] The Jesuit missionary, Fr. Nicholas Pimenta, who visited Coromandel, notes that large volume of ordnance, powder and shot were available at Gingee.[122] These instances show that the Arms Act was not unknown then and that the weapons of warfare were not allowed to fall into the hands of all and sundry.

Metal works were either smithies or jewelleries. Blacksmiths are called *kollar* and *karumar* in epigraphs. Iron, copper, brass, zinc and tin were generally used in the metal works,[123] for manufacturing vessels of various designs and use, as well as weapons like swords, battle axes, javelins, shafts, bows, arrows and spears. Duarte Barbosa records that copper was used on a large scale for manufacturing cooking pots and vessels.[124] Metal workers were engaged by Tiruvannamalai temple and paid one *panam* from the income of *Malaikaval*.[125] They were also engaged for making brass vessels for Tirupati temple in 1535.[126] Blacksmiths were hired to supply solid iron blocks—*tiruther irumbu mutti*—used to brake the temple car in its progress on ceremonial occasions.[127] Blacksmiths also manufactured bells and gongs used during ceremonies and festivals, a variety of brass lamp stands, bronze idols and metal sheet coverings over the stone steps, *sikharas* and thresholds of temples.[128] *Nayakas* levied a 'furnace tax' called *ulai bhattam* and *ulai kadamai* on the blacksmiths.[129]

Goldsmiths were known as *tattan, nagai asari* and *kammalar* in the Tamil inscriptions. Gasparo Balbi records a settlement of goldsmiths near Santhome in 1582.[130] Among their handiworks were silver and gold plated jewels for the foreheads of war animals, particularly horses and elephants;[131] women's ornaments such as earrings, nose studs, necklaces, bracelets, anklets, with fine coral beads and precious stones;[132] and jewels used for dance and decoration such as *yajnopavita*,[133] *talipadakkam*,[134] *kirta, sankha, chakara* and *abhaya hasta*.[135] Many donated these ornaments to temples. The temples in turn hired goldsmiths from time to time to renew and burnish the old jewels in their treasury. The *sthanattar* of the temple watched over this work and took custody of the repaired jewels.[136] The temples allotted a certain amount of money for repair of their jewels. *Nayakas* levied *thattava bhattam* taxes on goldsmiths.[137]

Sculptors—*silpis, koilsilpis* and *kalthachans*—carried out structural additions, alterations, renovation and repairs to the existing structure of temples, shrines, *gopurams, gopurams* built with *vimana*, flagstaff and stone car (*nilai ter*).[138] They also made new stone idols for the temples when required. Special types of *mantapas* with decorative pillars formed a salient feature of *nayaka* architecture.[139] Accordingly, sculptors were also called *mandapam seppanidugiria al*—people who repaired *mantapas*.[140] Well trained in the architectural traditions and texts, they exercised some freedom from canonical bonds, giving abundant expression to erotic and non-religious themes.[141] Architectural repairs were of ten kinds called *dasa-kriyai*, but details are not available,[142] although we know that sculptors carved stone carvings of the temple from base to top.

Carpenters (*thachan*) were engaged in making and repair of wooden vehicles, the pedestals and poles for carrying the deity in procession and the wooden handles used in the umbrella during the procession. The making of the huge wooden car with exquisite ornamental works was an exacting task.[143] Some carpenters were employed in painting the images of deities in Tirupati temple.[144] A piece of evidence suggests the various rights and privileges granted to carpenters of Tiruvaiyaru temple in Thanjavur district.[145]

Overall, metal, stone and wood works appear to have survived mainly with the patronage extended by temples rather than as independent crafts.

## PRODUCERS' GUILDS

Textile producers of Coromandel formed various communities such as *kaikolars, saliyars, devangars* and *pattunulkars*.[146] *Kaikolars* and *saliyars* were from Tamil-speaking areas. *Devangars* were Telugu speakers who migrated into Tamil country. *Pattunulkars* were from Gujarat and specialised in silk weaving. Each weaving community specialised in a particular type of textile at Kapistalam, Pattiswaram, Anniyur and Villiyanoor.

No direct references are found relating to the association of craftsmen and activities.[147] Some texts indirectly suggest that *kaikolars* and *devangars* assembled at *mantapas* erected after their community names such as *kaikola mandapam* and *devanga pahala mandapam* for meetings of their association.[148] Thus *saliyars* of Kapistalam,[149] *pattunulkars* of Pattiswaram,[150] *devangars* of Anniyur[151] and *kaikolars* of Villiyanoor[152] had an internal self-regulating unit laying down the conditions for production. These self-contained local systems were associations limited to specialised textile production. Not all textile producers of Coromandel were united by guilds: there were workers at home who kept themselves unattached to any organisation.

There were three categories of producers, namely master craftsman, journeyman and apprentice. The apprentice who had learnt the craft was under charge of the journeyman. The supervisor was responsible for producing the masterpiece and trained the journeymen.[153] Reasons such as heavy taxation and migration compelled the producers to unite for defence against the disorders and abuses to which they were victim. Thus objective of the guilds was to safeguard the equal independence of producers and the prosperity of the craftsmen.

Epigraphs refer to producers in metal, stone and wood works singly as *anju-jati-panchalattar.*[154] The earliest references to these five types of craftsmen are found as early as the eleventh century. Some scholars have studied the traditional account regarding their origin and identification under *idangai* caste.[155] *Nayakas* levied taxes such as *kanikkai* and *kattayam* on them.[156] *Kanikkai* was a constant burden on the producers. Many complaints are found in the epigraphs against imposition of *kanikkai*; even property had to be sold to pay up this demand.[157] *Kanikkai* formed a major constituent in a bunch of subsidiary taxes.[158] *Kattayam* also was a heavy burden,[159] and the producers had migrated in protest.[160] Many tax-related grievances of the producers of the place were settled in the presence of *nayakas.*[161] Reacting to widespread migration of producers in protest *nayakas* revised the tax rates and exempted *kammalars* of Villupuram,[162] Tindivanam[163] and Tiruvadigai,[164] goldsmiths of Thanjavur[165] and artisans of Ariyalur.[166] Since increased artisanal production implied growth in the revenues of *nayakattanams, nayakas* gave a privileged social status to the artisans. This strategy had the additional advantage of helping to pay revenue to the Vijayanagara centre. The revolts of producers probably would have led to temporary dislocation of crafts; and the development of craft economy was a decisive turning point in establishing the nature of crafts and craftsmen.

Although goods were manufactured with utility value, they were to some extent aimed at exchange value. There existed a neat professional division among artisans in craft production. Some products were labour-intensive and some capital-intensive. Artisans wanted to safeguard equality of terms of production among their fellow professionals in different parts of Coromandel, which policy was not inimical to growth.

## NOTES AND REFERENCES

1. A.I. Chicherov, (trs.) Don Danemanis, *Indian Economic Development in the 16th-18th Centuries: An Outline History of Crafts and Trade,* Moscow, 1971.
2. Noboru Karashima, Y. Subbarayalu & P. Shanmugam, op. cit., pp. 8 and 20.

3. *A.R.E.*, 144 of 1977-78, 278 of 1911, 627 of 1909, 253 of 1907, 275 of 1978 (1404), 311 of 1968-69, 152 of 1928-29, 203 of 1928-29, 88 of 1914-15, 59 of 1914-15 (1429), 283 of 1911 and 508 of 1922-23; *S.I.I.*, vol. IV, No. 524, vol. III, No. 22, vol. V, No. 176, vol. II, No. 66 and vol. XVII, No. 452; *I.M.P.*, vol. II, No. 996 A (1542).
4. P.V. Somasundaranar, *Agananuru,* Madras, 1974, lines 133-35.
5. P.V. Somasundaranar, *Pattupattu,* Tirunelveli, 1971, I, 82-83.
6. Joseph J. Brenning, "Textile producers and production in late seventeenth century Coromandel", *Indian Economic and Social History Review* (hereafter *I.E.S.H.R.*), vol. XXIII, No. 4, Oct.-Dec. 1986, p. 342.
7. Ibid., p. 334.
8. Vijaya Ramaswamy, *Textiles and Weavers in Medieval South India,* Delhi, 1985, pp. 70-71; Duarte Barbosa, *The Book of Duarte Barbosa,* vol. II, Delhi, 1989, p. 132.
9. Ibid., pp. 71-72.
10. P.M. Joshi, "Textile Industry and Trade of the Kingdom of Golconda", in Satish Chandra, ed., *Essays in Medieval Indian Economic History,* New Delhi, 1987, p. 132.
11. U.V. Swaminatha Iyer, ed., *Purananuru* (Anthology), Ancient Commentary (Anon), 5th edn., 1956, verse 274.
12. George Watt, *A Dictionary of Economic Products of India,* vol. IV, London, 1890, p. 10.
13. Duarte Barbosa, vol. II, pp. 152 and 170.
14. *A.R.E.* 193 of 1940. For details see H. Yule and A.C. Burnell, ed., W. Crooke, *Hobson-Jobson,* New Delhi, 1968, p. 518.
15. *S.I.I.*, vol. IV, 524(a). See also Joseph J. Brenning, *Textile Producers,* p. 334.
16. P.M. Joshi, pp. 131-32.
17. F. Hirth and W.H. Rockhill, *Chau-Ju-Kua: His Work on the Chinese and Arab Trade in the Twelfth and Thirteenth Centuries, entitled Chu-Fan chi,* St. Petersburg, 1911, p. 96.
18. Samuel Purchas, *His Pilgrims,* vol. X, Glasgow, 1905, pp. 625 and 711.
19. K.A. Nilakanta Sastri, *Foreign Notices of South India From Megasthenes to Mahuan,* Madras, 1972, p. 306.
20. John van Linschoten, *The Voyages of John van Linschoten to the East Indies,* ed. by A.C. Burnell and P.A. Tiele, vol. I, London, 1885, p. 91.
21. *A.R.E.,* 272 of 1912 (1436); *S.I.I.*, vol. III, No. 128.
22. Ibid., vol. I, No. 446 (1586); *A.R.E.,* 50 of 1900 (1532).
23. Ibid., 193 of 1940.
24. Vijaya Ramaswamy, p. 7.
25. *S.I.I.,* vol. I, No. 446 and vol. VI, No. 21; *A.R.E.,* 430 of 1921-22, 247 of 1916, 622 of 1915, 81 of 1913, 346 of 1959-60, 240 of 1906, 140 of 1915-16 and 490 of 1937-38.
26. *A.R.E.,* 697 of 1921 (1534), 60 of 1711 (1538), 424 of 1928-29 (1565) and 282 of 1932-33 (1574); *E.I.,* vol. VI, pp. 232-37; K.A. Nilakanta Sastri and N. Venkataramanayya, *Further Sources of Vijayanagar History,* vol. III, p. 87.
27. Ibid., 403 of 1914 and 1916, p. 142.
28. Ibid., 368 of 1917.

29. Ibid., 454 of 1916 (1513), 357 of 1939-40 (1563), 107 of 1941 (1552), 133 of 1941-42, 452 of 1913 (1532), 356 of 1912 (1533), 346 of 1923 (1563) and 218 of 1931 (1601); *S.I.I.*, vol. IX, Pt. II, No. 531, No. 516 (1525).
30. Ibid., 258 of 1967-68.
31. Ibid., 1 of 1921-22. See for details *S.I.T.I.*, vol. II, glossary.
32. Ibid., 263 of 1928-29 (1439), 34 of 1919, 207 of 1935, 220 of 1935, 300 of 1928-29, 104 of 1935-36, 356 of 1912, 294 of 1910 (1418), 41 of 1922 (1546), 208 of 1912, 622 of 1915, 62 of 1935 (1507), 207 of 1922 (1430), 252 of 1917 (1463), 248 of 1911 and 623 of 1934-35.
33. Ibid., 356 of 1912 (1533) and 372 of 1912 (1510).
34. Ibid., 307 of 1913.
35. Ibid., 376 of 1923 (Krishnappa Nayak of Gingee period).
36. Ibid., 423 of 1919 (1574).
37. *T.V.M.T.I.*, No. 375 (1506), No. 414 (1548), No. 428 (1568-69).
38. *A.R.E.*, 104 of 1935-36 and 52 of 1888. The text of Vrinchipuram Inscription records as follows *"Neyykira Tharikku Matham Arai panamum"*; *S.I.I.*, vol. V, p. 516; *A.R.E.*, 31 of 1905 and 300 of 1928-29.
39. Ibid., 409 of 1913-14 (1513) Attur Taluk, 247 of 1916 (1504).
40. Tiruppangadu Inscription of A.D. 1383 in *S.I.I.*, vol. XXII, p. 191 and another inscription of A.D. 1510 in *S.I.I.*, vol. XXII, p. 190; *A.R.E.*, 88 of 1921 and 294 of 1910 (Puliparakoyil, Madurantakam Taluk). Although the temples collected loom taxes they seem to have retained a portion and the balance was paid to the controller of tolls on behalf of the Vijayanagara King. See *A.R.E.*, 207 of 1922 (1430) and 693 of 1919.
41. *A.R.E.*, 81 of 1913.
42. Ibid., 376 of 1923.
43. Ibid., 622 of 1962-63.
44. Ibid., 507 of 1938.
45. Ibid., 486 of 1938 (1535).
46. Ibid., 293 of 1928-29 (1574).
47. Ibid., 207 of 1922 (1430) and 693 of 1919.
48. *S.I.I.*, vol. XXVI, pp. 216-17 (1498), Tirukkachur.
49. *A.R.E.*, 1937-38, p. 102 (1437) Iraivasanallur.
50. Ibid., 318 of 1910 (1489); *S.I.I.*, vol. XVII, No. 221 (1486-91).
51. Ibid., 207 of 1922 Sriperumpudur.
52. Ibid., 240 of 1906 (1510), 294 of 1897 (1524), line three of the Manimangalam inscriptional text runs as follows: *"Pala pattadai Kudimakkal"*.
53. Sixteenth century inscriptions record *Pattadai*. *T.V.M.T.I.*, No. 415 (1551); for *Pattarai* see *T.V.M.T.I.* No. 418 (1551). The term *Pattadai* in the inscriptions had been misread as *Pattu Adai* (silk cloth) by some scholars like T.N. Subramanyam and Vijaya Ramaswamy. *S.I.T.I.*, vol. III, Pt. 2, glossary p. li; Vijaya Ramaswamy, op. cit., pp. 86, 88 and 104. For a detailed discussion see also P. Shanmugam, "Pattadai and Industries in the Tamil Country under the Vijayanagara Rule", in *Journal of Asian and African Studies*, No. 37, 1989, pp. 33-34.
54. *A.R.E.*, 112 of 1924; *S.I.I.*, IV, 524.
55. Ibid., 367 of 1923; 11(a) of 1934-35.

56. Ibid., 160 of 1935.
57. Ibid., 364 of 1912 (1532-33) and 240 of 1916 (1510); *S.I.I.*, XXII, No. 24.
58. Vijaya Ramaswamy, "Weaver folk traditions as a source of history" in *I.E.S.H.R.*, XIX(1), p. 55.
59. *A.R.E.*, 216 of 1917 (Korukkai).
60. Ibid., 246 of 1916 (Srimusham).
61. *T.T.D.E.S.*, IV(112).
62. Ibid.
63. Duarte Barbosa, vol. II, p. 153.
64. Ibid., pp. 77-78, 132 and 162.
65. R.H. Major, *India in the Fifteenth Century*, London, 1857. See travels of Nicolo Conti, p. 78.
66. *S.I.I.*, IX, Pt. II, No. 516, p. 53. Some scholars opine that master weavers did not seem to have altered the mode of production. Vijaya Ramaswamy, "Master weavers in South Indian Textile Production", *Journal of the Economic and Social History of the Orient* (hereafter *J.E.S.H.O.*), vol. XXVIII, 1985, p. 300.
67. *A.R.E.*, 365 of 1912; *S.I.I.*, XVII, No. 758.
68. Ibid., 308 of 1913 and 96 of 1919.
69. Ibid., 16 of 1935.
70. *S.I.I.*, XXII(24); *A.R.E.*, 240 of 1906 (1510), line five of the Tiruppangadu inscriptional text runs as follows: "*Tiruppangadu kaikolar pala pattadaiyil undana pattadai nulayam undanudum*".
71. *A.R.E.*, 16 of 1935.
72. Ibid., 59 of 1914, *Saligar nilait tari.*
73. Ibid., 91 of 1918, *parait tari.*
74. Ibid., 59 of 1914, *seniyat tari.*
75. Ibid., 247 of 1916, 486 of 1938, 622 of 1915, 88 of 1921 and 314 of 1912.
76. P. Shanmugam, p. 38.
77. *T.T.D.E.S.*, IV (112).
78. Ibid.
79. Irfan Habib, "Potentialities of capitalistic developments in the economy of Mughal India", *Journal of Economic History* (hereafter *J.E.H.*), XXIX, March 1969, p. 68.
80. *T.T.D.E.S.*, IV(112).
81. Tapan Ray Chaudhuri, p. 11.
82. Antonio Baio, *Historia quinhista in edito do segundo cerco de Dio, Ilustrada com a correspondencia original tambem in edita de D. Joao de Castro, D. Joao de Mascarenhas e outro,* Coimbra, 1925, p. 308.
83. Karl Marx, *Capital,* Moscow, 1971, vol. III, p. 596. The supposition that merchant capital was employed more and more in usury and brought misery to weavers must be proved by further research in analysing inscription. We must also find out evidence to agree with Marx that usury did not alter the mode of production.
84. Frank Perlin, "Proto industrialization and pre-colonial South Asia", *Past and Present,* XCVIII, 1983, p. 33.
85. *A.R.E.*, 342 of 1950-52.

86. H. Yule and A.C. Burnell, p. 446.
87. Duarte Barbosa, vol. I, p. 185.
88. *A.R.E.*, 103 of 1918 (1404).
89. Ibid.
90. Ibid., 655 of 1919.
91. Ibid., 103 of 1918.
92. *A.N.T.T.* (MSS.), *C.C.*, Pt. IA, 11-50 (1512).
93. *A.R.E.*, 103 of 1918.
94. Ibid.
95. Fernand Braudel, *Civilization and Capitalism, The Wheels of Commerce*, London, 1982, vol. II, pp. 190-4.
96. Vasundhara Filliozat, op. cit., p. 20.
97. *A.R.E.*, 1912, paragraph 72. *Sekkuvaniyar* corresponds to oil merchants who possessed oil press called *sekku*.
98. *T.V.M.T.I.*, Nos. 375 (1506), 402 (1537), 405 (1538), 414 (1548), 428 (1568-69), 440 (1590), 441 (1591).
99. *I.P.S.*, No. 722.
100. *T.V.M.T.I.*, No. 440.
101. *I.P.S.*, No. 722.
102. *A.R.E.*, 607 of 1919.
103. Ibid.
104. *I.P.S.*, No. 722.
105. *A.R.E.*, 607 of 1919.
106. A. Narayanaswami (ed.), *Natrinai Nanuru*, Madras, 1967, verse 345, line 8.
107. Ibid.
108. *A.R.E.*, 367 of 1911 (1424).
109. Ibid., 520 of 1919.
110. Ibid., 25 of 1919 (1499) and 27 of 1919 (1520).
111. *S.I.I*.V, 375 (1535).
112. *A.R.E.*, 367 of 1911.
113. *S.I.T.I.I*, pp. 498-99.
114. *A.R.E.*, 367 of 1911.
115. *E.I.*, VI, p. 232.
116. *A.R.E.*, 27 of 1919 (1520).
117. Ibid., 225 of 1916 (1521).
118. Gaspar Correa, tom. III, p. 578.
119. *A.R.E.*, 129 of 1921 (145-57).
120. *A.N.T.T.* (MSS.) *C.C.*, Pt. II, maco 118, doc. 38, 40, and 41.
121. S. Singaravelu, "The Ambassadorial mission of Lakshmana Hang Tuha from the kingdom of Malacca to the kingdom of Vijayanagar in South India", *Tamil Studies*, II(1), 1982, pp. 32-3.
122. Purchas, vol. X, pp. 218-19.
123. *A.R.E.*, 340 of 1926; *S.I.I.*, IX(439).
124. Duarte Barbosa, vol. I, p. 191.
125. *A.R.E.*, 423 of 1912 (1574).
126. *T.T.D.E.S.*, IV(67) (1538) and VI(3); *A.R.E.*, 535 of 1919.
127. *A.R.E.*, 380 of 1919 (1572).
128. Ibid., 459 of 1919. For *ulai kadamai* see *T.V.M.T.I.*, No. 396 (1534).
129. *S.I.T.I.* II, p. 637.

130. Purchas, vol. X, p. 148.
131. Robert Sewell, *A Forgotten Empire,* New Delhi, 1970, pp. 276-77.
132. *A.R.E.,* 150 of 1924 and 180 of 1922; *T.T.D.E.S.,* IV(16) and III (16 and 64).
133. Ibid., 430 of 1919. This jewel is called sacred thread.
134. Ibid., 136 of 1942. This ornament called *tali* is worn around the neck at the ceremony of wedding.
135. *S.I.I.,* IV(54). Crown, conch, discus and other weapons of God are the jewels generally kept as one set of ornaments.
136. Sadhu Subrahmanya Sastry, p. 216.
137. *S.I.T.I.,* p. 637.
138. Robert Sewell, *List of Antiquarian Remains in the Presidency of Madras,* Madras, 1882, p. 209; Kalyana-Venkateswara temple was erected at Narayanavanam during 1541; *A.R.E.,* 194 of 1965-66, 352 of 1913, 47 of 1906, 359 of 1911, 563 of 1904 and 55 of 1900; *T.T.D.E.S.,* II(135), IV(19 and 39), V(10 and 147) and III(168).
139. *T.T.D.E.S.,* IV Nos. 40 (1545), 125 (1530-42) and 31 (1534), III(113) (1516), V(64) (1545) and VI, Nos. 7 (1586) and 168 (1561).
140. *A.R.E.,* 535 of 1919.
141. Ibid., 563 of 1904 and 55 of 1900.
142. Ibid., 188 of 1909.
143. T.A. Gopinatha Rao, *Copper Plate Inscriptions Relating to the Sankaracharya Math of the Kamakoti Peeth,* Madras, 1916, pp. 15-17; *A.R.E.,* 380 of 1919 and 535 of 1919.
144. *T.T.D.E.S.,* V(25).
145. *A.R.E.,* 142 of 1918.
146. Ibid., 372 of 1912, 59 of 1914-15 (1429), 201 of 1936-37 and 257 of 1926-27.
147. *I.M.P.,* II(996A) (1542). This epigraph speaks of *devangapahala mantapam* erected by *devangars; A.R.E.,* 257 of 1926-27 mentions *pattunulkar* settlement at Pattiswaram. During field visit to Anniyur it was observed that *devangars* were the only weaving community in the village.
148. *T.T.D.E.S.,* VI(6) (1584), Tirupati.
149. *I.M.P.,* II(996A) (1542), Kapistalam.
150. *A.R.E.,* 257 of 1926-27.
151. Ibid., 622 of 1915 (1560).
152. Ibid., 201 of 1936-37 (Achyutadevaraya Period).
153. Ibid., 161 of 1956-57.
154. Wood, metal and stone industries flourished separately and artisans were also classified individually. They were grouped together and called *anujati-panchalattar* in epigraphs. Chicherov interprets this to mean that artisans of Vijayanagara period simultaneously worked as carpenters, blacksmiths, goldsmith, which view seems to be incorrect, Chicherov, p. 32.
155. N. Arokiasamy, *The Kongu Country, Madras,* 1946, p. 273; Edgar Thurston and K. Rangachari, *Castes and Tribes of Southern India,* vol. II, Madras, 1909, p. 117.
156. *A.R.E.,* 246 of 1911 and 680 of 1917; *T.V.M.T.I.,* No. 396.
157. *S.I.I.,* XXIII(151); *I.P.S.,* No. 726.

158. *A.R.E.*, 59 of 1914. An inscription records that new taxes such as *karuvi panam* and *tirigai ayam* were levied on artisans by Ramaiyar at Iraivasanallur in 1520. The names of taxes suggest that they were levied on barbers; see 495 of 1937-38.
159. *T.V.M.T.I.*, No. 396; *A.R.E.*, 352 of 1916.
160. *S.I.I.*, VI(72), p. 39. The inscription belongs to Krishnadevaraya period and it reads: "*Kanmalar purapattu pogaiyile*".
161. *A.R.E.*, 273 of 1939-40 (1546) Kodangi and 293 of 1928-29 (1574); *S.I.I.*, VIII, p. 47.
162. *S.I.I.*, VI(72), p. 39.
163. *A.R.E.*, 118 of 1897 (1528).
164. Ibid., 294 of 1910 (1527).
165. *E.I.*, XII, p. 343; *A.R.E.*, 22 of 1897 (1517).
166. *A.R.E.*, 493 of 1938 (1543).

4

# Rural and Urban Linkages of Internal Trade

Market, like trade, is generally assumed to involve some kind of exchange. But theoretically market and trade are not the same: they were linked with each other at some point of time.[1] Trade in the past did not occur in marketplaces alone. The historian's use of the term market thus conveys a broader sense than the economist's.

Some historians use the term local trade in a wider sense to mean the movement of goods between town and country; this underlines the importance of demand and supply in various towns.[2] In our context, local trade also included the movement of goods between various rural localities. Considerable commercial activity seems to have been attached to *nagaram, pettai, sante* and *ankadi* in the Coromandel hinterland. The present chapter studies how these local units commanded a hierarchy of local exchange, transacting regional commerce and inter-regional trade and became the foci of commercial wealth for the zones of economic activity they served.

## MARKETS AND OVERLAND TRADE

Kenneth R. Hall's study has shown that each *nadu* in Tamil country had its own marketing institution called *nagaram*, confined to certain well defined parts of a town and occasionally, also located outside the town walls. Hall believed that commerce flourished in these *nagarams*; they established rules and regulations besides dominating trade within a series of lesser and subordinate markets.[3] We have discussed earlier that *nadu* units declined with the coming of Vijayanagara kingdom in Tamil country and they were converted into *parru* and *simai* divisions.[4] If so, what happened to *nagarams* in *nadus*? *Nagarams* were important urban wholesale market centres. They functioned as trading bases with a guild—*nagaram* of resident mercantile community—*nagarattar*. Arani,[5] Puttur, Agaram, Mullandram,[6] Ponnilpadi,[7] Kanchipuram, Tirupati,[8] Chandragiri,[9] Padaividu,[10] Devikapuram,[11] Uttiramallur,[12] Sriperumbudur,[13] Tirumylapore[14] and Tiruchengattankudi[15] were famous as *nagarams*. They were nodal meeting points for merchants.

As discussed earlier, the growth of *palayams* led to the emergence of *pettai* as rural trading centres.[16] *Pettai*, used generally as a suffix to a place name, connoted marketing activity. Several such *pettai* existed, either newly established or old ones revived with the encouragement of the rulers. Thus Achyutappa *nayaka* established a *pettai* at Tiruvannamalai;[17] Kamakappa *nayaka* did so at Manalur area near Tirukoyilur;[18] another *pettai* existed at Verur;[19] Vaiyappa *nayaka* created a *pettai* at Vachchanayakanallur, near modern Arakandanallur, in his own name;[20] Immadi Tulukka *nayaka* established a *pettai* north of Aragalur;[21] Achyutadevaraya created Siddhara *pettai* at Alampundi;[22] another market was established at Venkatadrinayakan *pettai* in his time at Vadakkulittai.[23] It may be noted that the suffix *ur* in these place names conveys a peasant settlement.

Royal orders were issued regarding the affairs of *pettai*. Kamakappa *nayaka* decreed that all who traded with Manalur *pettai* were exempt from market taxes for the first three years.[24] Another *nayaka* granted special concessions only to natives of the marketplace,[25] possibly with the intention of attracting merchants to settle down in this *pettai*. Another piece of evidence suggests that in spite of the unfavourable terms issued in 1579 many merchant families settled down at Unnamalaiyamma *pettai* in Polur taluk.[26] During Surappa *nayaka's* rule, a tax called *talayarikkam* was collected as protection fee from Kugaiyur *pettai*.[27] This amount was in 1562 donated to the local temple.[28] Taxes were also levied in *pettai* on the handicrafts of rural producers.[29] The granting of market privileges by the local *nayakas* alone and imposition of taxes by them implies that the central government at Vijayanagara did not exercise absolute control over distant localities.

The temples also encouraged the establishment and development of *pettai*. As many as seven *pettai* existed around Tiruvannamalai and they received encouragement from the temple *sthanattar*.[30] Two markets, called Tilainayakan *pettai* and Chidambaranathan *pettai* near Chidambaram, were extended with

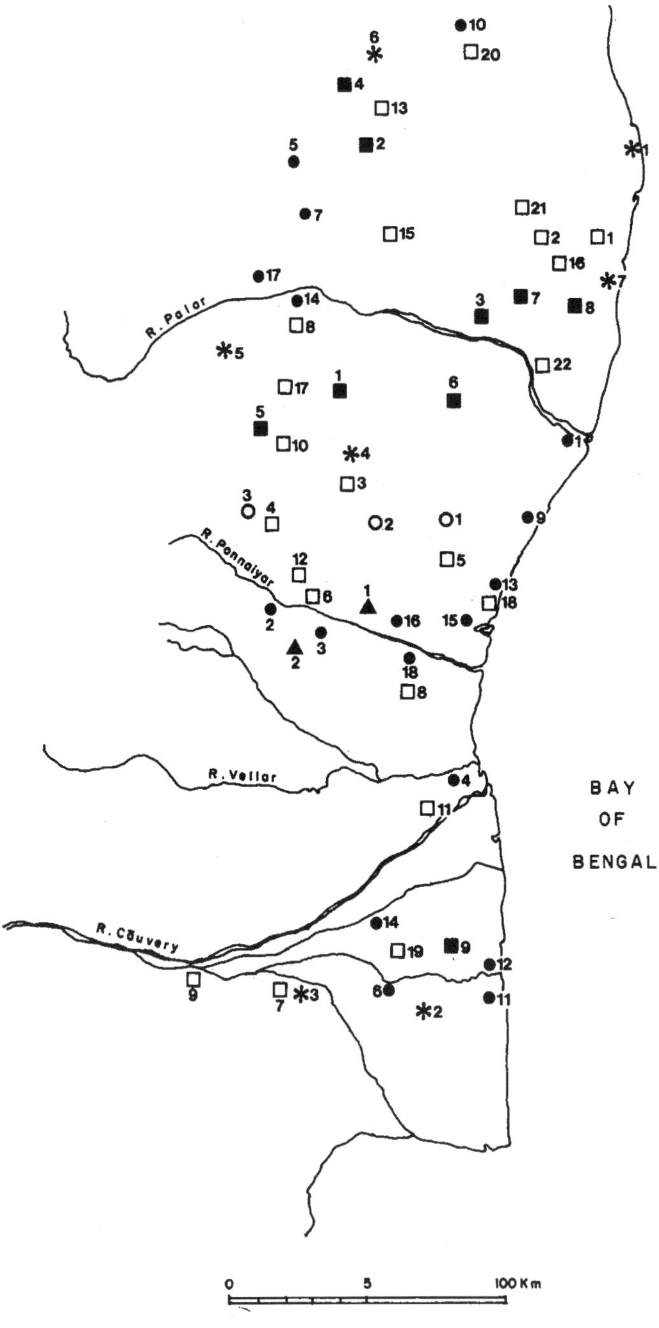


MAP 3. COROMANDEL: MARKETS AND URBAN CENTRES, 1500-1600

(For details see page 229)

additional space of six *ma* of land donated for the development of *pettai*.[31]

We may therefore conclude that *pettai* were permanent markets near the rural production centres. They were subsidiary feeder centres of local supply catering to the needs of *nagarams* and regional collecting centres called *sante*. *Pettai* flourished with the encouragement extended by *nayakas* and temple officials who benefited from the tax potential of *pettai*.

*Sante*, signifying internal trade, flourished at various places. *Sante* in Tamil means market; prefixed with *vara* it means weekly. Markets were held on particular days of the week at different places. Wednesday was market day in Tindivanam, the market being held at a hamlet called Gidangil,[32] which now is a suburb of Tindivanam town. Wednesday was market day also for Manamadi[33] and Friday for Gingee.[34] Gingee's Friday market continues even today at Chettipalayam. Thazhandhondi in the hinterland of the port of Tirumullaivasal in Shiyali taluk had its market on Saturdays.[35] Sunday was market day for Tenmahadevimangalam.[36] The market in Tiruvannamalai was held on Tuesdays or Wednesdays,[37] the day probably changing in a cyclic order.

Being regular affairs, these weekly markets attracted merchants from far and wide. Merchandise was brought for sale from areas of different extensions: from eighteen *simai*[38] in Tindivanam market and fifty-six *nadu* in Tiruvarur[39] and Tiruvannamalai[40] markets. P. Shanmugam suggests that the number mentioned did not signify much, being merely a conventional usage[41] which is not borne out by epigraphical evidence. It is possible that the epigraphs neglected to list the whole range of places from which merchants came to the weekly markets, on account of the length of the list. *Vara sante* was one of the biggest local markets in the hinterland and it became a trading point for surplus products brought by peasants and artisans. The *nayaka*, who controlled these markets, charged a levy on whoever traded in them.[42]

*Tirunal sante* were another important events of regional commerce, these being held during festivals and fairs. The dates of these periodic fairs being fixed, merchants could plan much in advance to assemble there whether monthly, annually or periodically. The fame of regional fairs at Padaividu, Kanchipuram, Sadurangapattinam and Chandragiri is indicated by the fact that an inscription at far away Belur in modern Karnataka describes them vividly.[43] Tirupati *sante*, held during its various festivals were another important affair. People from many places came to Tirupati a fortnight before the festival; it used to be so crowded that someone with murder on his mind could get away with the crime.[44] *Tirunal sante* created a wider economic system by providing an opportunity to have direct access to regional buyers.

Tamil literary sources mention 108 Vaishnavite *sthalas* and 274 Shaivite sacred complexes in Tamil country; saints celebrated these in their hymns. The *Nayaka* rulers extended their patronage to Vishnu temples[45] and made endowments to protect Srivaishnavas[46] who lived in separate quarters of the sacred towns.[47] Some temple towns grew into powerful commercial centres. With the numerous grants bestowed for the celebration of festivals, they attracted crowds of pilgrims by conducting *pooja* and holding festivals.[48] These centres carried out multiple functions.[49]

*Tirunal sante* were celebrated according to the Tamil calendar. Annual festivals such as *Deepavali* and *Yugadi* helped to develop periodic markets.[50] The celebration of *Muharam*, a festival of Muslims, was stopped in 1524 because it became a nuisance.[51] In 1534 it caused annoyance to Hindus.[52] Some temple festivals lasting nine days were celebrated in Chingleput.[53] Among festivals lasting as long as eighteen days were *Mula Tirunal* celebrated in the Tamil month of *Avani*, *Brahmotsavam Tirunal* during the month of *Puratassi, Periya Tirunal* during *Markazhi* and *Uttaram* in the month of *Punkuni*.[54] This long festivals considerably helped to increase marketing activities in Tirupati. The festivals at Tirupati lasted a total of 153 days in a year, which attracted merchants and pilgrims.[55]

Gaspar Correa, the Portuguese writer, gives an eyewitness account of a Tirupati fair. The market covered approximately eight leagues. Merchandise of all varieties was available in the number of small tents pitched in a plain. Coins of many regions were accepted in payment.[56] Correa describes the traffic in shaving of heads: the items covered the actual shaving of the head of pilgrims, changing of copper coins for payment, purchase of heaps of cut hair, and turning this into puffs of various kinds for sale at the same fair for the use of women. The temple levied *perayam* on all dealers[57] and charged twelve *rekhai pon as* land rental for shops.[58]

A certain area in the heart of the town became the centre of trade. Thus, for instance, Putlapati Timmaraja constructed a trade centre on *Periya Raja Vidhi* running east-west in the heart of Tirupati town.[59] Trade centres, called *ankadi* or *nalankadi* in Tamil and *ankaras* in Telugu epigraphs, had rows of permanent shops on both sides of the streets.[60] Caesar de Federici, a traveller of this period, calls such a marketplace *bazaro*.[61] The shops opened daily, as may be inferred from the prefix *nal* in *nalankadi*, which means a daily shop. Merchants of *ankadi* specialised in a particular commodity and its allied products.[62] Dealers in a particular craft item tended to have shops close to one another. In the trade centre at Tirupati, there was a gold market called *kasukkadai*.[63] In the trade centre of Agaram in North Arcot district merchants sold emerald and bronze.[64] The merchants of Devikapuram sold rubies, pearls, diamonds and emeralds openly in the *bazaars*.[65]

The establishment and development of *ankadi* would have been linked with the process of urbanisation of towns. Merchants in the *bazaars* had to pay tax in cash.[66] Men, shopkeepers[67] in general and particularly women shopowners in the *ankadi* at Tiruvannamalai paid three-eighths of a *panam* as tax.[68] At Tirupati, shopkeepers with permanent shops paid thirty *rekhai pon* as land tax,[69] which was double that paid by keepers of temporary stalls.[70] The highest tax—ten *rekhai pon*—was realised from pearl merchants, which indicates that taxation to some extent depended upon the nature of the commodity.[71]

It would appear that Coromandel *bazaars* specialised in trade in jewels, metals, pearls, precious stones and bullion. Some recent scholars have held that there is little sign of dense structure of periodic marketing in South India; they might have concluded otherwise, had they been able to analyse the epigraphical evidence.[72] From the evidence available to us it becomes clear that there was a remarkable development of organised rural and urban markets, both temporary and permanent, their periodicity varying from daily, weekly and cyclic.

## COMMODITIES OF EXCHANGE AND TRADE ROUTES

Standardisation of commodities brought for sale to the market was attempted by stamping them with *hamsa mudra* or swan mark.[73] A duty called *mudrayam* was levied for the purpose.[74] The royal emblem of the swan suggests market control to prove that

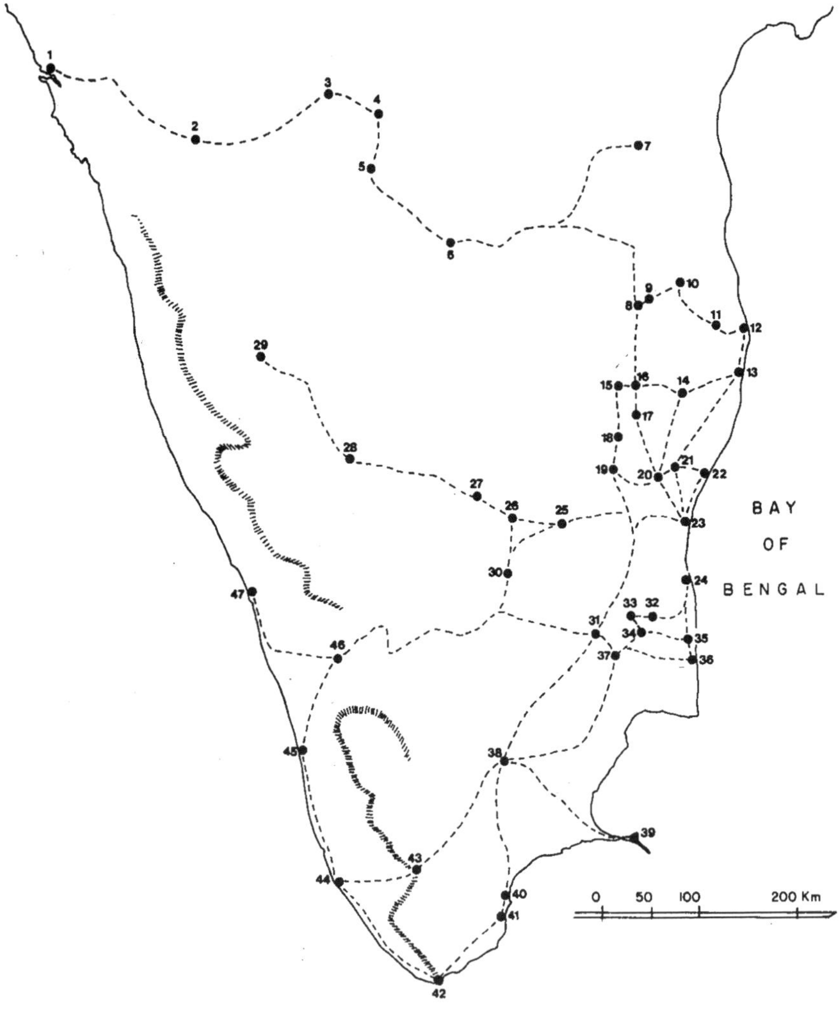


MAP 4. OVERLAND TRADE ROUTES OF COROMANDEL, 1500-1600

(For details see page 230)

goods were pure, the swan being a mythical symbol of purity.[75] Godowns existed in marketing centres; in one such case Nagama *nayaka* purchased godowns at Chidambaram.[76] All this indicates that marketing had developed with advanced systems.

Certain commodities of exchange like yarn, oil, betel leaf and textiles were to a large extent traditionally monopolised by some merchant groups.[77] Epigraphs provide a list of agricultural and non-agricultural commodities sold at various markets, primarily produced by peasants and artisans in addition to imports from various regions.[78] The markets of Tirupati, Kunimedu, Tiruvannamalai and Tiruppunduriti primarily dealt in agricultural produce like sesame, paddy, turmeric, arecanut, gallnut, cumin and ginger. Tamarind was available at Kunimedu market; the Portuguese purchased it for making vinegar.[79] Tirukoyilur and Tiruvannamalai were centres of horse trade.[80] Buffaloes were sold at Putalapattu. Vrinchipuram, Kanchipuram,[81] Karaikal,[82] Tiruppunduriti,[83] Kenkondan, Arasur, Tenkaraikoyilur, Kavanur, Alishukattu and Erumbur[84] were centres of trade in pepper, probably supplied from the Malabar coast. Raw cotton, silk and cotton yarn and finished cotton goods were brought by weavers to markets in Avur, Tindivanam, Vrinchipuram, Putalapattu, Tirupati and Chandragiri.[85] Manufactured goods such as salt, ghee, palm jaggery and sugar also were sold in these markets. Goods generally used for worship in temples, such as camphor, civet, musk, scent and *kumkum* were sold at markets of Kanchipuram and other temple towns.[86]

Thirteen main overland routes connecting the major towns and ports of South India, including the royal city of Vijayanagara, may be traced from various sources such as inscriptions, literary sources, Portuguese records and travellers' accounts. These were:

- Tiruvadigai to Sendamangalam.[87]
- Chandiragiri to Srirangam via Tirupati, Kalakhasti, Kanchipuram, Tiruvannamalai.[88]
- Pulicat to Vijayanagara.[89]
- Kanchipuram to Vijayanagara.[90]
- Bidnur to Gingee.[91]
- Mylapore to Vijayanagara via Penugonda, Udayagiri, Chandragiri, Tirupati, Pulicat.[92]
- Santhome to Chandragiri via Tiruvallur.[93]
- Santhome to Goa.[94]
- Vijayanagara to Rameswaram via Chandragiri, Tirupati,

Kanchipuram, Tiruvannamalai, Chidambaram, Madurai.[95]
- Mylapore to Cochin via Attur, Palghat.[96]
- Cochin to Mylapore via Cape Comorin, Tuticorin, Punnaikayal, Talaimannar, Nagapattinam, Tranquebar, Chidambaram, Gingee.[97]
- Quilon to Coromandel via Shenkottah, Ariyankavu, Pudukottai.[98]
- Vellore to Kunimedu via Marakkanam.[99]

It would be expected that these routes fostered internal trade by linking commercial centres with various destinations in South India. Trees were planted on both sides of the roads during 1530,[100] most likely to give shade to the travelling merchants. These overland routes made travel possible round the year from the Coromandel region to Malabar coast and further up to Goa and the west coast. The time taken would have been a minimum of twenty-seven days and a maximum of four weeks.[101]

## MEANS OF TRANSPORT AND TYPES OF MARKET TAXES

Goods were transported in various ways. Sadasivaraya, for example, donated 200 bulls for transporting provisions such as ghee, oil and vegetables to Tirupati temple, which suggests that bullocks were the chief means of transport.[102] Supporting this view is another piece of evidence which states that merchandise was brought to markets chiefly on pack bullocks. Epigraphs provide an exhaustive list of means of transport such as *kavadi*, head loads, pack asses and horses used for trade.[103] This evidence supports the view of W.H. Moreland and T.V. Mahalingam that carts were not used for transport of market goods in this period.[104]

Two types of duties were collected in internal trade: *sthala ayam* at the place of sale, and *margadayam* on goods in transit. Taxation practices changed from place to place. The sale of merchandise and collection of market revenue in *parru* and *simai* had to be registered. The explanation in an epigraph about the transfer of market revenue from the smaller territorial division of *parru* to the larger division of *simai* indicates pooling of revenue by *nayakas* in their *nayakattanams*.[105] Ayyakaran was the tax collector appointed by *nayaka* to collect market levy on articles during market days. He also saw to it that no secondary taxes were collected.[106] Chinna Virappa *nayaka* fixed a scale of market taxes for the Tindivanam market.[107] There is also evidence that details of market levies were communicated between various *nayakas* of the *simai*, probably to provide the merchants with market information. Some evidence points out that the temples purchased the right to collect market fees by paying a lumpsum to the local leader.[108]

Market taxes were collected in cash. Arulandiya devapandaram, appointed by *nayaka*, collected a monthly market tax called *tirvai* from the merchants of Tiruvannamalai. This tax, ranging between three-eighths to half *panam*, appears to have been a tax on manufactured and miscellaneous goods.[109] Various stone records mention a tax called *magamai*, generally collected in kind. *Magamai* taxes were collected at specific rates in kind and given to local temples of the market centres.[110] *Magamai* was an additional source of revenue to temples. *Nayakas* granted market taxes to temples.[111]

To a large extent, markets contributed to the revenue of *nayakas*. The local ruler of Kunimedu collected transit taxes called *tundappidari* on textiles which passed through Kunimedu.[112] Portuguese sources also corroborate that merchants carried textiles called *beatilhas* from Pulicat to Goa by land, and paid duty at certain places during transit. The local market customs of the Vijayanagara kingdom were introduced in the Portuguese territory of Goa as well. The period of the Portuguese governor Martim Affonso de Sousa witnessed an increase in transit taxes of Goa, which brought substantial revenue to the king of Portugal. These taxes existed even as late as 1577.[113]

Various secondary taxes were collected in certain localities on goods coming from certain specified regions. Thus, secondary taxes such as *anuppu* and *allu* used to be collected in the Tiruvannamalai market.[114] Secondary taxes like *ullayam, perayam, mulaivisam, melakai* and *kodai* were charged on goods which came to the Tirupati market from all over South India.[115] Commodities which came from various *nadus* and *simai* divisions of Padaividu *rajya*, Tiruvadigai *rajya* and Tanjore region[116] to Tirupati market were charged and tax on nine types of aromatic merchandise, called *navarasaya vargam,* was levied. Other secondary taxes like *nattu ayam* and *udiri tirvai* were collected at Kunimedu market on goods from Vellore and Marakkanam.[117] It would appear from this evidence that secondary taxes on markets were collected by *nayakas* and the king of Vijayanagara did not exercise control in the local markets.

Gold coins of various types served as an important medium of exchange since gold was available in plenty. The coins had various names such as *gadyana, varahan, pagoda, pon, pratapa, kati* and *haga*. Gold *varahans* had a standard weight of fifty-two grains; half *varahans* weighed twenty-six grains and quarter *varahans* thirteen grains.[118] Emperor Krishnadevaraya introduced a double *varahan* of about 120 grains. Another coin introduced in this period, called *pratapa*, was equal to half *gadyana* or *varahan*.[119] Gold of three types with the fineness of eight, eight and a half and nine carats existed. Its quality was examined by the goldsmith on the touchstone.[120] Gold was preserved after being melted and cooled.[121] This *kati varahan* block of gold had a higher value than the ordinary *pon, rekhai pon* and *varahan*.[122] Kati, another gold coin in ciruculation, was equal to one-fourth of *varahan*.[123]

Silver coins were less in currency. Silver was weighed in *ara manai padikkal* and *koyil padikkal*,[124] which suggests that two different weights of the royal palace and the temple prevailed in weighing silver.[125] Considering that silver weighed in terms of *tukkam* was gifted to temples it is likely that the metal must also have been abundantly available although not as currency.

*Panam* was a copper coin used in trade. The prefix *nar* indicated that the coin was not debased. It appears that the amount of copper in *panam* gradually decreased between the early sixteenth and early seventeenth centuries.[126] Some of the copper coins found at Vallam fort near Thanjavur were issued by King Achyutadevaraya. Caesar Federici makes it out that all *nayakas* issued copper coins in their territory. The coins found at Varadarajan *pettai* in Udayar Palayam taluk on 5 January 1989 corraborate this fact. Known as *veerarayar panam*, they contain less both of silver and copper.[127]

## MERCHANT GUILDS AND URBANISATION

The literary source *Amuktamalyada* refers to the existence of merchant guilds[128] which regulated commerce in the Coromandel hinterland. Two guilds are mentioned in inscriptions, namely *ayyavole* and *nagarattar*.

The *ayyavole* merchants, who hailed from Aihole in present-day Karnataka, conducted vast hinterland trade in South India.[129]

Their guild, consisting of members of fifty-six countries, controlled trade in raw cotton, yarn and dyes even during 1531.[130] Even in the closing years of the sixteenth century they monopolised the sale of raw cotton, thread and cloth in the Kanchipuram region.[131] The *ayyavole* trade guild facilitated the collection and supply from various parts of South India of goods necessary for weaving. It was an itinerant trading corporation.

*Nagarattars,* on the other hand, were resident merchants, since membership of the guild was open only to members resident in a *nagaram.*[132] Merchants from the community of *chettis, manradis* and others formed part of the guild.[133] Its president—it is not known whether he was elected or nominated[134]—was generally a *chetti* merchant.[135] *Chettis* also dominated the rest of the guild: five of the six signatories of a guild in the Kalakhasti region were *chettis.*[136]

*Nagarattars* watched over market transactions in the *nagaram* to ensure fair trade practices. Meetings, which were frequent, were usually held in the front hall of a temple. One subject of discussion was assignments of market taxes to various temples.[137] The guild was directly responsible for payment of market taxes to the government. The president collected and remitted them through his officers. *Nagarattar* guild exercised certain administrative powers in matters of taxation in *nagaram*. *Nagarattars'* consent was considered necessary if market taxes of *nagarams* were to be gifted to temples, which indicates their local importance.[138]

*Nagarattars* actively participated in hinterland trade and made large endowments to local temples.[139] In one case, the *nagarattars* of Sriperumbudur lent 210 *varahan* to the temple and allowed the interest to be spent on the temple.[140] *Nagarattars* of Chandragiri built two *mantapas* in the temple of Nagalapuram[141] and those of Devikapuram built a tank and a temple.[142] Thus, *nagarattars* carried out various acts of charity.[143] Presumably, the funds for these religious and charitable contributions came from the *nagarattars'* lucrative commerce in the *nagaram.*

Though the two guilds of *ayyavole* and *nagarattar* helped to some extent to mobilise and organise merchants, they did not unionise on a regional level, probably hampered by the wide variety of local market practices. A general tendency for growth as independent merchants is noticed both in epigraphs and Portuguese sources. When *nayakas* took necessary steps to revive the extinct markets and establish new markets in their *nayakattanams*, their driving goal was revenue farming, which would have been better realised by the instigation of independent merchants than by organised trade guilds. This consideration would have led to the growth of independent merchants at the cost of decline of the guilds.

The Coromandel region was covered by a network of urban centres with appellations such as *puram, pattinam* and *kottai. Puram* (lit.: outskirts of place) in the present context indicated the marketplace situated within the urban centre. Virarajendrapuram[144] in Jambai, Ulagamadevipuram[145] near Tindivanam and Marudanodayapuram[146] in Tirukkachiyur were well known. *Pattinam* was a coastal town, or sometimes an inland town on a river bank with a flourishing market. Some well known *pattinams* were Rajanarayanapattinam[147] in Rishivandiyam, Bhuvanekavirarayanpattinam[148] in Adhivarahanattam and Krishnabhupalanpattinam[149] near Tiruvarur. *Pattanam* also denoted big urban centres in the hinterland which functioned as markets. *Kottai* meant fort, several of which developed as markets.

Towns of the Coromandel had many stages of growth depending upon the political apparatus, economic system and the societal network at its base. Each category of town had its own distinct factor pushing its growth, depending on which towns came to be classified as political capitals, craft production centres, and religious places of pilgrimage. When these basic factors declined, the urban centre itself declined. Though commerce underlies urban growth anywhere, and trade became the backbone of the urban centres of the Coromandel, it is difficult to determine the main or the more important factor that led to urbanisation.

## INLAND TOWNS AND TOWN PLANNING

Urban growth is a complex process, open to debate among scholars. Some like Henri Pirenne linked the rise of towns with the tendency of the trading elements to seek protection within the fortresses.[150] Some have argued that the opportunities and inducements available at the great pilgrimage sites in the vicinity of shrines attracted the local conglomeration of traders to develop commerce.[151] Some others subscribe to the view that surplus agricultural produce rather than trade was the chief factor of urbanisation.[152]

In Coromandel, the dividing line between town and village was quite sharp since the village had a strong agrarian base. Although the English word town and the Russian *gorod* only mean a fortified place or one surrounded by walls, we may classify all towns as either open towns or fortified towns. Some of the open towns like Srirangam,[153] Kumbakonam[154] and Tirupati[155] attracted pilgrims by conducting *pooja* and festivals with the numerous grants bestowed on the temples and thus grew into powerful urban centres. The absence of fortification in these sacred centres does not make them ineligible to be treated as towns, considering that they have all other urban features.

We shall examine the town planning aspects of two towns, namely Thanjavur and Tirupati. Thanjavur town consisted of an *ullalai,* an inner quadrangle around the Brahadiswara temple, along with a *purambadi,* described as an outer circuit.[156] Tirupati, too, had similar town planning features, with *ulmandalam* (inner division) and *puramandalam* (outer division); each division consisted of separate living quarters for the temple priests and administrators and streets of other professional groups including merchants.[157] Thus the two temple towns of Thanjavur and Tirupati both had divisions distinctly demarcated for religious and commercial purposes. The inner circle covered a small area around the *sanctum sanctorum* and various small shrines in the temple. The outer division extended to many *pettais* and *purams* in the suburbs. Both showed the evolving pattern of town plan radiating from a temple in the middle and marking the four directions along with the street names[158] with chess board pattern of square or rectangular blocks.

Although the Pallavas constructed temples in a big way in the sixth and seventh centuries, till the last quarter of the tenth century temple towns did not develop much of trade and artisanal production.[159] The Chola and Vijayanagara rulers took great interest in constructing temples and temple towns developed with clear characteristics of trade and urbanisation. Inscriptions and Jesuits' letters mention that merchants resided in towns and conducted trade.[160] *Nayakas* collected taxes from these merchants who traded in their *nayakattanams*.[161] Merchants generally resided in the heart of the town probably to improve business prospects.[162] Separate streets existed for various castes, merchants and other artisans and were exclusively named after them.[163] Street names such as *vyapari vidhi* or *vyapari theruvu* indicated the exclusive business they catered for.[164] Some towns had a separate merchants' colony. Thus Krishnarayapattinam, a suburb of Chandragiri, was a settlement exclusively of *chetti* merchants;[165] and Narasingarayapuram, a suburb of Tirupati, had a colony of *chetti* merchants.[166] The urban development in these places is seen from various angles. The town limit of Chidambaram extended over fourteen hamlets in its neighbourhood.[167] In Tirupati, various colonies had emerged. Narasingarayapuram became the settlement of Tirupati merchants[168] and Achyutapettai emerged as the marketing centre feeding the main *nagaram* of Tirupati.[169] Krishnarayapuram formed a suburb of Bhuvanagiri town.[170] The hamlets of Vitalapuram and Vaipakkam were included in the urban limits of the temple town of Tirukalukunram.[171]

As new colonies emerged various types of houses began to be constructed. Each type was taxed differently.[172] *Nayakas* constructed new streets in their names. Bhogayadeva Chola Maharaja opened a new street called *Bhogaraja Peru Tiruvidhi* in Tirukoyilur town.[173] Ananda Tandava Perumal Tondaimar laid out a street called *Ananda Tandavar Tiruvidhi* at Iraivasanallur in 1539.[174] Adappa Timma *nayaka* established new streets in the town of Bhuvanagiri.[175] Muthu Krishnappa *nayaka* laid out a new street in Chidambaram.[176] Several orders relating to urban developmental activities issued by the rulers for the settlement of merchants and others are found in epigraphical texts.[177] One text, from Chidambaram, an open town, conveys the assurance of a *nayaka* that whoever came and settled in the street should not be afraid of anything other than the fury of the wind and heat of the sun,[178] which implies that people preferred not to live along the streets. Although commerce flourished in these open towns and urban development had taken roots, merchants and other settlers seem to have preferred fortified towns for the protection they afforded.

*Kottai* was suffixed to a fort town.[179] The *Silpa sastra* laid down the guidelines and principles for construction of forts, which were generally classified as *jala durga, giri durga* and *sthala durga*. The *mayamata* and the *mansara* also were followed in the construction of forts.[180] The design, whether square, rectangle, triangular, octagonal, circular, undulating or any other form, was chosen according to the site.[181] Kamaiyappa *nayaka* revived an old market at Adhamankottai, which had become extinct for quite some time, and he levied market fees on merchants who traded there.

This. indicates that fort towns combined their marketing functions.

Coromandel regional urbanisation began with focus on the protection provided by the rulers in the forts. Chingleput fort was built by the minister of King Krishnadevaraya;[182] Arni fort by his brother.[183] Similarly Timmaraya erected a fort at Tirupalaivanam near Pulicat.[184] Various literary sources like *Rayavacakamu*, *Jaimini Bharatamu* composed by Pillalmrri Pinarira Bhadra, *Thanjavur Andhra Rajulu Charitramu* and *Vasu Charitra* of Ramaraja Bhushana mention the forts of Chandragiri,[185] Vallam, Sathyavedu, Narayanavanam,[186] Bhuvanagiri, Gingee[187] and Thanjavur.[188] Inscriptions mention the forts at Padaividu,[189] Uttiramerur[190] and Kalathur.[191] Thus many forts had come into existence.

Two copies of the map of Thanjavur fort are preserved in Saraswati Mahal Library at Thanjavur. One copy is a rough one containing corrections with all four directions of Thanjavur town. The names are written in modi script belonging to the Maratha period of the seventeenth century. There is an interesting note in one corner of the smaller fort which mentions the year 1560.[192] When the fort was probably built, the gates were marked in addition to the moat. Walls were carefully depicted with the large fort and a small fort in this map. This evidence suggests that Thanjavur became a fortified place with the coming of *nayaka* rule.

Vellore fort is a perfect specimen of a *jala durga*. Surrounded on all sides by an excavated moat full of water, it is rectangular with a small projection towards the gate and conforms to the principles of Hindu *sastras*.[193] According to local tradition it was built by Bommu *Reddi*, a native of Bhadrachalam. Later, when Vellore became the seat of power under *nayakas* and the capital of Vijayanagara empire, the fort underwent many improvements.[194] Krishnadevaraya erected the *rajamahal*, a tank and other buildings. The temple of *Jalakanteswara* located inside the Vellore fort was built by Venkatapatidevaraya II. The limits of Vellore fort also extended over the hamlets of Arapakkam, Ariyur and Saddupperi situated in its evirons[195] and still later, over the hamlets of Sattuvacheri, Samanginallur and Perumai when Vellore became the Vijayanagara rulers' capital.[196]

Gingee fort was a typical example of *giri durga* (mountain fort). Gingee was the Sanskrit equivalent of *Srinji*, which means a fortress on a hill. The fort was under Gopanaraya, a subordinate ruler of Vijayanagara, in the fourteenth century. Fr. Nicholas Pimenta, who visited Gingee, described it as the Troy of the East built on three hills forming a triangle; he compared it with the other towns in Portugal except Lisbon.[197] Many buildings of Gingee fort such as the fortification at the top of *Rajagiri*, *Kalyana mahal*, granaries, bastioned walls and ditch enclosing three mountains were attributed to the works of Tubaki Krishnappa *nayaka*.[198]

Vallam fort was a *sthala durga,* meaning a fort built on plain land. Situated on the low Vallam tableland eleven kilometres south of Thanjavur, it was surrounded by a man-made moat and it had two temples.[199] King Achyutadevaraya made some territorial adjustments as a consequence of which Vallam fort was taken away from Madurai *nayakas* and handed over to Thanjavur *nayakas*.[200] A local proverb conveys that this fort was a great protection to Thanjavur. The proverb runs: "If one can capture the fort of Vallam, the fort of Thanjavur will fall of its own accord."[201]

These forts must have essentially grown as political power centres and administrative headquarters of the rulers. They emerged as urban centres in course of time, when trade and crafts combined and increased the process of urban development. The Friday market at Gingee, of which we have spoken earlier, attracted merchants probably owing to the security afforded by the fort. The progressive urban development of fort towns can be attested by various suburban areas around forts. Chandragiri fort had Krishnarayapattinam,[202] Krishnarayapuram[203] and Gopidevipalayam[204] as its suburban areas. Many politico-administrative towns did exist but not all of them were urban. To develop as urban centres, these towns had to have the lasting patronage of the rulers as their capital cities.

Urbanisation of open towns with religious importance or fortified towns with political significance was catalysed by trade and crafts to some extent. Kanchipuram, although its religious importance endured as before, was described as the best town in an inscription, probably owing to its textile production too.[205] This corresponds to the view of Abul Fazal and W.H. Moreland that towns were centres of craft production.[206] In this light, Arjun Appadurai's view that the dual classification of towns led to a series of disorders in the Vijayanagara towns, may be reconsidered.[207] Frank Perlin terms the process of urbanisation as "urban" owing to its mixture of rural and urban characters.[208] Although emphasis could be placed on various factors, trade was the stimulus behind the process of urban development.

## EVOLUTION OF PORTS

For various reasons, our knowledge of medieval Coromandel ports and maritime trade has been a dark area. To begin with, most valuable sources on the subject are in Arabic and Chinese. What indigenous sources exist throw little light on the subject. Also, the Portuguese sources have not been adequately tapped. In the absence of detailed scientific works it is difficult to be categorical about the overseas trading pattern and changes that occurred in the structure of maritime trade.

Coromandel ports conducted active internal trade with ports on the eastern and western coasts during the medieval period. The availability of goods and the flourishing hinterland trade made it possible to bring commodities to these ports. To some extent the growth of maritime trade also contributed to the bifurcation of particular coastal towns.

Tamil classics roughly indicate the layout of the coastal towns. It comprised two main divisions called *ur* and *pattinam*.[209] This type of well defined division existed in many places. The division called *ur*, situated a little further interior of the coastal town, was inhabited by peasants and artisans. Hindus generally lived in the interior of *ur* while Muslims remained on the coastal area. *Pattinam* was a mercantile settlement close to the seashore where marketing and exchange by foreign merchants flourished. Thus the *pattinam* became a major town and *ur* an ancillary town. Custom duties collected in *pattinams* on imports and exports were assigned to temples[210] in *ur*.

The division of coastal towns is supported by the fact that twin names are generally found in epigraphs applied to one and the same port town. Thus Pulicat is also called Anandarayapattinam; Sadras as Rajanarayanapattinam; Marakkanam as Eyirpattinam; Cuddalore as Nissarikammalanpattinam; Porto Novo as Krishna-pattinam; and Tranquebar as Kulasekharapattinam.[211] Conversion of some coastal villages into new centres of maritime trade brought about the suffix *pattinam*. The names of founder rulers of these port towns also formed part of the name of ports such as

Rajanarayananpattinam, Tirumalairayanpattinam and Krishnarayapattinam.[212] These *pattinams* which emerged as port-towns were different from the coastal villages; the Nagalapuram inscriptional text distinguishes the coastal villages by the usage of *karai* and *turai,* which meant a landing place on the coast.[213]

Port towns called *pattinams* developed due to the significant role of maritime trade. They went through a cyclical process that comprised emergence, growth and decline. Some ports responded and adapted themselves to changes, benefiting from the new opportunities while maintaining continuity with change. These changes were necessitated with the coming of Muslims, Chinese and the Portuguese merchants in addition to the rule of local powers such as the Samburvaraya kings and the Vijayanagara emperors.

The port of Sadras (Rajanarayananpattinam) was founded by the King Rajanarayana Samburvaraya (A.D. 1339-63).[214] An inscription dated 5th February 1353 mentions various tolls and duties on articles of merchandise collected in this port where merchants from many places conducted trade.[215] Sadras was in 1376 also called Sadiravachakanpattinam; it conducted maritime trade in pearls, long cloth and bales of variety of textiles.[216] During the early Vijayanagara rule in Tamil country, Kumara Kampana consolidated the payment of *kaikolars* of Tirukalukundram who took the cloth to Sadras for sale and export.[217] With the advent of Muslim rule in the south during the later decades of the fourteenth century Sadras began to decline. The early Muslim expansion in Tamil country had encouraged the settlement of Muslim traders at Kunimedu, a neighbouring coastal village situated little south on the coast. Vasco da Gama's diary notes that Kunimedu had emerged as an important centre of maritime trade in the late fifteenth century where Muslim traders were very powerful.[218] The fact that the Italian traveller Girodamo di Santo Stefano sailed from Kunimedu shows that it became the port of embarkation and a famous harbour in the early sixteenth century. Tome Pires mentions port of Kunimedu (11° 56' N) as *Cunjmeyra.*[219] This port is also identified with *Collim* of Fernao Nuniz, the Portuguese chronicler.

The Muslim occupation of South India in the medieval times encouraged the Islamic traders to settle down at Nagore (10° 45' N; 79° 50' E) situated at the mouth of Kudavaiyar. Nagapattinam was then flourishing but declined in the fourteenth century and in its place Tirumalairayanpattinam emerged as an important centre of country trade in the following century. Throughout, the Muslim merchants of Nagore conducted maritime trade with ports of South-East Asia. Vasco da Gama's diary describes Nagore as a port city where Muslim traders flourished in the late fifteenth century.[220] Tome Pires mentions that Nagore continued to flourish in the second decade of the sixteenth century.[221] Later when Nagapattinam emerged as an international trading mart in the 1520s, the Muslim merchants of Nagore began to participate in the overseas trade at Nagapattinam along with the Portuguese merchants.

The emergence of Pulicat as an important port may be attributed to the decline earlier of a neighbouring port. According to the Arab geographers who furnish detailed information on the port towns on the east coast, Pulicat did not figure as an important centre. Port Mottupalli was the famous international trading centre under the Kakatiya ruler Ganapatideva (A.D. 1200-50) who gave *abhaya sasana* to foreign merchants.[222] This charter was renewed in 1358 by Annapota Reddy who inscribed this inscription both in Tamil and Telugu languages fixing the payment of duties on articles of imports and exports. Maritime trade of Mottupalli flourished in the subsequent years. Another trade charter was issued at Mottupalli based on the model of Ganapatideva and Annapota Reddy by the Vijayanagara king Devaraya I in A.D. 1390 to develop overseas trade.[223] Krishnapattinam, located in the present Nellore district little north of Pulicat, was another active seaport as early as A.D. 1256. The Telugu Chodas of Nellore, who were subordinates of the Kakatiyas, patronised trade in this port.[224] This port also flourished under the Reddis (A.D. 1325-1448) who were the political successors of the Kakatiyas. These ports witnessed decline in overseas trade slowly and it appears from epigraphs that Pulicat emerged during the heyday of Vijayanagara ruler Devaraya II (A.D. 1422-46) who appointed Anandaraya as a governor in this region.[225] Anandaraya developed this port which was named after him as Anandarayanpattinam.[226] Pulicat was anglicisation of its local Tamil name Pazhaverkadu.[227] A Telugu inscription found at the southern wall of the Adinarayanaswamy temple at Pulicat reveals that this port was also called *Pralaya Kaveri* since the port was often flooded with sea water comparable to the floods in the river Kaveri in those days.[228] The port of Pulicat situated on the mouth of river Araniyar (13° 29' N; 80° 50' E) greatly facilitated sailing during floods, serving as a protected harbour. The Portuguese, when they came to know about the flourishing commerce at the port began trading with it. They mention it as *Palleaquate* and *Paleacate.*[229]

*Corpo Cronologico* is a valuable collection of manuscripts preserved in the National Archives of Lisbon, which throws ample light on the port of Pulicat. The manuscripts contain orders issued by the Portuguese captain of Coromandel to purchase and deliver rice and other commodities at Pulicat along with acknowledgements signed by those who exported them.[230] The names of ships, officers, estimate of exports, ports of destination and other related details of coastal economy in the age of Portuguese expansion are also found. Various travellers like Abdul Razzack (1420), Nicolo Conti (1443) and Athanasius Nikitin (1470) have described how the Vijayanagara rulers encouraged significant trade in diamonds, pearls, rubies and precious stones at the capital city.[231] They sought to develop Pulicat as an outlet of bullion, jewels and precious stones. Ludovico di Varthema was the first western traveller to notice Pulicat and its immense trade in precious stones during the early sixteenth century.[232] These precious stones found their way to the city of Vijayanagara where

PORTUGUESE EXPORTS FROM COROMANDEL PORTS TO THE WESTERN COAST, JULY-DECEMBER 1524*

| *Ship* | *Rice (Cottai)* | *Butter (Marakal)* | *Salt (Cottai)* | *Iron (Pipa)* | *Timber (Ratal)* | *Cannon Balls (Nos.)* |
|---|---|---|---|---|---|---|
| Santiago | 3266 | 25 | 6 | 4 | 13 | 150 |
| Conceicao | 14160 | - | - | - | - | - |
| Anunciada | 56 | 2 | 9 | 2.15 | 4715 | - |
| Sao Thome | - | - | - | - | - | 50 |
| Antonio | - | 12 | - | - | - | 50 |
| Pantaliao | 63 | 500 | - | - | - | - |
| Catarina | 2880 | - | - | - | - | - |
| Other Ships | - | 14 | - | - | - | - |

*For details on *Navio Santiago, A.N.T.T.,* CC IIa-115-67, 117-43, 117-170, 118-14, 118-41, 118-72; *Navio Conceicao, A.N.T.T.,* CC IIa-117-194, 125-2; *Navio Maria Anunciada* CC IIa-118-69, 119-12, 121-41; *Parau Santhome,* CC IIa-118-38; *Parau Antonio,* CC IIa-118-40, 2a 119-104; *Fusta Pantaliao,* CC IIa-118-46, 118-47, 119-107; *Fusta Catarina,* CC IIa-118-31. For other ships see IIa-120-25 (8 October 1524).

a capital market existed for jewels and gems. The Portuguese exported from Pulicat rice, textiles, salt, iron, timber, butter and cannon balls.

Owing to this flourishing commerce, Pulicat became the site of the earliest Portuguese trading station on the coast. Manuel de Frias, appointed as the captain of the Coromandel coast in 1522, resided at Pulicat.[233] A letter written to the King of Portugal mentions the existence of an office at Pulicat till 1530 to issue *cartazes*. The letter said that since the expenditure incurred exceeded the income of the Portuguese Crown at this port, it was advisable not to have a fort at Pulicat.[234] The seat of the captaincy of Coromandel was therefore shifted from Pulicat to Santhome at Mylapore when the next captain Miguel Ferreira took up his residence in 1530.[235] Although Portuguese contacts with Mylapore developed after the tomb of St. Thomas was discovered there in 1517 many Portuguese had already settled down before the church of the Apostle was rebuilt in 1524.[236]

Nagapattinam (10° 36' N; 79° 55' E) at the mouth of Uppanar flourished as a port under the Cholas in the eleventh and twelfth centuries. The Chinese traded with it in the thirteenth century and called it *Na-Kia-Po-Tan-Na*,[237] but in the fourteenth century stopped visiting it, preferring to trade with the ports of the Malabar coast like Quilon, Cochin and Calicut. With the advent of Vijayanagara rule in the Tamil country, Tirumalairayan-pattinam (10° 53' N) gained prominence as a port in the fifteenth century. Going by Portuguese sources, it became the main port of country trade.[238] Saluva Tirumalai Devamaharaya, a governor of Vijayanagara kings who ruled the Thanjavur region comprising Papanasam, Pattisvaram, Tirukattupalli, Srimushnam, Kudu-miyanmalai and Srirangam areas from 1450 to 1486, founded a new port town named after himself—Tirumalairayan-pattinam—situated between two rivers.[239] He excavated the Tirumalairajanar to the north of the town and the Puravudiyar in the south and connected the rice cultivating hinterland of the port by waterways to bring paddy and rice for export.[240]

A letter written by the Portuguese viceroy to his king describes the large volume of trade conducted from Tirumalairayan-pattinam with Cochin.[241] Two hundred vessels, big and small, sailed from Tirumalairayanpattinam to Cochin in 1506.[242] The merchants from Cochin paid a levy to the Portuguese on each *navio* and as *cartaz* for trade with Tirumalairayanpattinam.[243] Rice, which was available in plenty in the Cauvery delta, was the main attraction for the merchants. Some unpublished manuscripts preserved in the National Archives of Lisbon contain orders issued by the captain and factor of Coromandel coast to purchase rice at Tirumalairayanpattinam and despatch orders signed by the Portuguese officials who transported rice from this port to Cochin and other ports on the Malabar coast even during 1524.[244]

## COASTAL TRADE

The abundant availability of rice in Coromandel was a factor that greatly contributed to its export commerce.[245] Chinese accounts of the fourteenth and fifteenth centuries, particularly *Tao-i Chi-hlioh* (1349) and *Hsing-Ch'a Shenglan* (1436) note the flourishing rice trade of Coromandel with Malabar.[246] Coastal ports like Tirumullaivasal, Tirumalairayanpattinam and Nagapattinam, being situated in the agrarian based hinterland of Cauvery delta, served as the best market centres where the physical environment of the port and its hinterland determined the pattern and volume of trade.

Coromandel and Malabar had flourishing country trade. The *Marakayars* of Coromandel generally dominated the rice trade, particularly with Calicut in the early years of the sixteenth century; they sailed in their own vessels.[247] Three leading Hindu merchants of Mylapore also engaged in rice trade.[248] Many Muslims and Hindus of Malabar sailed to Coromandel in their own ships for purchase of rice.[249] Merchants of Cannanore too traded with Coromandel in rice.[250] The rice trade of Quilon with Coromandel is well known. The Portuguese captain, Duarte Pacheco Pereira, describes the rice carrying ships.[251] The region from Tanur to Quilon received abundant supply of rice from Coromandel coast,[252] Coromandel rice being four times cheaper than rice of Canara region.[253]

The Portuguese settled in Cochin, when they learnt that spices were exchanged for Coromandel rice in the Malabar coast, stipulated that all rice-carrying vessels sailing from Coromandel to Calicut should carry *cartazes*.[254] They also maintained an armada in Coromandel to protect ships against pirates and to curb the movement of ships sailing without *cartazes*. The *orcamento da Estado da India* records that soldiers of the armada were paid thirty-six *pardaos*.[255] As early as 1503, some Portuguese traders like Duarte Pacheco and Manuel Pessanha sailed from the Coromandel coast for Cochin with a cargo of rice. Fearing an attack by *Marakayars*, they arranged for an escort,[256] which implies that domination by *Marakayars* of seaborne rice trade in Coromandel. The town of Calicut[257] heavily depended on regular rice supply from *Marakayars*.[258] The Portuguese probably blockaded rice supply to Calicut in order to force King Zamorin to sign a better contract for the purchase of spices. The Portuguese began actively participating in rice trade after the Portuguese Viceroy, Dom Duarte de Menezes gave the green signal by appointing Manuel de Frias as *Feitor da Costa da Choromandel* in 1522 to organise the provision of rice and other commodities to the west coast.[259]

The export of rice from Coromandel to Cochin in 1527 was 124 *gantas*[260] and in 1547, 717 *gantas*.[261] Cochin also emerged as a rice distribution centre to Maldives. The viceroy, Lopo Soares, encouraged private Portuguese barter trade with rice exchanged for spices, especially pepper.[262] The *Casados* of Cochin were the first to respond, taking an active role in the procurement of rice from Coromandel. The Portuguese required rice also for themselves, since the soldiers were paid partly in cash and partly in rice. We have confirmation of this in the writings of *Almoxarife dos Mantimentos* of Cochin, who reports that rice of Coromandel was necessary for military payments.[263] Some of the Portuguese traders who came to Coromandel to procure rice later settled down at various ports. Nagapattinam thus emerged as a great centre of rice trade replacing Tirumalairayanpattinam. Correa observed as many as seven hundred boats loading rice at Nagapattinam to supply various ports.[264] Barros states that thirty private Portuguese traders settled at Nagapattinam and conducted brisk trade in rice with Cochin.[265] Later, fifty *Casados* of Cochin who traded in Coromandel rice made huge profits in this activity.[266]

The growing Portuguese rice trade from Coromandel was not to the liking of the rulers of Malabar. The *Casados* had participated in the military actions taken against the ruler of Porakkad by the Portuguese viceroy; in retaliation, Porakkad began to hamper Portuguese trade in rice.[267] The Portuguese attacked and prevented ships of the *Marakayars* carrying rice to Calicut, which antagonised the Zamorin of Calicut against

RECORDED DEPARTURES FROM PULICAT TO MALABAR PORTS, 1502-24*

| *Period* | *Destination* | | | |
|---|---|---|---|---|
| | *Calicut* | *Cochin* | *Quilon* | *Cannanore* |
| 1502 | 7 | - | - | - |
| 1503 | - | 1 | - | - |
| 1505 | 1 | 1 | - | - |
| 1508 | 1 | 1 | - | 1 |
| 1510 | - | 1 | - | - |
| 1511 | - | 1 | - | - |
| 1513 | - | - | 1 | - |
| 1515 | - | 1 | - | - |
| 1518 | - | 1 | - | - |
| 1524 | - | 10 | 2 | - |

*See A.D. 1502, Correa, vol. I, pp. 300-4; Biker, tomo I, p. 23; F.C. Danvers, p. 85. (1503), Correa, tomo I, Pt. I, pp. 429-30. (1503), Correa, tomo I, Pt. II, cap. VIII, p. 594, Correa, I, pp. 609-15. (1508), Correa, I, pp. 301-2, *A.N.T.T.*, CC-II-15-129. (1510) Barros, II, liv. II, cap. III. (1511), Barros, liv. III, cap. XIV. (1513), CC-II-41-144. (1515), CC-II-61-157. (1518), Correa, tomo II, Pt. II, cap. VIII, p. 594. (1524), CC-2a-113-176, 2s-1187-137, 2a-118-32, 2a-120-113, 2a-121-34, 2a-120-110, 2a-120-111.

Portuguese trade in rice. Another reason for the Zamorin's antipathy was that Portuguese trade posed a fierce competition to Muslim traders.[268]

The *Marakayars'* trade in rice does not seem to have been seriously affected by the entry of the Portuguese. Pate *Marakayar* from port Kunimedu in Coromandel took up residence at Cochin because of its lucrative trade.[269] At Kunimedu, the brothers and relatives of Pate *Marakayar* and Kunjali *Marakayar* helped in procurement of rice and organisation of trade. Correa records that rice trade was carried on by *Marakayars* all of whom had partnership with their friends. Kunjali *Marakayar* died at Kunimedu in 1534 but his family members continued rice trade.[270]

Faced with hostilities from the Portuguese in the sea, the *Marakayars* began to avoid the sea route and continued their rice trade often on bullocks crossing the ghats to unload it in the Malabar region.[271] Mamale *Marakayar* was the chief of all *Marakayar* monopoly holders in rice trade and continued to dominate Coromandel rice trade.[272] With their knowledge of the local inland routes *Marakayars* began to penetrate through the hinterland. The Portuguese attacks at sea also paved the way for the emergence of *Marakayars* as retail distributors of rice in Malabar in addition to their earlier wholesale business. They went to the hinterland, sold rice and collected pepper. Mamale *Marakayar* had an agreement with the local Malabar rulers under which Mamale *Marakayar*, his brother Cherina *Marakayar* and allied partners had the exclusive right to sell rice on the Malabar coast.[273] Thus rice trade from Kunimedu with Cochin, Calicut and Quilon flourished and continued to be dominated by *Marakayars* towards the end of the 1520s.

Circumstances of later years, however, favoured the Portuguese. Coromandel was severely distressed by drought and famine in those years and rice production declined drastically. The Portuguese began to import rice from Bengal and other regions into Coromandel. The Vijayanagara emperor Achyutadevaraya, in appreciation of their services sent an *ola*.[274] The competition in rice trade continued and the *Marakayars* sought the help of the Zamorin. A letter written at this time records that *Marakayars* of Coromandel paid one hundred *pardaos* while Hindu merchants paid fifty *pardaos* for purchase of a *cartaz* to trade in rice.[275] The *Marakayars* gave whatever the Portuguese asked, so that their business voyages did not become a total loss. Some Portuguese also began to trade with *Marakayars* in Coromandel. The armada of Coromandel, which was supposed to guard the Coromandel ships, oppressed the merchants and caused them annoyance. There had to be administrative intervention to stop this.[276]

A number of factors may explain the changing attitudes of the Portuguese. It is possible that the Portuguese had learnt from their experience with the western coast that compromise with native merchants in country trade paid off. The native merchants, on their part, began to collaborate with private Portuguese traders, since this assured them better protection from piratical attacks.

The leading *Marakayar* merchants, who had enough resources, began to resist the Portuguese attacks under the patronage of rulers. M.N. Pearson holds that the Muslim reaction against the Portuguese attacks was one of self-defence.[277] When the *Marakayars* were defeated at Vedalai near Rameswaram, the Portuguese *casados* were overjoyed. They celebrated their success with a victory march at Cochin.[278] When the viceroy prohibited voyages of the *casados* of Cochin to Maldives, their rice trade suffered, and so did the import of coir and cowries from Maldives.[279] The *casados'* trade in rice from Coromandel to Cochin and Maldives began to decline in the middle of the sixteenth century notwithstanding a letter eight prominent Portuguese rice traders wrote to their king in 1548, seeking new concessions and authorisation to engage in rice trade with Maldives.[280]

Some organised rice trade by the Portuguese seems to have taken shape when Cosmo de Paiva became captain of the Coromandel coast. He retained monopoly of rice trade and exported rice from Coromandel to the fishery coast and Malabar, which he sold at a price of his choice.[281] This was, quite likely, a personal enterprise.[282]

The continuing conflict in rice trade between the Portuguese and the *Marakayars* hindered the supply of rice from Nagapattinam to Cochin, Quilon and Cannanore in mid-sixteenth century.[283] An increasing number of Portuguese vessels were engaged in rice trade.[284] The Portuguese also employed the twenty-one vessels of the *Marakayars*, which were captured and taken as booty in 1568.[285] The Portuguese defeated the *Marakayars* at Talaimannar in 1577 and used their captured vessels, numbering fifty ships big and small, for shipping rice.[286] Various native vessels such as *fragata, fustas, sampans, caturs, paravu* and *toni* were used for transporting rice.[287] Compared to the number of Coromandel vessels employed in rice trade in 1577, the number of ships seems to have definitely increased.[298]

Nagapattinam emerged as the main port of rice trade in the Cauvery delta. Trigo de Almeida, captain of Nagapattinam, procured rice from the hinterland areas.[289] Merchants like Diogo Fernandez Pereira supplied rice regularly from Nagapattinam in 1586.[290] The domination of Nagapattinam-based Portuguese and Kunimedu *Marakayars* in rice trade is clear from contemporary records. Boccaro narrates that with the enormous profits derived from rice trade conducted from Nagapattinam with various ports in 1594 the Portuguese built houses of stone.[291] As part of country trade in rice between the eastern and western coast of India, Portuguese ships carried more than 20,000 measures of rice (equivalent to 470,000 bushels) annually from Nagapattinam.[292]

The Portuguese predominance in rice trade brought to an end the established practice of bilateral visits and investment in rice trade by merchants of Malabar and Coromandel, and towards the end of the sixteenth century the mode became that of one-way traffic by visit and investment between native traders and Portuguese settlers in Coromandel. Francisco Maneiro, employed in the Portuguese factory at Cochin, left his service and began to trade with Coromandel.[293] Many *casados* like Pedro Goncalves and Braz Alvares resided at Santhome and traded in rice and encouraged *Parava* converts to participate in country trade.[294] Even a Sinhalese Christian, Duarte de Miranda, participated in country trade and later settled down at Santhome. He owned a *nau* and two *catamarans*.[295] Other *casados* of Santhome, who had *fustas* and ships, also traded in rice with Malabar.[296] An inventory of the merchandise received by the factor of Cochin mentions cotton textiles from the Coromandel coast, which were also probably used to exchange for spices.[297]

Pepper was smuggled from Quilon to Coromandel coast through Vilinjam, Aryankavu and Puthura. To prevent its smuggling the Portuguese maintained an armada which seems to have been effective.[298] Provisions for the armada were regularly sent from Cochin. Large quantities of pepper were also smuggled into Coromandel over the ghats, particularly through Palghat in Coimbatore district via Pudukottai. Unauthorised traffic was also carried on via Aramboly pass in Kanyakumari district.[299] The armada, with captains specially appointed by the king of Portugal, was expected to curb this clandestine trade.[300] The lucrative

PORTUGUESE TRADE IN IRON EXPORTED FROM COROMANDEL TO COCHIN, 1524-47*

| *Date* | *Ship* | *Volume* |
|---|---|---|
| 17 May 1524 | Navio Santiago | |
| 20 August 1524 | Navio Sta. Maria Anunciada | 2 pipas &15 arcos |
| 4 September 1524 | Navio Santiago | 3 pipas |
| January 1547 | Navio... | 1 arb, 3 art, 6 arcos |

*A.N.T.T., *CC* 2a-115-67, 2a-118-69, 2a-118-172 (1524) Elaine Sanceau, Cartas de Dom Joao de Castro, XLIII, IV, fl. 329 (1547).

business of importing pepper into Coromandel from the Malàbar region[301] lured even many Portuguese traders to it, among whom was Antonio Mendes, living in Cochin and trading with Nagapattinam.[302] Joao Fernandes Correa left Cochin permanently to settle at Nagapattinam.[303] Francisco Toscano, a *casado* resident of Santhome, owned a *navio* engaged in pepper trade in 1547.[304]

The Portuguese tried their best to purchase the entire stock of pepper in Malabar and blockade its supply to other regions like Coromandel, but failed. Pepper trade was too lucrative to be so artificially constrained, attracting some Portuguese themselves to illegal trade in it.

Besides pepper, the *naus* from Cochin supplied arecanuts to Coromandel. Merchants from Cannanore traded in other commodities such as coconuts, jaggery and palm sugar with the Coromandel coast.[305] Iron from the hinterland of Pulicat and Kunimedu was exported to Cochin.

In 1527 twenty-two quintals, three arrobas and twenty-two arratels were exported from Coromandel to Cochin,[306] and, apparently, re-exported to Lisbon. The Portuguese exported mutton, pork, other varieties of meat, fish and timber from Coromandel to ports on the western coast. Copper was the main import from Cochin to Coromandel.[307]

Coromandel trade with Bengal flourished during the late sixteenth century. Early sixteenth century sources record that Satagon, called *porto pequeno de Bengala,* and Chittagong, called *porto grande*, were the chief ports of Bengal coast. From about 1580 Hooghly became the chief port. As early as 1526 ships of Bengal traded with Coromandel. A ship sailing from Bengal to Coromandel without *cartaz* was captured by the Portuguese captain of Coromandel,[308] who sold off all its merchandise including its *nakhoda.*[309]

The king of Bengal had friendly commercial relations with Coromandel and this encouraged Bengal trade.[310] After the Portuguese conquest of Diu, the viceroy rewarded the officials and granted permission to eighteen persons to undertake voyage to Bengal from Coromandel, which encouraged the Portuguese to trade there.[311] Damio Bernaldes, a leading merchant of the time, was given special licence to sail to Bengal and was later arrested at Nagapattinam for his misdeeds.[312] Antonio de Lemos, trading from Santhome with Bengal, was a rich merchant.[313] The Portuguese factor and captain of Coromandel, Diogo Rebello, took Coromandel guns and arrived at Satagon in his own vessel. He sent Diogo de Spinolla and Duarte Dias as messengers to the king of Bengal. They were received well at Satagon and were asked to construct their factory in Chittagong.[314]

The main attraction for the Portuguese in Bengal trade was the huge demand for *chanks* produced in the pearl fishery coast. The *chanks* were brought to Coromandel and exported to Bengal for making bracelets; in return, sugar was imported into the Coromandel coast.[315] Boats also sailed from Nagapattinam to Pipli on the Orissa coast to bring back a large volume of sugar. There was a Portuguese settlement at Pipli. The English traveller Ralph Fitch records that ships from Nagapattinam arrived at Hooghly in 1586 to load sugar.[316] Some ships from Nagapattinam sailed only to the ports of Orissa, mainly Pipli.[317] Among the traders sailing from Coromandel to the Orissa and Bengal coasts were Duarte Pinheiro,[318] Cristovao Cortes, Duarte de Panha, Jose de Silveira, Estevao Roiz, Gaspar Costa, Inacio Macedo and Simao Melo.[319]

After the Portuguese arrived, Coromandel established trade contacts with the ports of Canara coast and further up to Diu in Cambay. Inter-coastal trade was chiefly in butter, meat and timber found in abundance on the Coromandel coast.[320] Quality timber, available in Coromandel, was probably used for building ships and sea-going vessels. The technique of shipbuilding seems to have been specialised to carry particular commodities, such as rice, timber and horses.

Early Portuguese sources record that goods from Cambay were brought to the Coromandel coast by the Malabar merchants; no direct trade existed either between Coromandel and Canara or Coromandel and Cambay.[321] Dyes were an important import from Cambay to Pulicat.[322] Portuguese traders exported butter and meat from Pulicat and Nagapattinam to Bassein, which was a major settlement of the Portuguese on the western coast.[323] Chaul was another port of importance. Horses from Ormuz and West Asia were imported to Chaul, which induced many Portuguese traders to trade in horses with Coromandel. Among Portuguese merchants at Chaul were Fernao Jorge, who traded with Pulicat[324] and Antonio Dias who traded with Santhome of Mylapore.[325]

Coromandel trade with Goa began as early as 1522 from Pulicat.[326] The Portuguese also traded with Goa in 1524 from Tirumalairayanpattinam.[327] After Goa became the capital of the

*Estado da India* in the 1530s, Coromandel was linked with Goa and commerce flourished. Rice brought in *champanas* from Coromandel to Goa by the Portuguese on the crown account came handy in the upkeep of soldiers.[328] Adao Lourenco from Goa frequently sailed to Pulicat and conducted regular trade with that port.[329] His partner, Antonio Cordoso, who traded in rice, later settled down at Santhome.[330] Tristao de Paiva was an honoured citizen of Goa who traded with Mylapore, where he settled down.[331] Many Portuguese abandoned Goa and other ports of the western coast to settle down in Coromandel to participate in country trade, as a result of which the number of Portuguese country traders in the Bay of Bengal region went up to 1,000 in 1546.[332]

According to the *Regimento do Mandovim*, the *navios* of the king of Portugal sailing from Coromandel paid one-fifth value of their cargo on arrival at Goa in October 1522. Viceroy Dom Duarte de Menezes ordered that the ships of native merchants would pay one-twentieth value of their cargo at the customs house of Goa.[333] This provision was made chiefly to attract the Asian merchants.

Coromandel-to-Goa trade, however, did not flourish. Textiles from Pulicat were subjected to multiple taxes at Goa, introduced by the viceroy Martim Affonso de Sousa. When this was brought to the notice of the king of Portugal, he asked the viceroy, Dom Joao de Castro, to revive the Pulicat textile trade and to find ways of raising customs profitably. The viceroy in his reply said that he was looking forward to receiving supply of textiles from other Coromandel ports where they were available in plenty.[334] Later, between 1568 and 1577, the tax rates were increased. On any merchandise landing at Goa from anywhere six per cent duty was to be paid.[335] This was in addition to the customs charged at Cochin port.[336] The Portuguese also collected anchorage fee according to the type of vessel at several ports of the western coast,[337] ranging from one *pardao* of gold to half a *tanga*, which the traders found excessive.[338] Coromandel merchants therefore preferred to sell their commodities at Cape Comorin, which was tax free.[339]

The traders received some relief when the viceroy ordered on 21st September 1577 that tax on *beatilha* textiles of Pulicat, if taken by land, would be one-third that charged for transport by sea. The merchants were thereby encouraged to favour the land route to Goa,[340] and coastal trade between Coromandel and Goa began to decline while trade by land flourished.

Broadly speaking we may mention that overland trade in the Coromandel region was carried on in relatively large number of conspicuous and substantial market centres in diverse sets of commodities throughout the year. Many places had specific given market days catering to the needs of the buyers and sellers and the organisation of internal trade itself differed in several points from that of the trade before the creation of *nayakattanams* and the appointment of *nayaks* in Coromandel. Land-bound commerce resembled also in some respects the features of the previous Chola period set up where merchants from different parts of South India flocked together at the Coromandel markets. It is evident that barter was not feasible as the inflow of cash assumed unprecedented proportions during the sixteenth century. More and more coins had been issued from the minting houses of the Vijayanagara rulers and the *nayaks*. As noted by the Portuguese all these types of coins were in circulation at the markets. Seeking the cooperation of the *nayaks,* markets came to be linked to the administrative centres. Although coastal trade was seasonal the presence of the Portuguese really added change in the patterns of country trade during the sixteenth century which was quite different from the one that existed in the previous centuries.

## NOTES AND REFERENCES

1. Karl Polyani, *Traders and Trade,* New York, 1975.
2. Irfan Habib, *The Agrarian System of Mughal India 1556-1707,* Bombay, 1963, p. 75.
3. K.R. Hall, *Trade and Statecraft in the Age of the Colas,* New Delhi, 1980; K.A. Nilakanta Sastri, The Colas, Madras, 1975, vol. II, p. 294.
4. *S.I.T.I.,* III, pp. 1077-79. Some *nadus* mentioned in the inscription of 1513-14 have attained the status of larger division called *simai.* They are Kunrattur, Kottur, Virabhadhra, Palaiyur and Perukanchi *simai.* The inscription of 1514 menions eighty-five *nadus;* but only eighteen *nadus* existed at end of the century.
5. *A.R.E.,* 58 of 1900.
6. Ibid., 398 of 1911.
7. Ibid., 180 of 1963-64.
8. Sadhu Subrahmanya Sastry, p. 248.
9. *A.R.E.,* 623 of 1904.
10. Ibid.
11. Ibid., 405 of 1912.

12. Ibid., 302 of 1904; *S.I.I.*, XVII, p. 154.
13. Ibid., 198 of 1922 (C).
14. Ibid., 235 of 1903.
15. Ibid., 54 of 1913.
16. Ibid., 470 of 1938; 81 of 1943.
17. *T.V.M.T.I.*, No. 436 (1587).
18. *A.R.E.*, 470 of 1937-38 (1560).
19. Ibid., 450 of 1920 (1524).
20. Ibid., 164 of 1935.
21. Ibid., 409 of 1913.
22. Ibid., 138 of 1942.
23. Ibid., 170 of 1966.
24. Ibid., 470 of 1937-38.
25. Ibid., 450 of 1920.
26. Ibid., 87 of 1943 (1579).
27. Ibid., 106 of 1918 (1562).
28. Ibid. The protection fees appear to have been collected from the entire region of Tenkarai *simai*.
29. *A.R.E.*, 423 of 1929 (1574).
30. Ibid., This *pettai* was established by Urattatupappu *nayaka* in 1546 who demarcated the boundaries of market within which the people were to be settled; see also ibid., 312 of 1918.
31. Ibid., 369 of 1913 (1596).
32. Ibid., 30 of 1905 (1583).
33. Ibid., 221 of 1931.
34. Ibid., 240 of 1904 (1550); *S.I.I.*, XVII, pp. 104-5.
35. K. Deivanayagam, *Dharumai Adheena Seppedugal*, Dharmapuram, 1988, *C.P.* No. 6, line 6 (A.D. 1513).
36. *A.R.E.*, 45 of 1934.
37. Ibid., 427 of 1928-29 (1569).
38. Ibid., 240 of 1904.
39. Ibid., 19(a) of 1946-47.
40. *T.V.M.T.I.*, No. 440 (1590).
41. P. Shanmugam, "Pattadai and industries in the Tamil country under the Vijayanagara rule", *Journal of Asian and African Studies*, No. 37, 1989, p. 42.
42. *T.V.M.T.I.*, No. 413 (1548).
43. *Epigraphia Carnatica*, V, Pt. I, b.L. 75.
44. Gaspar Correa, tomo IV, ch. XXI, p. 282.
45. A *nayaka* granted more lands to the Vishnu temple and less to Siva temple in Kanchipuram; Achyutadevaraya settled the matter through equal distribution of lands to both temples.
46. *A.R.E.*, 301 of 1965-66.
47. *T.T.D.E.S.*, V(55), The Srivaishnavas lived at Kulasekharapuram in Tirupati.
48. *A.R.E.*, 301 of 1965-66.
49. *Sthala* in Indian traditional usage is a place where a famous shrine or temple exists. Temples could be divided into various groups such as *murti* of Tiruvarur, *sthala* of Mylapore and Kaṇchipuram, and the nucleating

type of Srirangam, with a cluster of temples related to one another by a nexus of legend and lore.

50. *S.I.T.I.*, I, p. 318 (1521).
51. *T.T.D.E.S.*, III(91), p. 195 (1524).
52. *T.V.M.T.I.*, Nos. 395 and 397 (1534).
53. *S.I.T.I.*, I, p. 343 (1534).
54. *T.V.M.T.I.*, No. 440.
55. T.K.T. Viraraghavacharya, *History of Tirupati* (The Tiruvengadam Temple), Tirupati, 1954, vol. II, pp. 565-66.
56. Gaspar Correa, tomo IV, ch. XXXI, pp. 282, 299-304 and 324-25.
57. Sadhu Subrahmanya Sastry, p. 304.
58. *T.T.D.E.S.*, V(367) (1547).
59. Sadhu Subrahmanya Sastry, p. 258.
60. Some inscriptions mention the names of bazaars. The bazaar at Putalapattu was called *Navalan Perunthеruvu* where merchants and sundry traders assembled from various places in the Chittoor region during 1516; *S.I.I.*, XXIII, pp. 32-3.
61. Purchas, vol. X, p. 105.
62. *A.R.E.*, 442 of 1906.
63. *T.T.D.E.S.*, V, p. 66 (1554).
64. *A.R.E.*, 282 of 1977-78 (B).
65. Ibid., 442 of 1906.
66. *S.I.I.*, I, pp. 88-9.
67. Mackenzie Manuscripts 15-6-8; for details see T.V. Mahalingam (ed.), Mackenzie Manuscripts: Summaries of the Historical Manuscripts of the Mackenzie Collection (Tamil and Malayalaṁ), vol. I, Madras, 1972.
68. *T.V.M.T.I.*, No. 425 (1569).
69. *T.T.D.E.S.*, V(367) (1547).
70. Ibid.
71. Sadhu Subrahmanya Sastry, p. 304.
72. Sanjay Subrahmanyam, *Merchants, Markets and State in the Early Modern India*, Delhi, 1990.
73. Sadhu Subrahmanya Sastry, pp. 251-52.
74. *T.V.M.T.I.*, No. 425 (1569).
75. The swan is believed to separate water from milk. It is a symbol of unadulterated state. *Pattinapalai* mentions the seal of the Chola State with the tiger mark used in the marketing of commodities. See *Pattinapalai*, Indian Antiquary (hereafter *IA*), 1912, p. 149.
76. *A.R.E.*, 331 of 1913 (1475). The temples such as Srirangam possessed big godowns for storage of provisions and not for marketing. There are other pieces of evidence cited in this reference to show that godowns existed for commercial purposes.
77. Ibid., 221 of 1929-30, 261 of 1909, 201 of 1936-37. We find references to oil merchants such as *ayira vaishyar, vanigar, sekku vanigar*, see 91 of 1918 (1427). This oil monger community originally consisted of one thousand *gotras*. See also, *A.R.E.*, 1912, para 72. *Sekku vanigar* is compared to oil merchants who possessed *sekku* (oil press). For details see also *T.T.D.E.S.*, IV(112).
78. Ibid., 697 of 1921-22 (1534), 60 of 1911-12 (1538), 282 of 1933 (1564)

and 430 of 1909-10; *E.I.*, VI, pp. 232-39.

79. Ibid., 18 of 1935, 54 of 1907 (1517) and 119 of 1937; *S.I.I.*, XVII, p. 105; *S.I.T.I.*, II, p. 995; *A.N.T.T.*, *CC*-I-19-102.
80. *S.I.I.*, XXII, p. 144; (1531) Kachchirayar (Tirukoyilur); *A.R.E.*, 175 of 1906; 111 of 1933-34 (Rishivandiyam) Kudirai kanikkai is mentioned (Timmappa *nayaka*); 423 of 1929 (1574) Kudirai Viladam called horse stables are mentioned at Tiruvannamalai.
81. *A.R.E.*, 193 of 1939-40.
82. *A.N.T.T.* (MSS.) *N.A.*, No. 808, fl. 2v.
83. *S.I.T.I.*, II, p. 995; *A.R.E.*, 119 of 1931.
84. *A.R.E.*, 348 of 1913, as early as eleventh century we find some aspects relating to a regulated market existed in Chidambaram, see K.R. Hall, p. 102.
85. *I.M.P.*, I, Nos. 620 and 512; *A.R.E.*, 18 of 1915, 53 of 1907 and 241 of 1904; *S.I.I.*, XVII, p. 105; I(446); and IV, 524(a), 30 of 1905, 193 of 1940, 295 of 1919.
86. *S.I.T.I.*, I, 446 (1586).
87. *A.R.E.*, 407 of 1921.
88. N. Venkataramayya, *Studies in the History of the Third Dynasty of Vijayanagara*, Madras, 1939, pp. 30-1.
89. Duarte Barbosa, vol. II, p. 130.
90. N. Venkataramanayya, p. 297.
91. K.N. Chitnis, *Socio Economic Aspects of Medieval India*, Poona, 1979, p. 332.
92. J. Wicki, *Documenta Indica* (1583-85), Roma, 1975, vol. XIII, pp. 46-8.
93. R.H. Major, *India in the Fifteenth Century*, Delhi, 1974, p. 7.
94. Schurhammer, *Francis Xavier: His Life His Times*, Roma, 1977, vol. II, p. 57 and vol. III, pp. 204 and 321(f.n.); J. Wicki, *Jesuit Residence of St. John in Santhome-Mylapore 1549-98;* Anand Amaladass (ed.), *Jesuit Presence in Indian History*, Anand, 1988, pp. 54 and 61.
95. Ibid.
96. Ibid.
97. Purchas, vol. X, pp. 217-19.
98. K.S. Mathew, *Portuguese Trade with India in the Sixteenth Century*, Delhi, 1983, p. 27.
99. *A.R.E.*, 241 of 1904.
100. Ibid., 295 of 1897 (1530); the text of the epigraph reads: "Irandu puramum salai maram vaithu".
101. Gaspar Correa, II, p. 725. For Santhome-Goa overland trade route, see Joseph Franz Schuttle, *Valignano's Mission Principles for Japan*, 2 vols., John J. Coyne (tr.), The Institute of Jesuit Sources, St. Louis, Missouri, 1985, vol. I, p. 121.
102. *T.T.D.E.S.*, V(154), pp. 407-8; *I.M.P.*, I, Nos. 620 and 512; Sadhu Subrahmanya Sastry, pp. 251-52.
103. *A.R.E.*, 18 of 1915.
104. Moreland, *India at the Death of Akbar*, Delhi, 1962, p. 7; T.V. Mahalingam, Administration . . . , p. 153.
105. *S.I.I.*, XXII, p. 115. The text reads: *Palangur parrutil kumiliser chola pandya purathil kudirai . . . engal simaiyil rekai padincha pon muppatharu panam.*

106. *A.R.E.*, 427 of 1929 (1569).
107. Ibid., 30 of 1905 (1583-84).
108. Ibid., 231 of 1910.
109. Ibid., 241 of 1904; the text of the epigraph mentions *"cilarai sarakkundana tirvai"*.
110. *S.I.T.I.*, II, p. 995; *A.R.E.*, 64 of 1907; 11(A) of 1934-35; *T.V.M.T.I.*, Nos. 438 and 440.
111. *A.R.E.*, 47 of 1938, 106 of 1918 and 360 of 1913.
112. Ibid., 241 of 1904.
113. *Biblioteca Nacional de Lisboa* (hereafter *BNL*) MSS. *Fundo Geral*, No. 2702, Livro do registos da Alfandega de Goa, fl. 7 v.
114. *A.R.E.*, 427 of 1929. *Annupu* was levied on goods sent out; and *allu* on goods that were picked up or selected by the consumers.
115. Sadhu Subrahmanya Sastry, pp. 251-52. *Ullayam* (local taxes), *perayam* (per person), *mulai vesam* (one-sixteenth on capital).
116. *T.T.D.E.S.*, V, pp. 407 and 408.
117. *S.I.I.*, XVII, p. 105.
118. G.S. Dikshit (ed.), *Early Vijayanagara Studies in its History and Culture*, Bangalore, 1988, p. 163.
119. Ibid.
120. *A.R.E.*, 494 of 1921; *S.I.I.*, II (71).
121. R. Nagaswamy, *Tamil Coins*, Madras, 1981, p. 64.
122. Sadhu Subrahmanya Sastry, p. 268.
123. *I.A.*, vol. XX, pp. 7-8.
124. *S.I.I.*, XXIV (1538), p. 415.
125. *A.R.E.*, 43 of 1938-39 (1538).
126. R.S. Panchamukhi, "Some Vijayanagara coins", *Journal of the Numismatic Society of India*, V, June 1943, pp. 58-9.
127. The coins were 3/4 cm in diameter and 350 mg weight. The ninety-three coins together weighed 36 grams.
128. For details see, A. Rangaswami Sarasvati, "Political maxims of the emperor poet, Krishnadevaraya" *The Journal of Indian History*, VI, (1925), pp. 61-88.
129. Meera Abraham, *Two Medieval Merchant Guilds of South India*, New Delhi, 1988, p. 41.
130. *A.R.E.*, 200 of 1937-38 (1531).
131. Ibid., 377 of 1911 (1544); the ayyavole merchants by common consent gifted toll income to the temple at Tirupati.
132. Ibid., 378 of 1928-29.
133. Ibid., 235 of 1903 (1599) and 59 of 1939.
134. Ibid. The President was called *pattanaswami;* he took care of specific aspects of administration. *Pattanam* means town; *swami* may be interpreted as chairperson. *pattanaswami* is almost an equivalent of *nagarsheths* of Gujarat.
135. Ibid. Chinna Nattichiyala *chetti* was the *chetti pattanaswami* of Mylapore *nagarattar*. Mylapore had merchant trade guilds even during the time of Rajendra Chola I. See *A.R.E.*, 321 of 1922.
136. *S.I.I.*, XVII(326); *A.R.E.*, 623 of 1904 and 59 of 1939.

137. *A.R.E.*, 59 of 1937(1547) and 1 of 1931-33, Pandanallur *simai* resident merchants agreed to pay certain rates of taxes per head load of grains and articles of merchandise to the Mudaliyur temple in Kumbakonam taluk.
138. Ibid., 681 of 1922.
139. *T.T.D.E.S.*, III(338), pp. 72-80.
140. *A.R.E.*, 198 of 1922 (C) (1596).
141. Ibid., 623 of 1904.
142. Ibid., 405 of 1912.
143. Ibid., 302 of 1904 and 54 of 1913.
144. *S.I.I.*, XXII, 103.
145. *A.R.E.*, 133 of 1919.
146. Ibid., 318 of 1909.
147. Ibid., 118 of 1944.
148. Ibid., 538 of 1963, 539 of 1963.
149. Ibid., 19(a) of 1946-47.
150. Henri Pirenne establishes the striking differences between the empire of trade and rise of cities. According to him no city in any circumstance evolved independently of commerce or industry; Henri Pirenne, *Medieval Cities, their Origins and the Revival of Trade* (tr.), Princeton, 1949.
151. Burton Stein in his study of Peasant State emphasises the role of temples and sectarian movements in urban development.
152. Lewis Mumford, *The City in History: its Origin and its Transformants and its Prospects*, London, 1961, pp. 35 and 235-54. Sociological theorists like Mumford and Sjoberg overemphasised the role of political power in the rise of urban towns.
153. Srirangam was an island town where river Cauvery encircles. Mythology places Cauvery on par with the Ganges in terms of taking a holy dip on *Adipperukku* festival. This place attracted pilgrims to its famous temple where Lord Vishnu reclines; it was sung by Tirumalisai Alvar in the eighth century.
154. *A.R.E.*, 293 of 1926-27; Kumbakonam was a famous pilgrimage centre where *Mahamagam* festival was celebrated. Merchants and people from Telugu region visited Kumbakonam and made endowments.
155. T.K.T. Viraraghavacharya, vol. II, 1954, pp. 565-66.
156. The name Thanjavur appears for the first time in the inscription of Rajaraja, *S.I.I.*, II, Pt. II, No. I. This town suffered a decline when Rajendra Chola I shifted his capital to Gangaikondacholapuram.
157. *T.T.D.E.S.*, III(159), pp. 331-32.
158. *T.V.M.T.I.*, No. 38; *A.R.E.*, 140 of 1915-16.
159. R.S. Sharma, *Urban Decay in India c.300-c.1000*, New Delhi, 1987, p. 107.
160. *T.T.D.E.S.*, V, p. 166; *A.R.E.*, 257 of 1930 (1511), 69 of 1938-39 and 260 of 1930 (1534); *Chennaimanagara Kalvettugal*, 81E of 1967; R. Sewell, *Antiquarian remains*, vol. I, p. 172; *D.I.*, V, p. 671.
161. *A.R.E.*, 532 of 1919.
162. Sadhu Subrahmanya Sastry, p. 219.
163. Ibid., p. 319.
164. Ibid.
165. *T.T.D.E.S.*, IV, pp. 166-67 (1537), pp. 179-81 (1575).

166. Ibid., III, No. 599 (1507), No. 266 (1512), No. 244 (1527); IV(55) (1533); V(396 ) (1544).
167. *A.R.E.*, 1914, part II, para 13.
168. *T.T.D.E.S.*, II(22).
169. Ibid., V(366).
170. *A.R.E.*, 538 of 1962-63 (1561).
171. Ibid., 117 of 1932-33 (1518).
172. Ibid., 623 of 1904 (1521) and 585 of 1919.
173. Ibid., 356 of 1922 (B).
174. Ibid., 1937-38, p. 106.
175. Ibid., 538 of 1962-63 (1561).
176. Ibid., 352 of 1913 (1598) and 11(A) of 1934-35.
177. Ibid., 356 of 1922 (B).
178. Ibid., 352 of 1913.
179. Akkappa *nayaka* paid *birangi vari* (cannon tax) to King Venkatapatidevaraya, which shows that the Arms Act was not unknown. The inscription is from Nellorepet which forms a suburb of modern Guidyattam town; *A.R.E.*, 121 of 1921.
180. P.V. Jagadisa Ayyar, "Construction of forts", *Quarterly Journal of the Mythic Society*, vol. XII, 1921-22, p. 368.
181. Ibid.
182. C.S. Srinivasachari, *History of the City of Madras*, Madras, 1939, p. XXV.
183. R. Sewell, p. 168.
184. T.V. Mahalingam, *Mackenzie Manuscripts*, vol. I, MSS. No. 13, p. 97.
185. *T.T.D.E.S.*, V, p. 281 (1540) Chandragiri became the capital of Vijayanagara empire under Srirangaraya and Venkatapatidevaraya from 1576.
186. N. Venkataramanaya, pp. 170-71.
187. S. Krishnaswamy Ayengar, p. 86; *E.I.*, XXV, p. 302.
188. Ibid., p. 323.
189. *T.T.D.E.S.*, IV, pp. 150-51 (1536) and IV(197) (1536).
190. *A.R.E.*, 376 of 1922 (1536); *T.T.D.E.S.*, I, p. 202 (1509-29).
191. *E.I.*, XIV, 1917-18, pp. 168-77 (1528).
192. The fort at Uttiramerur had a Brahmin street; *A.R.E.*, 376 of 1922 (1536).
193. Virginia Fass, *The Forts of India*, Delhi, 1985, p. 250.
194. Vellore was known as Paramesvaramangalam in the eighth century; *S.I.T.I.*, I(110), p. 130; R. Sewell, *List of Antiquarian Remains in the Presidency of Madras*, Madras, 1882, p. 154. See also Dinsha Aaleshir, "The legend of Vellore Talayarkan"; *I.A.*, II(172), p. 154. For details of the legend and the construction of Fort Vellore see, Lieut, H.P. Hawkes, "Memorandum of the fort and Hindu temple at Vellore and over its neighbourhood as recorded in 1815 October-March", *The Madras Journal of Literature and Science* (hereafter *M.J.L.S.*), No. 8, New series, p. 274.
195. *A.R.E.*, 41 of 1887 and 42 of 1887; *S.I.I.* I, pp. 73-5.
196. Ibid.
197. Purchas, vol. X, pp. 217-19.
198. Heras, *The Aravidu Dynasty*, p. 405.
199. Y. Subbarayalu, *Vallam Excavations*, Tanjore, 1984, p. 13.

200. R. Sathiyanatha Aiyar, *History of the Nayaks of Madura*, Madras, 1980, p. 37.
201. Y. Subbarayalu, p. 13.
202. *T.T.D.E.S.*, IV(238).
203. Ibid., No. 152, 175, 198 and 365.
204. Ibid., No. 386.
205. *A.R.E.*, 259 of 1911.
206. See for details, Abul Fazal, *Aini-i-Akbari*, Delhi, 1978, vol. III, p. 443; W.H. Moreland, *India at the Death of Akbar*, Delhi, 1962, p. 150.
207. Arjun Appadurai, "Right and Left Castes in South India", *I.E.S.H.R.*, 11, Nos. 2 and 3, 1974, pp. 216-60.
208. Frank Perlin, "Proto industrialization and pre-colonial South Asia", *Past and Present*, 98, 1983, p. 33.
209. Silappadikkaram in its *Valuvur edutha Kathai* states that *Kaveripoom-pattinam* consisted of two main divisions called Maruvur and Pattinapakkam. See also *Annals of Oriental Research*, Madras, 1960, vol. XVI, 1959-60, Pt. I, p. 1.
210. *A.R.E.*, 256 of 1912, 342 of 1912, 103 of 1933 (1353) and 170 of 1933 (1374).
211. *S.I.I.*, XVII, pp. 311-13; (Sadras) *A.R.E.*,103 of 1933 (1453), 173 of 1932-33 (1376); (Cuddalore) *A.R.E.*, 1944-45, p. 61 (1303); (Marakanam) *A.R.E.*, 30 of 199; (Tranquebar) *S.I.I.*, IV, p. 120.
212. T.V. Mahalingam, *Reading*, p. 169.
213. *A.R.E.*, 623 of 1904.
214. Ibid., 103 of 1933 (1353).
215. Ibid.
216. *S.I.T.I.*, I(66); *A.R.E.*, 173 of 1932-33 (1376).
217. *A.R.E.*, 70 of 1932-33; *S.I.T.I.*, I(165) (1374).
218. *Diario da Viagem de Vasco da Gama*, Porto, 1945, vol. II, pp. 291-95.
219. Tome Pires, vol. II, p. 271.
220. *Diario da Viagem*, pp. 250 and 301-3.
221. Tome Pires, vol. II, p. 221.
222. For details see Mottupalli pillar inscription in *E.I.*, XII(29).
223. V. Yasodha Devi, "Andhra's contribution to Indian culture: trade and commerce", *S.V. University Oriental Journal*, Tirupati, 1973, vol. XVI, p. 105.
224. See *Journal of the Andhra Historical Research Society*, vol. XXV, pp. 118ff. See also *A.R.E.*, 78 and 79 of 1964; *N.D.I.*, I, Gudur, 39.
225. *A.R.E.*, 357 of 1928-29, 369 of 1928-29, 374 of 1928-29, 202 of 1923 (Devaraya period).
226. *S.I.I.*, XVIII, pp. 311-13, lines 23-4.
227. Ibid.
228. During the field visit to Pulicat this inscription was observed. It records that Pangajavalli repaired this temple and erected the *kalyana mandapam*. Donations were made by one Balavantakulu.
229. *A.N.T.T.*, *C.C.*, II-117-22, *C.C.*, II-118-32.
230. Ibid., II-118-32.
231. R.H. Major, *India in the Fifteenth Century*, London, 1857.
232. Varthema, pp. 195-96.

233. Correa, vol. II, Pt. II, ch. 9, p. 721.
234. *A.N.T.T.*, Gavetas, XV-19-11.
235. Correa, vol. III, pp. 448-49.
236. Achilles Meersman, *The Franciscans in Tamil Nad*, Schoneck-Beckenried, 1962, pp. 16-29.
237. K.A.N. Shastri, *Foreign Notices of South India: from Magesthenes to Mahuan*, Madras, 1972, p. 115.
238. *A.N.T.T.*, - MSS. *C.C.*, Pt. 2a-119-103; 2a-119-104 (1524).
239. T.V. Mahalingam, *Readings* . . . , p. 169; see also *A.R.E.*, 448 of 1922, Papanasam (1453). 524 of 1920 (1450) Pattisvaram, 456 of 1922, Kudumiyanmalai (1458); *S.I.I.*, VI, 4, Tirukattupalli (1460); 238 of 1916 Srimushnam (1486).
240. Ibid.,
241. *A.N.T.T.*, *Gavetas da Torre do Tombo*, 20, maco 4, doc. 15, fl. 2. See Braganca Pereira, APO, 27 December 1506, doc. 19, p. 163.
242. Ibid.
243. Ibid.
244. *A.N.T.T.*, *C.C.*, Pt. 2a - 119-103, 2a - 109-104 (1524).
245. Gaspar Correa, vol. I, p. 593.
246. W.W. Rockhill, "Notes on the relations and trade of China with the eastern archipelago and the coast of the Indian Ocean during the Fourteenth century" in *Toung Pao*, vol. XVI, 1915.
247. Correa, vol. I, pp. 300-4.
248. J. Biker, *Collecao de tratados e concertos de pazes que o Estado da India, Portuguesa Fez com os reis e Senhores*, Lisboa, tomo I, pp. 21-3.
249. Duarte Barbosa, vol. II, p. 97.
250. Ibid., vol. I, p. 81.
251. Castanheda, vol. II, p. 97.
252. Tome Pires, vol. I, pp. 76-7.
253. Barros, vol. II/1-4, Castanheda, liv. VI, capit 91.
254. Correa, tomo I, p. 298.; H.A.G. Mss Codex No. 3027, *Provisoes Alvares e regimentos*, Pt. I, fl. 21v. The *cartaz* listed the name and tonnage of the ship, age and name of its captain, port of embarkation, disembarkation, approximate date of departure, name of the writer, the issuing authority and the date. The *cartaz* served more as an instrument of control than as a means of raising revenue after 1522 in Coromandel. For details see K.S. Mathew, "Trade in the Indian Ocean and the Portuguese system of cartazes" in Malyn Newitt (ed.), *The First Portuguese Colonial Empire*, Exeter, 1986, pp. 69-84; Tome Pires, vol. I, pp. 76-7.
255. J. Biker, p. 22.
256. Correa, tomo I, Pt. I, pp. 428-30.
257. Ibid., tomo I, Pt. II, cap. VIII, p. 594.
258. Ibid., p. 559. The date recorded by Correa is October 1518.
259. Silva Rego, *Documentacao Para Historia das Missoes do Padroado do Portugues do Orient, Lisboa*, 1947, vol. I (1500-42), p. 417.
260. *A.N.T.T.*, *C.C.*, I-38-50.
261. *A.N.T.T.*, Cartas de Dom Joao de Castro, XLIII, IV, fl. 329.
262. For details see, R.S. White Way, *The Rise of Portuguese Power in India, 1497-1550*, Patna, 1979, pp. 179-98.

263. *A.N.T.T., C.C.*, Pt. 2a-30-196 (February 1512).
264. Correa, tomo IV, pp. 131-32.
265. Barros, tomo IV, Pt. I, chap. 25, pp. 517-19.
266. Correa, tomo III, p. 820.
267. Correa, tomo I, pp. 279-81 (1528).
268. Ibid., pp. 335-36.
269. Ibid., tomo III, p. 820.
270. Ibid., tomo I, p. 610, tomo III, pp. 553-57.
271. Castanheda, tomo V, 7; Correa, tomo II, pp. 558-9; letter of Nuno de Castro to Dom Manuel, Cochin, dated 31.10.1520, R.A. Bulhao Patao, *Cartas de Affonso de Albuquerque*, Lisbon, 1884-1935, tomo VII, pp. 175-76.
272. Correa, tomo I, pp. 428-32 and 481; Castanheda, liv. I, p. 121.
273. Ibid., tomo I, p. 430. They also had trade in spices, particularly cloves; see *A.N.T.T., C.C.*, I-13-113.
274. Ibid., tomo IV, pp. 131-32.
275. *A.N.T.T., C.C.*, I-30-36 (October 1523).
276. Ibid.
277. M.N. Pearson, *Coastal Western India: Studies from the Portuguese Records*, New Delhi, 1981, p. 31.
278. Correa, tomo III, p. 831.
279. Armando Cortesao and *Luis de Albuquerque, Obras* Completas de D. Joao de Castro, Coimbra, 1976, p. 543.
280. Ibid.
281. G. Schurhammer, vol. III, p. 520.
282. Ibid.
283. *A.N.T.T., C.C.*, I-77-26, fl. 1v. (Nov. 1545).
284. Correa, tomo II, 569 and 680.
285. Ibid.
286. S. Mohamed Husain Nayinar, *Tuhfat-ul-Mujahiddin*, Madras, 1942, ch. IV, sec 14, p. 89.
287. *Catamarans* were used for shipping rice from Nagapattinam to Jaffna, *Collecao Sao Lourenco*, III, 335; *tonis* were used for shipping rice, *A.N.T.T., C.C.*, II-114-21, 117-22, 119-103 and 120-17; *fustas* were used for carrying rice to Cochin *As Gavetas da Torre do Tombo*, IV, p. 134; Barks sailed from Quilon to Coromandel carrying pepper in exchange for rice *Mandado de Lourenco Moreno to Alvaro Lopes*, Cochin, 7.9.1513; *A.N.T.T., C.C.*, II-41-144; Champanas seem to have specially used for movement of cargo of rice Duarte Barbosa, vol. II, pp. 111-12; Tome Pires, see Portuguese version, tomo II, fol. 160R-160V.
288. Correa, tomo I, p. 301.
289. *A.N.T.T., Chancellaria de D. Filipe*, livro 2, fl. 174-174v.
290. F.C. Danvers, *The Portuguese in India*, London, 1966, vol. II, pp. 32 and 76.
291. *A.N.T.T., C.C.*, I-112-51, letter dated 17 Dec. 1588.
292. Antonio Bocarro, *Livro das Plantas de todos as fortalezas cidades e povacoes do Estado da India Oriental*, Bragacana Pereira, Arquivo Portuguez Oriental, Bastora, Goa, tomo IV, vol. II, Pt. I.
293. A.*N.T.T., C.C.*, I-9-92 (1520).

294. Armando Cortesao and Luis de Albuquerque, vol. III, p. 437, Doc. 580.
295. Ibid., p. 195. See also *A.N.T.T.*, Chancellaria D. Sebastiao and D. Henrique, liv 22, fl. 54, Collecao Sao Lourenco III, 354.
296. Ibid., p. 235.
297. *A.N.T.T., C.C.*, 2a-20-35-(1511).
398. R.A. Bulhao Patao, tomo VII, p. 175; *A.N.T.T.,C.C.*, II 41-144 (1513).
399. Correa, Pt. II, p. 559.
300. *A.N.T.T., Livro do registo de leis e regimentos de D. Manuel*, fol. 134v-136 (1520).
301. Correa, II, p. 559.
302. Armando Cortesao and Luis de Albuquerque, III, 74-5, 80, 90, 112, 202, 271, 494, 511, 545.
303. Ibid., p. 490. This casado is not be mixed up with another casado of the same name who was the captain of Nagapattinam in 1540.
304. B.A. Codice, 51-8-45- fl. 97.
305. *A.N.T.T., As Gavetas do Torre do Tombo,* gaveta 15, maco 21, doc. 30; see also *CAA*, IV, p. 42; Duarte Barbosa, I, p. 81.
306. Ibid., 1-38-50 (December 1527).
307. Ibid., 2a-114-41 (26 March 1524), 2a-118-49 (17 August 1524), 2a-118-172 (4 September 1524), 2a-120-110 (25 October 1524), 2a-121-41 (13 November 1524), 2a-120-111 (25 October 1524), 2a-114-41 (26 March 1524), 2a-118-69 (20 August 1524), 2a-118-172 (4 September 1524), 2a-120-25 (8 October 1524), 2a-122-130.
308. *A.N.T.T., Nucleo Antigo*, 808, fl. 2-3.
309. Ibid., fl. 2v.
310. *A.N.T.T., C.C.*, I-40-80 (1528).
311. B.A. Codice, 51-8-46.
312. Correa, III, 446. Castanheda, VIII, 46.
313. See the letter of Miguel Ferreira to D. Joao de Castro, 28 March 1546, in Sanjay Subrahmanyam, *Improvising Empire: Portuguese Trade and Settlements in the Bay of Bengal*, Delhi, 1990, pp. 241-44.
314. Barros, IV, Pt. II, p. 496; Correa, III, 649.
315. Correa, III, 820; G. Schurhammer, II, pp. 598 and 304.
316. Purchas, vol. X, p. 114.
317. *A.P.O.*, V, doc. 51.
318. *Chancellaria de D. Filipe I*, liv. 19, fl. 324.
319. Ibid., liv. 15, fl. 465v, liv. 28, fl. 75v, liv. 15, fl. 379v, liv. 31, fl. 183, liv. 18, fl. 3v, liv. 31, fl. 57, liv. 31, fl. 55v, liv. 4, fl. 292.
320. *A.N.T.T., CC,* Pt. IIa-120-25-(8 October 1524); see also Tome pires, I, p. 272.
321. Duarte Barbosa, vol. II, pp. 121 and 124.
322. Ibid., p. 132.
323. Adelino de Almeida Caldao, "Livro que trata das Coisas da India e do Japao", *Boletim da Bibiloteca de Universidade de Coimbra*, vol. 24, 1960, fl. 29v., p. 606; Archivo General de Simancas (hereafter A.G.S.), *Provincaelas Secretarias*, Codice, 1551, fl. 608-10v.
324. Armando Cortesao and Luis de Albuquerque, III, 184-88, 193-94 and 439-41.
325. Colecao Sao Lourenco, III, fl. 239.

326. Silva Rego, *Documentacao*, vol. I, p. 417, *C.C.*, 2a-121-41 (1522).
327. *A.N.T.T., C.C.*, 2a-114-45, 114-25 (1524).
328. Armando Cortesao and Luis de Albuquerque, doc. 633, pp. 471-72; see also *A.N.T.T., C.C.*, I-7-62, fl. 1v.
329. Ibid., III, Doc. 656.
330. Ibid., see also Correa, IV, pp. 227 and 403.
331. *A.N.T.T., C.C.*, I-7-62 fl. 1v.
332. Colecao Sao Lourenco, II, 354.
333. H.A.G., *Provisoes Alvares e Regimentos,* I, 77, 168-171, fl. 169.
334. *A.P.O.-CR,* liv. I, fl. 13v-15v; see the order of the king of Portugal issued from Almeirim, dated 25 March 1547.
335. B.N.L. *Fundo Geral,* No. 2702. *Livros das regimentos de Alfandega de Goa,* fl. 1v.
336. Ibid., fl. 3v.
337. H.A.G. *Livro Antigo de Registos,* fl. 56, 13 May 1598; *A.P.O.-CR,* Fasc.V, pp. 1512-13, doc. 1069.
338. B.N.L. *Fundo Geral,* No. 2702. *Livros das regimentos de Alfandega de Goa,* fl. 4v.
339. Ibid., fl. 7v; see also H.A.G. *Livros das Moncoes,* No. 4, 24-25-26 Codice 24-25-26/5-1, fl. 659.
340. H.A.G. *Livro Antigo de Registos,* fl. 56, 13 May 1598; *A.P.O.-CR,* Fasc. V, pp. 1512-13, Doc. 1069.

# 5

# External Trade of Coromandel

Historians' views on pre-modern Asian trade fall into three general categories. J.C. Van Leur formulated the idea of peddling trade in expensive goods and analysed the relationship between the agrarian state and peddling.[1] This concept is difficult to accept. To start with, Coromandel was not a centre of peddling; it became a transit trade centre where merchants secured local and foreign commodities and sold their goods on their way to South-East Asia. Secondly, Niels Steensgaard has observed that the Portuguese trading system was a redistributive one rather than a productive enterprise. Similarly Meilink Roelofsz explains that intra-Asian trade was predominantly not in luxury articles; on the contrary, bulk goods were transported over long distances.[2]

Another school of historians speaks of the involvement of the agrarian state in the long distance trade of Asia and its relationship with merchants.[3] Some of them go beyond the pure category of merchants and speak of producers who held substantial portfolios and wielded economic and political power. They emphasise the role of these portfolio capitalists in the early modern Indian economy and in the period of transition to colonialism.[4] The third model is the trade model derived from anthropological theory and stresses the pivotal role of trading communities.[5]

None of these approaches says much on the evolution, growth and possibly structural change that occurred in the trading world of Coromandel, which formed an essential component of the Asian economy. Recent attempts to trace the maritime history of Coromandel during the Portuguese expansion have done a useful service by throwing light on the writings of a few Portuguese scholars which were little known outside Portugal; but these studies have not concentrated on Coromandel and its commodity composition of overseas trade during Portuguese expansion. Rather, they have highlighted the distinction that existed between the formal structure of the trade of *Estado da India* and the informal Portuguese private trade.[6]

There is, therefore, a need to study what share the Portuguese had in the total trade of Coromandel and their impact on the various aspects of Coromandel economy. This chapter proposes to dwell on the merchants, ports, commodities and the trading pattern of Coromandel. It attempts to prove that Coromandel was commercially very fertile and it was actively involved in an ever increasing maritime trade with the ports of South-East Asia, South Asia and China.

## MERCHANT COMMUNITIES

It is gleaned from the inscriptions and Portuguese sources that the merchants at the ports of Coromandel conducted long distance trade as individuals rather than as groups. They had operated commerce for generations depending upon their individual financial capacity. The emergence of *Vellala Mudaliars,* a predominantly agrarian caste, as a group of Hindu merchants of commercial importance, who possessed enough financial resources to invest in long distance trade, was a new development.[7] Some of them traded with Malacca and settled there.[8]

When the Portuguese came in contact with the Coromandel coast they searched for trade partners from the local merchant communities whose expertise could be helpful. They found these *Mudaliars* with adequate capital to invest, who knew the local languages and distant markets. In the early sixteenth century, the Tamil-speaking *Mudaliars* came forward to help the Portuguese when they proposed to build a Portuguese fortress in Sunda where a large volume of pepper was produced.[9] In 1522 they guaranteed the annual sale and supply of 1,000 sacks of pepper.[10]

The *Mudaliars* also advanced loans to the Portuguese. In the beginning, aware of the social background of the *Mudaliars* Portuguese officials were prompt in repaying the loans. The *Mudaliars*, happy with such regular repayment of loans, appealed to the king of Portugal to appoint Jorge Cabral, who was then the Portuguese captain, as captain for life. Later in 1527, when the Portuguese began to default on the repayment of loans, Manoel Gomes wrote to the king of Portugal, at the request of the *Mudaliars*, complaining about the poor repayment of loans.[11] By helping the Portuguese to make fortunes the *Mudaliars*, who had functioned as merchant capitalists, must have lost some of their capital; these *Mudaliars* would not have been in overseas trading or shipowning to any degree in the seventeenth century.

The *chettis* were another group of Hindu merchants whose business has been well described in the writings of the Chinese travellers in the fifteenth century. *Yingyai Shenglan* described the *chettis* as brokers, which would imply that the *chettis* initially functioned as brokers in the fifteenth century.[12] Portuguese sources of the early sixteenth century speak of the emergence of *chettis* as traders, when the external trade of Coromandel was conducted by certain castes and groups of *chetti* merchants.

Tamil-speaking *chettis* were commonly identified with their place names such as Kalakhasti, Tiruppasur, and Kanchipuram.[13] The Tamil *chettis* were called *nagarattars* who resided in *nagarams*. Pulicat, Karaikal and Nagapattinam were the main *chetti* mercantile settlements.[14]

The Telugu *chetti* castes of *Komatis* and *Kavarai chettis* had migrated from the Krishna and Godavari delta regions of Andhra during the Vijayanagar period and settled down in Coromandel.[15] Various *chetti* merchant communities specialised in a commodity. *Kudiraichettis* specialised in horses.[16] *Kavaraichettis* dealt in precious stones, other metals and bullion; they also assessed and valued them. They fixed the price of pearls, precious stones, seed pearls, polished and rough corals according to their carats, beauty and goodness.[17] The *kavaraichettis'* dealing in valuable metals such as gold and silver, either coined or to be coined, gave them considerable control over money exchange. The sons of these *chetti* traders were trained in early ages to go about exchanging small coins.[18] They carried scales and weights with them. They were great clerks and accountants who reckoned all their sums on their fingers.[19] Their wealth was evaluated by *bahar* of gold and some *chettis* owned sixty quintals of gold. Thus the *kavaraichettis* emerged as shroffs in the early sixteenth century.[20] *Komatichettis* dealt in food items, and all kinds of fruits and vegetables.[21] *Berichettis* collected textiles from weavers and exported many varieties of textiles to Malacca.

An epigraph dated in the first half of the seventeenth century gives eight sub-castes of *chettis*. Various *gotras* of *chettis* such as *Purambalagotra, Shahstragotra* and *Guntakulagotra* also came into being.[22]

Among the leading *chetti* traders residing in the Coromandel ports, there is mention of Alagu *chetti*, Narayana *chetti*, Periya

Koneri *chetti* and Kavarai Kondu *chetti* of Pulicat, Chinna Nattichiyala *chetti* of Santhome of Mylapore, and Meyper Kariya *chetti* of Nagapattinam. Business was carried on along family lines, siblings being distinguished by the prefix *chinna* (younger) and *periya* (elder).[23]

Francisco de Albuquerque, in a letter to the king of Portugal describes Nina *chetti*, a native of Coromandel as the leading textile trader.[24] *Chettis* generally conducted trade with South-East Asia from Pulicat. Some had established resident quarters in northern Malacca, Upeh being a major settlement of Tamil *chettis*.[25] By and large, they sailed in Malay *junks* with consignments worth eighty or ninety thousand *cruzados* of coarse cloth of Pulicat,[26] which they exchanged for gold at Malacca. In this light, the opinion of some scholars[27] that Hindu *chetti* merchants regarded sea travel as religiously contaminating may safely be set aside.

When an expedition under Diogo Lopes de Sequeira reached Malacca in 1509 to look for trading facilities and was captured by the Sultan of Malacca, Naina *chetti*, an influential merchant from Pulicat intervened and the Portuguese were released.[28] Thus early commercial ties between the *chettis* and the Portuguese had commenced. Later some traders like Thiruvenkata *chetti* entered into commercial contacts with the Portuguese.[29] The Portuguese entered into trade contacts with a number of *chettis*[30] since the latter owned sailing ships of high quality, mainly operated between Pulicat and Malacca.[31] In 1547, some Portuguese vessels were pawned to *chettis*.[32] When the *chettis* did not allow these *navios* to sail, the Portuguese Viceroy was asked to intervene as the lack of transport jeopardised the Portuguese overseas trade.[33]

In this light, the views of W.H. Moreland and Surendra Gopal that in the sixteenth century Asian shipping and commerce had

DESTINATIONS OF *CHETTI*-OWNED SHIPS IN COROMANDEL,*
1512-59

| *Period* | *Destination* | | *No. of Ships* |
|---|---|---|---|
| | *From* | *To* | |
| 1512 | Pulicat | Malacca | 1 |
| 1514 | Pulicat | Malacca | 1 |
| 1559 | Pulicat | Malacca | 1 |

**A.N.T.T.*, .*C.C.* Ia-11-50(1512); *C.C.* I-14-51 (1514); H A.G. Provisoes Alvares, e Regimentos, Liv. 2. fl. 260·V(1559).

lost considerable ground to the Portuguese may be reconsidered.[34] From the evidence available, we can only conclude that the *chetti* commercial magnates rose from the status of brokers, money-lenders, shroffs and shipowners to a higher status that combined these various functions.

*Marakayar* were Tamil-speaking Muslims of Coromandel, particularly in the coastal regions. They were descendants of Arab merchant settlers who had mixed with the Tamils both culturally and in bloodline.[35] The earliest historical evidence of such Muslim settlements on the southeastern coast of India dates from the ninth century. A copper plate edict records that the ruler of Madurai granted asylum to a group of Arab Muslim immigrants in A.D. 875. These settlers integrated with the local community, married local women, and followed the local language and customs. Their population increased in many coastal villages of Coromandel. In the subsequent centuries too they continued to be chiefly traders.

The Portuguese distinguished the indigenous Muslim communities of Malabar trading in coconut, sugar and oil,[36] whom they called *Moplah,* from *Marakayars,* who were natives of Coromandel concentrated on the coastal region from Kunimedu to Nagapattinam. The ports of Kunimedu and Nagore were their chief settlements.[37] The *Marakayars* were not very great observers of Islamic laws. They are said to have learnt to write and speak several eastern languages and conducted trade in all the kingdoms of Asia. As early as 1509, the *Bendhahara* of Malacca, who was a Tamil Muslim, handled the matters of the merchants trading there. A ship's bell, now housed at the Wellington Museum in Newzeland has a Tamil inscription to the effect that it came from a ship owned by a *Marakayar.*[38]

The principal *Marakayar* merchants made large investments in maritime trade with various ports of the Indonesian archipelago. Native sources like *Tuhfat-ul-mujahiddin* depict the fall of the Muslim trade and the rise of Portuguese commerce. Frequent commercial clashes occurred between leading Muslim traders and the Portuguese, including attacks on ships and settlements in Coromandel, the intent being to dominate the maritime trade. The Muslims were disallowed from trading in any high profit-yielding goods; they were allowed to trade only in commodities for which the Portuguese had little interest.[39] They were forbidden to sail freely for commercial purposes and had to obtain

DESTINATIONS OF MARAKAYAR SHIPPING FROM COROMANDEL, 1506-50*

| *Destination* | *1506* | *1512* | *1513* | *1514* | *1517* | *1527* | *1537* | *1545* | *1550* |
|---|---|---|---|---|---|---|---|---|---|
| Malacca | 2 | 1 | 1 | 1 | 1 | - | 1 | - | - |
| Achin | - | - | - | - | - | 2 | - | - | - |
| Pegu | - | - | - | - | - | - | - | 1 | 1 |
| Macao | - | - | - | - | - | - | - | - | 1 |
| Pasai | - | - | - | 1 | - | - | - | - | - |

**A.N.T.T., C.C.* op. cit., I-5-117; *C.A.A.* III, p. 358; *C.C.* Ia-13-74; *C.C.* I-14-49; II-49-24; I-22-62. fl. 8v. *C.C.* I-22-80; *C.C.* I-60-17-fl. 8v.; *C.C.* I-77-18. l. 2v. Colecao Sao Vincente, vol. X. fl. 128.

*cartazes* from the Portuguese for the purpose. These curbs on travel induced some *Marakayars* to become pilots, sailors and navigators in the Portuguese ships trading from Coromandel, who received some *cruzados* and rice as payment.[40] Although frustrated by the Portuguese in maintaining their commercial monopoly, the *Marakayars* managed to survive in business, deriving special favours from the two Islamic sultanates of Johore and Achin in the Malay archipelago, who supported the *Marakayars* in their commercial rivalry with the Portuguese.

The Portuguese, who had established themselves on the western coast, desired to exploit the trade potential of Malacca. From Coromandel ships regularly sailed to South-East Asia, Kunimedu being the port of departure for the Malay archipelago. A team of Portuguese pioneers sailed from Cochin to Kunimedu in 1506 on way to Malacca,[41] in a *nau* belonging to Nina *Marakayar*. The team comprised the son of the Viceroy Francisco de Almeida, Francisco Pereira, Estevao de Vilhena and a son of Gaspar da gama.[42] At Kunimedu, when the *Marakayars* learnt that their Portuguese commercial rivals were being given shelter by Nina Marakayar's brother, they attacked the Portuguese and forced them to return to Cochin.[43] Obviously, the *Marakayars* did not want the Portuguese, who had established their overseas supremacy and control from the western coast, to trade from Coromandel ports. The view that Asian trade was blockaded by Europeans[44] seems to be exaggerated and gives inordinate importance to the naval superiority of the Portuguese and their place in Asian overseas trade.

Foiled in their attempt to reach Malacca, the Portuguese wished to commence trade with the flourishing port of Nagore, but when an exploratory team arrived near Nagapattinam they were arrested by the *Marakayars* and jailed.[45] When the news reached the Portuguese captain at Pulicat, he sent a letter to the captives through a 'dark person' from Coromandel, who handed it over to the *Marakayars,* for which he was rewarded.[46]

## COROMANDEL TRADE WITH MALACCA

In the second decade of the fifteenth century many Coromandel merchants traded with Malacca, encouraged by king Parameswara. When he was converted to Islam, Tamil Muslims of Coromandel, particularly *Marakayars* were attracted to trade with Malacca.[47] These *Marakayars* played a major role in the *coup d'etat* by killing an infant ruler of Malay blood and elevating his younger brother Muzaffar Shah, born to a Tamil mother, as the sultan of Malacca.[48]

Coromandel merchants generally unloaded their consignments of cloth at Malacca after paying customs to the sultan. Their merchandise was quickly sold out. But the Coromandel traders did not have a free hand in the sale of textiles. The system was that ten or twenty merchants of Malacca jointly met the owners of the merchandise and fixed the prices, which were divided among the consignment holders proportionately.[49]

In 1511 the Portuguese conquered Malacca and thereafter encouraged Coromandel merchants to trade there. The ships of Coromandel came with rice cargo; the trade conducted was voluminous, which brought good revenue to the Portuguese factory at Malacca.

The abundant supply of textiles from Pulicat to Malacca necessitated a *shahbhandar* exclusively appointed to look after the welfare of Coromandel merchants.[50] Although the sultan of Malacca lost his kingdom, he continued to trade with Coromandel. A junk which he owned was captured by the Portuguese while trading at Pulicat.[51]

Textiles formed an important commodity of maritime trade at Pulicat. The *chetti* merchants dominated the trade in textiles from Pulicat to Malacca in the years 1510 and 1511. Gujarati traders posed them tough competition with cloth brought from Cambay

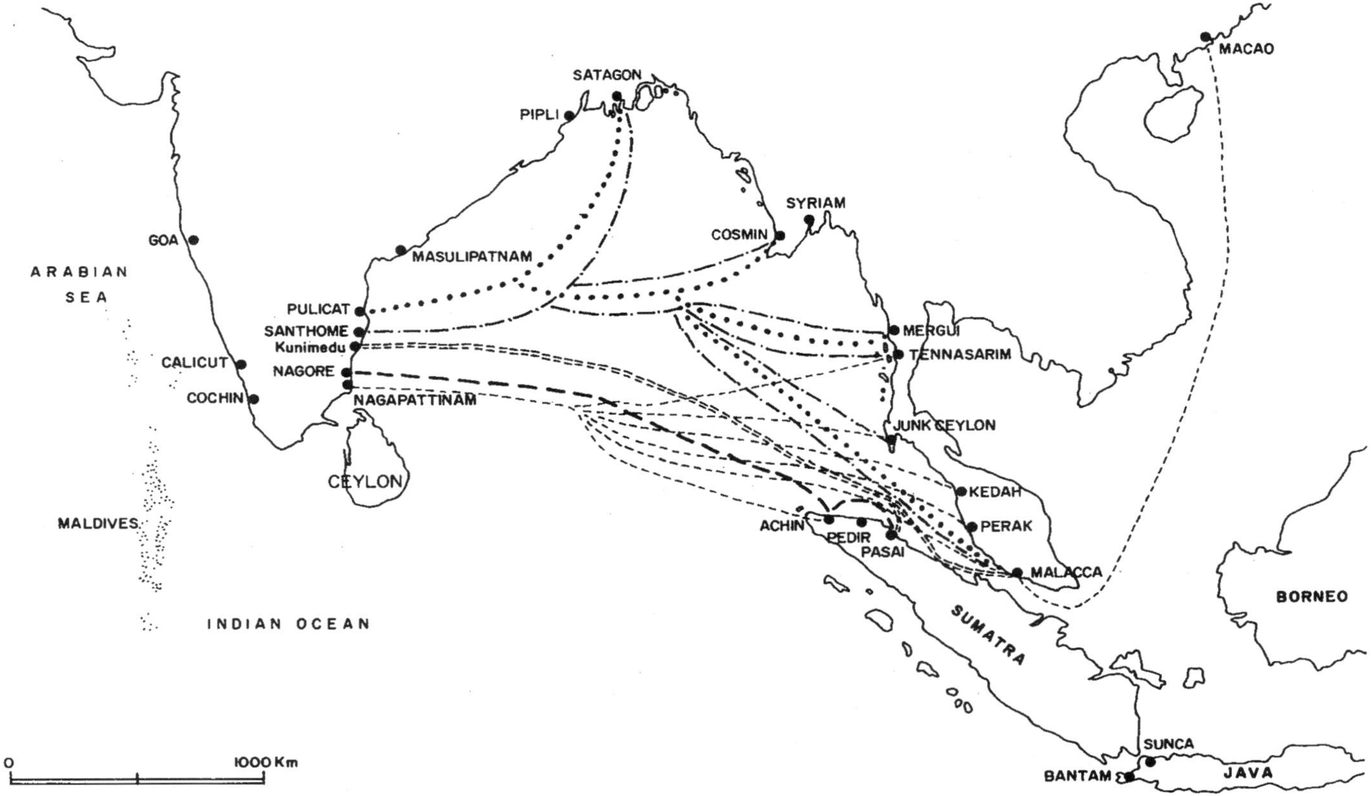


MAP 5. COROMANDEL: PORTS AND OVERSEAS TRADE ROUTES,

RECORDED PORTUGUESE SHIPPING FROM/TO PULICAT, 1511-28*

| Period | Departure from Pulicat | | Arrival at Pulicat | | | |
|---|---|---|---|---|---|---|
| | Malacca | Pasai | Malacca | Pasai | Pegu | Tenasserim |
| 1511 | - | - | 1 | - | - | - |
| 1512 | 1 | 1 | - | 1 | - | - |
| 1513 | 2 | 1 | 1 | - | - | - |
| 1514 | 2 | - | 2 | - | - | - |
| 1516 | - | - | 4 | - | - | - |
| 1518 | - | - | - | - | - | 1 |
| 1520 | - | - | - | - | 1 | - |
| 1524 | 2 | - | - | - | 2 | - |
| 1525 | 3 | - | - | - | - | - |
| 1527 | 2 | - | 1 | - | - | - |
| 1528 | - | - | 1 | - | - | - |

*Correa, op. cit., p. 216. *C.C.* Ia-11-50; *C.A.A.* vol. I, IX, pp. 29-65; *C.C.* II-53-93, fl. 319v; I-14-12; II-53-93, fl. 299v; Correa, op. cit., II, p. 545, p. 717; *C.C.* IIa-117-149, II-117-154, IIa-126-102, IIa-125-2, 126-87.

and Chaul.[52] Their assistance to the Portuguese at this time to conquer Malacca from the sultan brought for the *chettis* the position of sole textile traders at Malacca under the protection of the Portuguese. In return for the service he had rendered to them, the Portuguese appointed Nina *chetti* as *shahbandar* and *bendahara,* chief justice on all civil and criminal matters at Malacca and as the King's revenue collector.[53] *Chettis* and the Portuguese sailed together to Pulicat from Malacca in junks. In the second decade of the sixteenth century the Portuguese encouraged Pulicat trade with Malacca in order to increase their revenue at Malacca.

The Coromandel merchants were charged a concessional custom duty of six per cent while others were charged ten per cent. Jorge de Albuquerque, the Portuguese factor of Malacca, also promised great privileges to Coromandel merchants who settled there.[54] To facilitate Portuguese commercial activities the captain of Coromandel initially resided at Pulicat to supervise textile exports to Malacca. It would appear from the above that the Portuguese contribution to Coromandel textile trade with Malacca was relatively insignificant and Coromandel merchants dominated the scene.

PORTUGUESE EXPORTS OF RICE FROM PULICAT TO MALACCA, 1512-25*

| *Period* | *Ship* | *Captain* | *Quantity (in gantas)* |
|---|---|---|---|
| 26 March 1512 to 25 February 1514 | Navio... | - | 10946.429 |
| 6 August 1524 | Navio Santiago | Joao Rodrigues | 3240.00 |
| 10 August 1524 | Navio Conceicao | - | 14160.00 |
| 10 August 1524 | Nau Rui Marcos | Joao Correia | 3100.00 |
| 15 August 1524 | Fusta Sta. Catarina | Domingos Fernandes | 2880.00 |
| 8 April 1525 | Navio Conceicao | Joao Paes | 1575.00 |
| 10 July 1525 | Navio Trinidade | Joao Fernandes | 2000.00 |
| 15 July 1525 | Navio... | Luis Affonso | 15280.00 |

*Chancelaria de D. Joao III, Liv.18 fl.108$^{v}$ *C.C.* IIa-117-54, IIa-117-194; IIa-117-195; IIa-118-31; IIa-125-2; IIa-126-87; IIa-126-102.

PORTUGUESE EXPORTS OF TEXTILES FROM COROMANDEL TO MALACCA, 1511-48*

| *Period* | *Value (in cruzados/pardaos)* |
|---|---|
| 1511 | 9,000 cr. |
| 1512 | 5,000 cr. |
| 1515 | 12,000 cr. |
| 1522 | 90,000 cr. |
| 1540 | 4,000 cr. |
| 1548 | 84,840 par. |

**A.N.T.T. C.C.* I-77-18. fl. 2$^{v}$; *C.C.* Ia-11-50; II-53-93. fl. 319$^{v}$; II-46-98; I-16-106; I-60-17. fl. 8$^{v}$; I-68-86; Elaine Sanceau, Cartas de D. Joao de Castro, p. 213; Biblioteca Municipal de Elvas, Mss. 5/381.

PORTUGUESE TRADE IN BUTTER EXPORTED FROM PULICAT TO MALACCA, 1512-18*

| *Period* | *Quantity in Marakals* |
|---|---|
| 26 March 1512 to 25 February 1514 | 1209.00 |
| 1 November 1515 to 31 May 1518 | 300.10 |

*Chancelaria de D. Joao III, Liv. 18. fl. 108$^{v}$ ; Liv. 4. fl. 72.

Between 1531 and 1532 and from 1535 to 1540 Coromandel was laid low with continuous drought and famines, which probably impaired textile production. The textile trade with Malacca declined and Coromandel merchants gradually withdrew from cloth trade.[55] Whereas earlier there used to be an annual average revenue of 100,000 *cruzados*[56] from the sale of Pulicat textiles at Malacca, in 1540 the merchandise mainly consisted of black cloth worth 4,000 *cruzados* and sailings from Coromandel ports to Malacca had declined considerably.[57]

RECORDED SAILINGS FROM COROMANDEL TO MALACCA, 1537-98*

| *Period* | *Pulicat* | *Period* | *Santhome* |
|---|---|---|---|
| 1537 | 4 | 1547 | 3 |
| 1538 | 1 | 1563 | 2 |
| 1539 | 1 | 1564 | 2 |
| 1546 | 3 | 1565 | 1 |
| 1548 | 1 | 1567 | 2 |
| 1559 | 1 | 1591 | 2 |
| 1562 | 2 | 1592 | 1 |
| 1564 | 1 | 1598 | 1 |

**C.C.* I-60-17. fl. $8^{v}$.; I-7-62.fl. 1.; I-68-86; B.A. Codice 52-VII-63. No. 33. Schurhammer, op. cit., vol. II. p. 100; Chancelaria de D. Joao III, Liv. 64. fl. $39^{v}$.; H.A.G. Privilegos Alvares e Regimentos, Liv. 2. fl.$260^{v}$. Chancelaria de D. Sebastiao. liv 19. fl. $226^{v}$.; liv. 71. fl. 18.; Chancelaria de D. Joao, III. liv. 15. fl. 23.; *A.P.O.* fasc. V. 2. Doc. 542. pp. 592-93; Chancelaria de D. Sebastiao liv. 71. fl. $29^{v}$:; liv. 15. fl. 11.; liv. 71. fl. 29. BPADE, Reservados, 752, fl. $24^{v}$.; *A.P.O.* V. No. 633, p. 689. AHU, India Caixa, XI, Doc. 15; A.P.O. fasc. III. IIa pt. Doc. 325, pp. 801-4; H.A.G. Livros das Moncoes, No. 313. Codice 12-25.

At the end of the 1530s, crown shipping was introduced to revive Coromandel-Malacca textile trade. The ship left Pulicat in August-September and generally returned from Malacca in January.[58] A *fidalgo* was awarded the captaincy of the vessel, in reward for services rendered to the Portuguese crown.[59] He could load his textile cargo before other merchants, 150 bales of it free of duty and could charge freight and duties on the cargo of other merchants, making a profit of 3,000 *cruzados* on that account.[60] Later, with a view to revive the Coromandel-Malacca trade, he was granted additional privileges: he was paid a year's salary in advance, he could take along four merchants and he was allowed to take along on the return journey any merchants from Malacca.[61]

But this organisation of regular official Portuguese textile trade helped only the private income of the captain and brought no revenue to the king.[62] According to one piece of evidence the captain gained 12,000 *cruzados* in freight, realised in the form of gold from Minangkabu in Sumatra and Chinese silver. Because the business was highly lucrative many applications were made for the post of captain on the Coromandel-Malacca-Moluccas crown voyages, stating reasons of poverty, death of a family member in battle and to meet the marriage expenses of their offspring.[63]

Textiles were procured from various ports like Nagapattinam, Kunimedu, Santhome and Armagon. To ensure troublefree procurement, the Portuguese viceroy persuaded the king of Vijayanagara to sign a treaty on 19th September 1547 to the effect that all textiles in the kingdom of Vijayanagara, particularly from Coromandel would be offered for sale to the Portuguese.[64] The cargo was transported in the *navios* of Santhome, the *naus* of Moluccas routed via Coromandel and the crown ship sailing once a year from Pulicat.[65] Spices and drugs were imported from Malacca to Pulicat and cloves from Moluccas via Malacca.[66]

Whereas Pulicat was the dominant port in Coromandel-Malacca trade in the 1530s, in the 1540s Santhome of Mylapore replaced Pulicat in importance. The fall of the Vijayanagara empire in the battle of Talikota was only a secondary cause of the decline of Pulicat,[67] the primary reason being that the Portuguese had started trading with Malacca directly from Santhome. Pulicat only became a mid-point on the Malacca-Goa route, which suited the Portuguese very well but not the indigenous traders trading from Pulicat. The established custom for the Coromandel merchants trading with Malacca was to pay the freight in advance and make their return voyage on the same ship in which they had sailed out.[68] Since such facilities were made available at Santhome, they preferred to settle down at Santhome and trade directly with Malacca from there, abandoning Pulicat.

In the 1550s, Malacca's trade relations with Santhome came under strain on account of the many spiteful actions of the Portuguese captain of Malacca.[69] He had received an embassy from the Muslim merchants of Masulipatnam for commercial alliance. In the wake of their visit he ordered that the galleon of Muslims alone would be allowed to depart for Masulipatnam.

RECORDED COROMANDEL-MALACCA CROWN VOYAGES, 1560-65*

| *Voyage Completed During the Period* | *Name of the Captain* | *No. of Voyages Undertaken* | *Ratification Order issued on* |
|---|---|---|---|
| 19.2.1560 | Joao Rebello | 2 | February 1561 |
| 1561 | Luis Mendes Vasconcellos | 2 | 22 February 1562 |
| 12.3.1562 | Pero Henriques | 2 | 13 March 1567 |
| 22.3.1563 | Martim Castilho de Vasconcellos | 2 | 21 February 1564 |
| 6.3.1563 | Luis Christavao Lobo | 2 | 14 March 1564 |
| 15.1.1564 | Pedro de Sousa | 1 | 27 January 1568 |
| 1565 | Jorge de Menezes | 2 | February 1565 |

**A.P.O.* fasc. 5. No. 370, p. 472; No. 625, p. 657; and No. 542, p. 592; *R.C.I.* vol. I, p. 133; Chancelaria de D. Sebastiao liv.15. fl 29, liv. 15. fl.11; liv. 19. fl. 226[V.]

Goods from the *nau* of Coromandel, which was to set sail for Santhome, were seized and put to his private use. The twenty-nine merchants of Coromandel bound for Santhome were forced to travel to Masulipatnam. Among those thus arbitrarily forced to change their destination was Fr. Christovao da Costa, the Rector of the college at Malacca, about which the Bishop of Malacca protested.[70]

Among the other hostile actions of the Portuguese captain of Malacca, about which the resident captain of Santhome protested to the Portuguese viceroy, were that he forced the Coromandel merchants to return in a decrepit ship owned by him after

SANTHOME BASED GRANT OF CONCESSION VOYAGES TO MALACCA, 1577-87*

| *Buyer* | *1577* | *1584* | *1585* | *1587* |
|---|---|---|---|---|
| Simao Abreu Pereira | 2 | - | - | - |
| Andre Teles de Menezes | - | 2 | - | - |
| Francisco de Sousa | - | 2 | - | - |
| Nuno Pereira de Miranda | - | - | 2 | - |
| Affonso Delgado de Brito | - | - | - | 2 |
| Jorge de Menezes | - | - | - | 2 |
| Total | 2 | 4 | 2 | 4 |

*Chancelaria de D. Sebastiao, Doacoes, liv. 40. fl. 228; A.P. fasc. V. Document no. 452, No. 542; *R.C.I.* vol. I, p.141, p. 287, vol. I, No.1156, p. 272.

paying their passage and sometimes deported the native merchants in the ships of other traders based at Santhome, putting them to needless and malicious loss.[71]

The Portuguese official trading pattern underwent a major change in the 1570s and a system of farming out Santhome-Malacca voyages was introduced. The number of voyages generally allowed was restricted to two with the consideration that if the first voyage entailed a loss the second voyage could help recoup the loss.[72] These voyages consisted partly of exclusive routes on which none other than the concessionaire, not even the indigenous merchants of Coromandel, were permitted to operate, which was not to their liking.[73] Other developments, such as clashes between the functionaries in the region and disputes between the contractors and the purchasers possibly led to the decline of Santhome-Malacca trade.[74]

The concessionaire of the routes allowed other merchants to travel on his route for a share in the profit. Sanjay Subrahmanyam and Om Prakash have calculated the net average profit per Coromandel-Malacca concession to have been 6,000 *cruzados*, while the auction price was around 5,500 *cruzados*,[75] but the rates were not standard, the concession sometimes coming down to as much as 4,000 *cruzados*,[76] apparently because the demand for Malacca voyages had declined. Among the reasons for this decline was the enhancing of the duty collected at Malacca till 1574 from six per cent to eight per cent, levy of additional taxes on drugs and fortification of Malacca.[77]

The Javanese merchants trading in Coromandel textiles at Malacca also withdrew in 1574 for reasons of enhanced taxes. They formerly paid no tax but were now forced to pay exit duty.[78] The income of the Portuguese customs house at Malacca also declined in 1580 because neither were the Coromandel merchants allowed to sell nor could the Javanese merchants buy textiles.[79] When the residents of Malacca petitioned the king of Portugal to reduce the increased customs duty which was damaging the income of the settlement, King Dom Filippe–I asked for information from the Portuguese viceroy of India on the matter. He wanted to know whether relaxation of customs duty at Malacca would affect the royal treasury of Malacca.[80]

Facing a prospect of declining income, some Portuguese of Malacca in 1592 misinformed the Coromandel traders about the enhanced taxes and took them to the settlement without proper despatch orders.[81] When the matter was discovered, the captain of Malacca prohibited the ships from returning to Santhome without payment of increased duties.[82] When the matter was brought to the notice of the king of Portugal he passed a royal order to the Portuguese viceroy at Goa in 1594 to the effect that on merchandise passing between Santhome and Malacca duties should be paid at Santhome.[83]

With a view to augment the declining Malacca-Coromandel trade, the King of Portugal[84] in 1596 restored the customs duty from eight per cent to six per cent.[85] But this does not seem to have helped matters. It had been made mandatory in 1598 for the Coromandel merchants to obtain prior approval of the officials of the Malacca customs to sail to Malacca. When it was pointed out to the king that this would have a ruinous effect on Malacca commerce,[86] the viceroy countermanded the order in April the same year.[87] All the same, Coromandel merchants preferred to trade in ports other than Malacca such as Pegu, Tennasarim and Indonesia, where they would have a more peaceful time. The decline in Malacca-Coromandel commerce at the end of the sixteenth century is confirmed by the instruction of the king, dated 15 January 1601 to the viceroy of India, to look into the possibilities of promoting Malacca-Coromandel trade.[88] The overseas commerce undertaken by the merchants in this route, estimated by Tome Pires in 1510-11 to have been worth 80,000 or 90,000 *cruzados* which had flourished significantly in the later years, was at the end of the sixteenth century worth 300,000 *cruzados*.[89] The number of ships by the natives sailing from Coromandel to Malacca for trade every year had been seven at the beginning of the sixteenth century and it had been four at the end of sixteenth century under the Portuguese.[90]

The decline of Pulicat in the 1550s boosted the commerce of Masulipatnam located at the confluence of river Krishna with its rich hinterland producing rice and textiles. Masulipatnam attracted the Portuguese traders as early as 1546. A resident population of 150 Portuguese at Masulipatnam was mentioned by the captain of Mylapore.[91] The port gained greater importance with the rise of the Golkonda kingdom, as the Portuguese began to settle and trade there. The Qutubshahi ruler of Golconda, whom the Portuguese called *Cota malaquo*, took *cartazes* from the Portuguese captain of Masulipatnam. In 1589 he entered into commercial contracts with the Portuguese to supply each year

300 *candis* of rice at Masulipatnam.[92] This relationship was further strengthened in 1597 when the ruler of Masulipatnam sent an embassy to the viceroy of Goa, with a request to send a Portuguese captain. The viceroy's choice for the post fell on Antonio Rodrigues de Elhanas.[93] Being a port of a Muslim kingdom, Masulipatnam had established trade contacts with Achin. It also extended commercial alliance with the kingdom of Pegu. Two *naus* of Achin and one ship owned by the king of Pegu brought rich revenues, valued at 1,60,000 *cruzados*. The diversion of trade to and from Masulipatnam with Malacca began to affect the Portuguese trade of Mylapore, as noted by the Portuguese captain of Santhome in his letter to the viceroy at Goa.[94]

## COROMANDEL TRADE WITH INDONESIA

Early references of the sixteenth century record that the port of Pasai in Sumatra had trade contracts with Nagore in Coromandel. Pasai was a famous trading centre of raw silk brought by Chinese ships.[95] The *Marakayar* merchants supplied rice to Pasai, where food provisions were scarce, in exchange for raw silk which was in great demand for textile manufacture in the Coromandel hinterland.[96] Giovanni de Empoli estimated that seven hundred velas of rice came from Nagore to Pasai.[97] Muslim merchants of Pulicat also exported rice amounting to 10,000 *gantas* to Pasai,[98] but *Marakayars* dominated the rice trade with Pasai. The *Marakayars* also bought whatever textiles they could from the weaving villages of Kunimedu and transported them in their own ships to Pasai. In 1512, the sultan of Pasai in a letter written to the king of Portugal in Arabic offered to make a guaranteed sale of fourteen *bahars* of silk annually to the Portuguese.[99] The *shahbandar* of Pasai made direct purchases of Coromandel textiles sending his ships to Kunimedu.[100] Kunimedu continued trade with Pasai till 1537.[101] When Pasai came under Achinese domination, the *Marakayars* switched their trade to the new emporium of Achin.

The *Marakayar* traders of Nagore helped their co-religionists, the Gujarati Muslim merchants, in their trade with Achin. A merchant, whose *navio* was captured by the Portuguese in 1527, confessed that the Gujarati merchants took *cartazes* from the Portuguese to make purchases at Quilon and then sailed on to

Coromandel to trade with Achin. The Muslim merchants at Nagore, who had established stable commerce with Achin,[102] encouraged other Muslim merchants to try their hand at it.[103] Three ships left Nagore for Achin every year with the textile cargo of the *Marakayars*. The Portuguese captain Lopo Vaz de Sampayo was specifically asked to attack these ships[104] since they greatly hampered the growth of Portuguese commerce at Malacca and Nagapattinam.

The Portuguese trade in Coromandel textiles in South-East Asia was mainly in exchange for spices. A treaty, signed by the Portuguese traders with the suppliers of spices, records the sale price of textiles.[105] Long pepper, abundant and cheap in Sumatra, came to Coromandel.[106] In the 1560s, encountering difficulties in the trade with Malacca, the Portuguese merchants diverted their commercial attention to Achin.[107] With the decline of Malacca trade, the king of Portugal decided to procure pepper and spices from other regions of South-East Asia, particularly in order to deflect the spice trade from the Muslim traders at Achin. With a view to liberalise the royal monopoly of pepper, royal concession-voyages were introduced from Coromandel to Kedah.[108] The low cost of concessions, amounting to 1,000 *cruzados* for a voyage between Nagapattinam and Kedah,[109] encouraged private Portuguese traders at Nagapattinam but did not result in the deviation of pepper from Achin. For one thing, the Portuguese had no customs house at Kedah and the crown could not control the private traders.[110] Besides, Kedah was on the opposite side of the coast, quite far from Achin. It was a Muslim sultanate where the Muslim traders controlled the supply of spices.

In 1584, the Portuguese made serious efforts to collect textiles from the Coromandel hinterland for sale in Achin, the most noteworthy contribution to this effort being made by the captain of Nagapattinam, Artur Gallejo de Castelo Branco.[111] Captain Francisco Correa de Brito in his time encouraged lucrative commerce from Santhome with Bantam and Moluccas. Several merchants began to carry cotton textiles to exchange for spices and drugs in 1589-92.[112] One outcome of this booming trade was smuggling of pepper and spices from South-East Asia through the ports of Coromandel to West Asia. The sultan of Achin received three to four thousand pieces of gold from Mecca for thirty or forty thousand quintals of pepper sent.[113] The king of

Portugal, when he was informed of this trade, ordered the viceroy at Goa to block it.[114] Special privileges granted to Coromandel ships by the sultan of Achin strengthened the trade links between Coromandel and Achin, which continued to flourish as late as 1598.[115]

Amboina had indirect commercial relations with the Coromandel coast, functioning as the main redistribution centre for Coromandel textiles delivered at Malacca. Portuguese official contacts with Amboina began with the appointment of captain Antonio Pais in 1562.[116] In 1580 textiles were directly taken from Coromandel to Amboina. With the establishment of a Portuguese fortress at Amboina in 1591, commercial ties became stronger.[117] Strengthening of the trade links was hastened when the Dutch arrived in India in 1595 with a clear mission to explore the marketing of Coromandel textiles directly with Indonesia, Pulicat being the originating port. According to sources, sixty bales of *beatilhas* of Pulicat, purchased at the rate of fifteen *xerafins per* bale from the regional contractors of Coromandel, were exported to Amboina. Similarly forty bales of *beatilhas,* purchased at the same rate and sent to Amboina in 1598, were estimated to have a value of 3,192 *xerafins.*[118] But the Portuguese only sowed the seed of marketing Coromandel textiles with Indonesia; it was left to the Dutch to reap the fruits later during the seventeenth century.

Various commodities were imported into Coromandel from the ports of the Indonesian archipelago. Edible camphor was chiefly brought in cylinders made of reeds to Pulicat, for use in confectionery. Other imports included white benzoin, sandalwood and sulphur from Achin.[119] Portuguese traders like Pero de Ataide, who traded with Java in 1599, assisted the Dutch and advised them to purchase spices there and load their cargo of spices without the knowledge of the Javanese merchants who might cause trouble.[120]

## COROMANDEL-CHINA TRADE

There was no direct Chinese trade with Coromandel in the early sixteenth century. The *Marakayars* exchanged rice and textiles for Chinese silk at Pasai. Some Coromandel merchants also purchased Chinese goods at Malacca in the 1520s.[121] A letter by Diogo Pereira in 1539 notes that Chinese traders visited Nagapattinam and left Coromandel with rich cargo, which would indicate that direct trade contacts between China and Coromandel began in the 1530s.[122]

The Portuguese, who began to trade in the Far East, realised the importance of Macao and entered into a commercial treaty with the local Chinese in 1554. This treaty of peace affirmed that the Portuguese would trade with China as merchants and not as smugglers.[123] Some private Portuguese traders and native merchants of Coromandel began to trade with Macao via Malacca.

A ship owned by Khwaja *Marakayar* sailed regularly between Nagapattinam and Macao.[124] Portuguese ships from Macao destined for Goa and Cochin also traded with Nagapattinam where there was a great demand for Chinese goods. To be able to offload at Nagapattinam they delayed their departure at Malacca, blaming winds unfavourable for sailing.[125] By then monsoons commenced on the west coast and the Portuguese merchants could with impunity sell the Chinese goods, particularly silk, brocades and porcelain at Nagapattinam. The ship's crew colluded with the Coromandel merchants and the captain of Nagapattinam to carry on this illegal trade. In one such instance silk worth 14,000 *pardaos* brought from Macao was sold at Nagapattinam.[126] To avoid this flooding of Chinese merchandise at Nagapattinam the captain of Malacca was authorised to examine the cargo of merchants returning to Nagapattinam.[127]

One fallout of the flourishing Chinese trade with Nagapattinam was the emergence of piracy in the open seas near the Coromandel coast.[128] Junks returning to Nagapattinam from Macao, laden with rich cargo, were attacked.[129]

SHIP ARRIVALS FROM CHINA TO COROMANDEL, 1550-98*

| *Period* | *From* | *To* | *No. of Ships* |
|---|---|---|---|
| 1550 | Macao | Nagapattinam | 1 |
| 1583 | Macao | Nagapattinam | 1 |
| 1585 | Macao | Nagapattinam | 1 |
| 1598 | Macao | Nagapattinam | 1 |

**A.N.T.T.*, *Colecao Sao Vincente*, X. fl. 128; Couto, Decada, X. 1, 425; and X, 11, 116; A.P.O. fasc. I. IIa pt. Doc. 5, pp. 61-74, see also Hay, *Derebus Iaponicus et Pervanis*, Antwerp, 1615, p. 835.

An armada sent by the viceroy of Goa under captain Antonio de Sousa Godinho to foil piracy was not very effective.[130] At the request of the Portuguese traders at Nagapattinam the king of Portugal in 1587 approved the setting up of an armada to protect *junks* sailing from and to Nagapattinam.[131] In 1589 it was further ordered that ships on the Nagapattinam-Macao route could be provided additional protection by the Armada of Bengal till they could safely reach Nagapattinam. Such measures of safety and protection given by the Portuguese encouraged the Chinese merchants in 1597-98 to trade with other ports of Coromandel like Santhome.[132] Later the State Council of Portuguese India decided to give additional security to merchants trading with China and Coromandel and an armada of six galleons was sent annually at the end of August.[133] Thus Coromandel-China direct commercial contacts were revived chiefly because of Portuguese participation.

### COROMANDEL-PEGU TRADE

The Port of Cosmin, on the site of modern Yangon (Rangoon) in Myanmar (Burma) conducted regular trade with Pulicat in the early sixteenth century.[134] Antonio Dinis' letter of 15 August 1516 highlights this flourishing trade: four or five ships of Pulicat carried the textiles and returned with a cargo of gold and rubies besides lac, which was used for dyeing textiles.[135] Khwaja Ali, a merchant of Pulicat, travelled regularly to Pegu and was engaged in jewel trade in 1516.[136]

In 1519 the Portuguese concluded a treaty of peace with the king of Pegu, under which they were permitted to settle and trade at the ports of the kingdom.[137] When Antonio Dinis was appointed the Portuguese factor of Martaban, he initiated serious efforts to conduct commerce with the Coromandel ports.[138] Pulicat and Kunimedu on the Coromandel coast imported much lac from Martaban.[139] A great amount of silver came from the silver mines of Laos to Pegu, which finally reached Coromandel.[140]

Precious stones, available in plenty at Pegu were another important commodity of export exchanged for Coromandel textiles; this valuable merchandise was brought to Pulicat. Devikapuram and Tirupati emerged as jewel trading centres in the hinterland of Pulicat. Precious stones are abundantly available at Tirupati on account of donations made to the temple. Tirupati

GIFT OF PRECIOUS STONES MADE TO THE TIRUMALA-TIRUPATI TEMPLE* 1513-15

| *Item* | *1513* | *1514* | *1515* |
|---|---|---|---|
| Rubies | 1644 | 104 | 21075 |
| Emeralds | 160 | 83 | 754 |
| Sapphires | 16 | 121 | 530 |
| Topazes | 1 | - | 74 |
| Pearls | 3114 | 549 | 3933 |
| Catseye | 91 | - | 40 |
| Diamonds | 707 | 132 | 920 |

*S. Jeyaseela Stephen, "Pulicat based shipping and trade, 1500-30", in Purabhilekh-Puratatva, vol. IX, Pt. II, 1991, pp. 1-12.

also had a gold bazaar.

The people of Pegu were ignorant of the art of polishing precious stones. They sent their rubies and pearls to Pulicat which boasted of excellent craftsmen.[141] The precious stones found their way to the city of Vijayanagara where existed a capital market for jewels, gems and precious stones.[142] The jewel trade attracted many merchants, including Portuguese private traders like Joao Moreno, who conducted overseas trade with Pegu from Pulicat.[143] In the absence of the Portuguese factory at Pegu Portuguese traders preferred to trade with Pegu than with Malacca.[144] Malacca was collecting a special tax called *bulibuliao* from the ships of Santhome, which also was a factor in diverting trade to Pegu.[145]

The captain of Malacca sent an armada to watch the Pegu coast, where Coromandel ships traded bypassing Malacca. Manuel Falcao was in charge of this mission but failed to stop the merchants of Pulicat from visiting the ports of Pegu.[146] The Portuguese also were regularly and illegally travelling to Pegu from Santhome. In 1547 the writer of the Portuguese factory at Santhome was accused of giving false *cartazes* for illegal voyages to Pegu.[147]

Some Portuguese traders like Diogo de Almeida and Boas Varela illegally traded with Pegu after negotiating with the native merchants of Coromandel from Santhome.[148] A ship of Khwaja *Marakayar* sailed from Nagapattinam to Pegu trading in jewels without obtaining a *cartaz* from the Portuguese captain of

RECORDED SHIPPING FROM COROMANDEL TO PEGU, 1520-87*

| *Period* | *Port From* | *No. of Ships* |
|---|---|---|
| 1520 | Pulicat | 1 |
| 1524 | Pulicat | 2 |
| 1541 | Pulicat | 1 |
| 1543 | Santhome | 4 |
| 1545 | Pulicat | 1 |
| 1546. | Santhome | 1 |
| 1547 | Santhome | 6 |
| 1548 | Santhome | 1 |
| 1554 | Santhome | 1 |
| 1557 | Santhome | 5 |
| 1587 | Santhome | 1 |

*Correa, op. cit., II. p. 717; *A.N.T.T. C.C.* IIa-120-17; I-77-18. fl. $2^{v.}$; *R.C.I.*, No. 341. As Fazendas Armadas Portugueses op. cit., pp. 50, 52, 59, and 60-61; Armando Cortesao, op. cit., vol. III, pp. 195, 296, and 331-32. *A.P.O.* fasc. V. Doc. 376.

Nagapattinam.[149] When he came to know of it the captain cancelled the grant of other voyages to the *Marakayar*. The viceroy even issued orders forbiding certain private Portuguese traders like Gabriel de Ataide from sailing from Santhome to Pegu.[150]

The Italian traveller Caesar de Federici confirms the existence of regular trade from Santhome to Pegu. A great ship left for Pegu on the tenth or eleventh September from Santhome. On their return the merchants brought many rubies since precious stones were cheaply available at Pegu.[151] The Portuguese chiefly imported luxury articles such as precious stones, lac, benzoin and sealing wax. Merchants of Coromandel imported large volume of musk and rubies from Arakan.[152]

Coromandel-Pegu trade continued to flourish in the first half of the sixteenth century owing to the heavy demand for jewels and precious stones at Vijayanagara. Tiruvaiyaru in the hinterland of Nagapattinam emerged as a jewel trading centre.[153] Some features such as low taxation and favourable conditions encouraged the merchants to undertake Coromandel-Pegu voyages.

The Vijayanagara empire promoted jewel trade with Pegu. Cosmin was the sale market of gems to Coromandel merchants. The merchants from Santhome and Goa often stayed there for a whole season to complete their business transactions.[154] Buyers and sellers of rubies would join their hands under a cloth and they bid by touching fingers against knuckles.[155] This was done to discourage spying by other merchants. Even after agreeing to a price and paying it, the buyers were at liberty to change their mind and received full refund. Honesty in the jewel trade was a contributing factor in its development. There were several public agents, called *taraghee*, who arranged to buy quality gems in the quoted price range.[156] Their honesty was legendary.

Sources of the second half of the sixteenth century note that Santhome merchants trading with Cosmin were not interested in rubies; instead they demanded silver or gold.[157] The change in the commodities of exchange may be attributed to the destruction of the city of Vijayanagara in 1565 and the decline of its jewel trade in South India in the second half of the sixteeenth century.[158] Some *navios* of Coromandel traded with Siriao in 1588. Portuguese traders like Filippe de Brito had special interest in trade with Siriao because of its high profits.[159]

The Arakan invasion of Pegu in 1591 prompted the king of Portugal to prohibit the Portuguese of Santhome and Nagapattinam with Pegu from conducting their highly lucrative trade with Pegu.[160] Portugal's interest in passing this order was to maintain its healthy relationship with the king of Siam. The trade embargo was not lifted even in 1598, since the outcome of the war was still not decided.[161] Some official voyages granted to individuals like Mathias do Caravalho Pereira from Santhome to Pegu on 20 November 1590 were not undertaken, but his son Joao Pereira da Costa requested the king of Portugal in 1624 to permit him to undertake the voyage.[162] The private Portuguese traders of Santhome and Nagapattinam, however, carried on clandestine trade in precious stones with Pegu.[163]

## COROMANDEL TRADE WITH SIAM

Portuguese chroniclers describe the ports on the Siam coast and the availability of rich merchandise such as gold, silver, benzoin, lacquer and tin. These ports were frequented by the *Marakayar* merchants and *chettis* of Coromandel.[164] The Siamese had not liked the *Marakayars* who had settled down at the various ports of the Siam coast, because they exercised powerful influence in the administration of the kingdom.[165] These merchants brought a variety of textiles in cotton and silk, both printed and dyed,

RECORDED SHIPPING FROM COROMANDEL TO PORTS OF SIAM COAST, 1580-85*

| *Period* | *Mergui* | *Tennaserim* | *Junk Ceylon* |
|---|---|---|---|
| 1580 | - | 1 | 1 |
| 1582 | - | - | 2 |
| 1585 | 1 | - | - |

*Medez da Luz, op. cit., fl. 89; Chancelaria de D. Sebastiao and D. Henrique, liv. 45, fl. 34v-37v; *B.N.L. Fundo Geral*, MSS. 7, No. 91.

besides saffron and opium.[166] Mergui on the Siam coast conducted regular trade with Pulicat in the early sixteenth century.[167] Gold, silver and other metals came to the ports of Siam from the inland Laos. Many white elephants were sent to Coromandel. Siamese traders did not frequent Malacca for many years and the trade was increasingly concentrated on the ports of Bay of Bengal even in 1511.[168]

Native merchants of Coromandel, particularly the *chettis*, continued their trade, paying only two-ninths of the value of the merchandise as tax.[169] Coromandel-Siam trade was dominated by the native merchants of Coromandel in the first half of the sixteenth century. Sources indicate that concession voyages were established between Coromandel and Junk Ceylon in 1580.[170] Some Portuguese like Trigo de Almeida, residing at Nagapattinam, bought textiles from this region and traded with Junk Ceylon. It appears that the voyages were irregular, since documentation for the subsequent years is silent on the matter.

It may therefore be concluded that Coromandel trade links with various ports of Siam were not well developed as late as 1580, although the Portuguese conducted active trade in all other directions of the Indian Ocean.

The Portuguese merchants developed a special taste for trade with Tennaserim when sale of concession voyages were introduced. The Jesuit visitor Fernao Guerreiro states that the Portuguese merchants from Coromandel unloaded their cargo at the ports of Siam and the textiles were taken inland, particularly to the kingdoms of Cambodia and Laos.[171] The Coromandel ships in return took amber, sapanwood, benzoin, lac, and lead. The Portuguese traders of Coromandel generally conducted trade with the help of native merchants. Francisco de Aguiar owned ships and always sailed in the company of *Marakayar* merchants to trade with Tennaserim.[172] Voyages were undertaken by a union of native merchants, specially *Marakayars* trading from Nagapattinam.[173]

Four voyages sanctioned to Antonio da Cova, captain of Nagapattinam, were readily acquired by this union of merchants. He personally supervised the transportation of merchandise on these voyages, making a neat profit.[174] The Portuguese residents of Nagapattinam protested against such doings of the captain and there was disorder in Nagapattinam between 1595 and 1599 on that account[175] and the matter was referred to the king of Portugal. Later, when the concession system was abolished at the end of the sixteenth century, the position of the captain of Nagapattinam became less important.[176] This incident shows that concession voyages operated from the ports of Coromandel had much to do with the control exercised by the Portuguese captain.

Santhome also traded with Tenasserim, which was much closer than going to Macao via Malacca. The preference for Tenasserim was on account of its proximity and the abundant availability there of Chinese merchandise. Tennaserim was the terminal port and valuable Chinese goods such as porcelain, silk, damask and brocade were brought there from China through the lands of Cambodia and Laos.

NAGAPATTINAM BASED GRANT OF CONCESSION VOYAGES TO MALACCA, 1580-87*

| *Voyage* | *Buyer* | *1580* | *1582* | *1585* | *1587* |
|---|---|---|---|---|---|
| (a) | Nagapattinam-Tennaserim | | | | |
| | Joao de sousa de Ataide | 2 | - | - | - |
| | Bastiao Borges | - | - | 2 | - |
| | Fernao Goncalves | - | - | - | 2 |
| (b) | Nagapattinam -Junk Ceylon | | | | |
| | Carneiro | 2 | - | - | - |
| | Trigo de Almeida | - | 2 | - | - |
| | Joao Rebello de Azevedo | - | - | 2 | - |
| | Total | 4 | 2 | 4 | 2 |

*For Tennaserim see *R.C.I.*, vol. I, No. 918, p. 214. *A.P.O.* fac. V. No. 452; No. 480. For Junk Ceylon see, *R.C.I.*, vol. I, No. 13718, p. 327, Chancelaria de D. Filippe Liv 2. fl. 174-174v.; B.N.L. *Fundo Geral*, MSS. 7, No. 91.

The voyages to Tennaserim brought good revenue to the Portuguese in Santhome.[177] An idea of how profitable they were may be had from the following instance. Two voyages from Santhome to Tennaserim were granted on condition that the income from these voyages was to be spent towards the acquisition of ammunition for the defence of the Portuguese settlement at Santhome.[178] The Portuguese who participated in Asian trade acquired enough wealth and they took vigorous steps to fortify their settlements on Coromandel at the end of the sixteenth century.

## COROMANDEL-CEYLON TRADE

Inscriptions of Vijayanagara kings like Krishnadevaraya, Achyutadevaraya and Sadasivaraya, found in the hinterland of Coromandel at Thanjavur and Tiruttani, record their conquests of Ceylon.[179] It is possible that their sovereignty extended and the commercial contacts flourished. Tirumullaivasal in the Cauvery delta was the foremost port for trade with Ceylon in the early sixteenth century. A copper plate inscription belonging to the Dharmapuram *Adheena mutt* describes imports of arecanut, jaggery, dry fish, sandalwood and camphor from Ceylon in exchange of rice export from Tirumullaivasal in 1513.[180] Portuguese sources also mention Tirumullaivasal as a busy port of Coromandel.[181] Tirumullaivasal later declined in importance and its rice trade was diverted to Nagapattinam when the Portuguese settled there. According to the Portuguese sources 176 *cottai* of rice were exported from Tirumalairayanpattinam to Ceylon on 25 September 1524.[182] The Portuguese of Coromandel, as also the captain of Colombo, Fernao Gomes de Lemos, had urged the king of Portugal to blockade the rice supply from Coromandel to Ceylon because rice was generally exchanged for cinnamon.[183] Having no control over rice trade, the Portuguese could not purchase cinnamon. The Portuguese thereafter persuaded the king of Ceylon to issue an edict expelling the *Marakayar* rice traders from his kingdom to augment their purchase of cinnamon.[184] When famines broke out in Coromandel and paddy cultivation was affected in the 1520s the people of Ceylon suffered from want of rice. Complaints were made in Kandy about the scarcity of rice and the Portuguese captain pleaded for rice supply from Coromandel.[185] The Archbishop of Goa in 1569

RECORDED PORTUGUESE SHIPPING FROM COROMANDEL TO CEYLON, 1519-47*

| *Period* | *Number of ships* |
|---|---|
| 1519 | 2 |
| 1523 | 1 |
| 1524 | 1 |
| 1527 | 1 |
| 1530 | 2 |
| 1545 | 2 |
| 1547 | 1 |

*Bouchon, op. cit, pp. 186-88; Gavetas, IV, pp. 140-44; (1519) *Documentos Sobre os Portugueses em Mocambique e na Africa Central*, vol. VI, p. 204; *C.C.* II-114-21, (1523); *C.C.* I-38-1, fl. 6. (1530); Schurhammer, op. cit., vol. III, p. 317 and 324(1527); *Colecao Sao Lourenco*, III, 326 and 335 (1545); Armando Cortesao, *Obras Completas* op. cit., vol. III, pp. 88-9.

described Coromandel as the throat of Ceylon from where supply of rice and food provisions came.[186]

Another important commodity of Coromandel sold at Jaffna and Mannar in Ceylon was textiles, in exchange for cinnamon. These textiles were officially stamped and the right to collect the fee was auctioned to the highest bidder. The stamp duty (*renda da chapa*) was a source of income for the Portuguese.[187] Coromandel vessels at Mannar were kept under strict watch to ensure that the merchants had paid all duties, failing which they were taxed ten per cent duty. Also, because export of cinnamon from Ceylon was strictly a monopoly of the Portuguese crown, if any cinnamon was found in the ships coming from Ceylon to Coromandel all the merchandise was seized, one-third value of the cargo being paid as reward to the informant or to the person who made the seizure.[188]

The merchants of Coromandel also bought elephants from the king of Ceylon.[189] These elephants were eminently docile and were greatly esteemed by the Vijayanagara kings, who used them in their army. The best elephants were sold at 1,000 or 1,500 *cruzados*.[190] The Portuguese also collected dye roots in Mannar from a wild shrub called *chaya*, after the Tamil word meaning colour, for export to Coromandel. Seven *bahars* of dye roots were sent to Coromandel in 1582.[191] Commodities like arecanut from Trincomalee and Batticaloa came to Coromandel, on which the Portuguese collected export duties in the last two decades of the sixteenth century.[192] Luxury items such as sapphire, rubies, topazes and semi-precious stones also found their place among the commodities exported from Ceylon to Coromandel.[193] Although restrictions were placed by the Portuguese, it appears that the commerce between Coromandel and Ceylon flourished owing to the factors of demand and supply.

## INDIRECT TRADE OF COROMANDEL WITH WEST ASIA AND EUROPE

Portuguese documentation on the textile trade of Coromandel with West Asia is scanty, although textiles from Cambay played an important role because of its proximity. Ordinary cotton textiles were required by the Portuguese at Ormuz[194] and elsewhere in West Asia for the use of slaves in 1525. It is possible that the *Marakayars* and other Muslims of Coromandel introduced Coromandel textiles in West Asia during *Hajj* pilgrimage. *Beatilhas* of Pulicat textiles were greatly valued in Persia, and the Portuguese viceroy presented 600 pieces of them through the embassy despatched to Ismail Shah of Persia.[195] These textiles were entered in the records of Goa customs house and finally found their way to West Asia.[196] Horses were imported from West Asia to the western ports of India by the Portuguese. Some *casados* like Pedro Alvaro de Mesquita and Diogo de Lisboa had specialised in horse trade with Coromandel and they stayed at Cape Comorin for the convenience of knowing in good time the arrival of horses from West Asia to Cannanore, Chaul and Goa. They sailed and brought the horses to Coromandel ports.[197] Some *casados* of Cochin also exported horses.[198] The *nayaka* of Thanjavur sent his men in quest of horses from the Portuguese at Nagapattinam,[199] who sold to the *nayaka* horses which had been imported from West Asia. Portuguese sources record that some of these horses became sick due to unfavourable climate before sale from Nagapattinam. There was a Portuguese *casado* by name Marcos who was appointed by the Portuguese captain to treat these sick horses. He was paid four *pardaos* for this special services.[200] Metals such as iron which was much available at the ports of Pulicat and Kunimedu had been purchased by the Portuguese and exported to Red sea[201] via Cochin. Thus no direct commercial relations existed between Coromandel and West Asia.

The Portuguese who came to purchase pepper and spices at

first in the Malabar region, developed interest in Coromandel trade and in due course exported some Coromandel commodities to Europe through the ports of Cochin and Goa. Textiles constituted the principal item of export. The sailings from India to Lisbon in 1587[202] consisted of 401 bales of textiles including cotton and silk products; forming 10.5 per cent weight of the ship, which probably included the Coromandel, the proportion of weight increased to 12.2 per cent in A.D. 1600.[203] We may therefore say that the Portuguese connected the Coromandel trading world with Europe indirectly. The Dutch and the English later on exported textiles directly from Coromandel to Europe.

## BANKING AND FINANCE

The increasing maritime networks of overseas trade of Coromandel provided an advanced system of banking and finance. A system of bill of exchange existed for long distance trade. A letter of Sabapathi *chetti* directed a Muslim merchant to pay Jorge Cirugao a sum of 75 *cruzados* for having received fifty *cruzados* earlier. Another letter relating to Pulicat-Malacca trade described that 200 *cruzados* given to Tamil merchants as loan fetched 300 *cruzados*.[204] These two pieces of evidence suggest that investment in long distance trade earned an interest of 50 per cent on an average. It is further inferred that *chettis* and the native Muslims had mutual financial agreements. We do not find any bar based on Islamic law on taking interest on loans.

Coromandel inscriptions record various rates of interest charged in hinterland transactions. The temples generally gave loans at 12 per cent in Chittoor and Chingleput regions from 1535 to 1548.[205] The Srirangam temple gave loans to yield 15 per cent interest as laid down in the *Yajnavalkyasmriti* during Achyutadevaraya's period.[206] Some loans were repaid at 18 per cent interest.[207] These details may be compared with the long distance trade investment mentioned earlier.

Travellers who visited the Coromandel region remarked that the temples had accumulated large volume of gold, which they had stored in the treasury. The gold treasury was known as *pon bhandaram;* a special officer, called *karta,* was in charge of it.[208] Gaspar Correa, who visited Tirumala-Tirupati temple in 1548, noted that the amount of gold offered by the pilgrims prostrating before the deity amounted to a heap of 215$^1/_2$ bushels of wheat.[209] The Portuguese planned to plunder the gold from the treasury of this temple, but the project had to be given up: the king of Vijayanagara, when he learnt of the conspiracy to loot the temple, having made special security arrangements to foil it.[210] Gold appears to have been stored in plenty and it had been also circulated.

## IMPORT-EXPORT DUTIES

Gold and silver were imported into Coromandel and they were used as marketable merchandise in exchange.[211] Coromandel received its supply of gold mainly from Malacca and Sumatra. As early as 1506, the Portuguese came to know that Coromandel owed a lot to Malacca for gold.[212] Malacca was the biggest gold emporium in Asia, which received its supply chiefly from Minangkabu through the ports of Indragiri and Panshar in Sumatra and also from Siam and Patani. The poorest quality of gold came from Borneo.[213] Minangkabu traders brought six, seven or eight *candils* of gold at a time and exchanged it for Coromandel textiles. It was gold dust of excellent quality in different particles and sizes, which when melted had a gold content of twenty and twenty-three and a half *carats*.[214] Each *katti* of gold at Malacca, exchanged for goods worth 200 *cruzados*, was sold for 280 *cruzados* at Pulicat in 1540.[215] Coromandel possessed an abundance of gold stock owing to its free flow of gold. According to Portuguese sources of the seventeenth century, the *atikari* of Santhome of Mylapore levied duty on gold imported from Malacca in 1626 and the merchants of Santhome wrote to the King of Portugal to help them.[216] The king instructed the viceroy to see that no duty was collected on gold imported from Malacca to Santhome.[217] This would lead to the conclusion that there was no restriction and levy of import duties on gold.

Krishnadevaraya in his *Amuktamalyada* described the development of ports of the Vijayanagara kingdom through a policy of importing merchandise and allowing decent profit in maritime trade.[218] Taxes were levied on imports and exports at the ports.[219] An inscription from Kariamanikka Perumal temple of Nagalapuram mentions that as on 1 January 1521 the *chettis* of Padaividu and Chandragiri *rajya*, who exported textiles in ships, paid one *panam* as duty at Pulicat.[220] Export of rice and other commodities were charged a quarter *panam* as duty in the same port.[221]

Import and export duties, called *etrumati* and *irakumati* in the epigraphs, were collected from various coastal villages such as Engonavellore, Modanellore, Anjur, Anjambedu, Karkartharpadi, Mendur, Godalikoti, Oongadu and Durgarajapattinam, as mentioned in another epigraph from Kalakhasti temple.[222] Duties were collected at the ports of Coromandel by the port officials. Pulicat,[223] Mylapore[224] and Nagapattinam[225] were administered by its own *shahbhandar* in the early sixteenth century. The *nayakas* of coastal regions appointed *atikaris* to collect import-export duties at the ports.[226] The *atikaris* of Mylapore resided close to the Portuguese settlement of Santhome and they collected these import-export duties. Some of the *atikaris* also leased the collection of import-export duties in Coromandel ports.[227]

The Portuguese paid custom duties to the *nayaka* in whose jurisdiction they traded in the ports. There is some controversy about a Portuguese revenue collector having been appointed to collect the customs revenue for Santhome in March 1589.[228] The fact that this appointment did not materialise shows that the Portuguese did not virtually control the ports of Coromandel but conducted trade depending more on the local situation and manners.

The present study of the Coromandel region, dealing with the growth of the Portuguese settlements and ports, enables us to assess the degree of dominance of the Portuguese. We have seen how the Portuguese contributed to Coromandel commerce, although they depended on the economic power of the native merchants. The Portuguese did not attempt to monopolise either the rice trade or the textile trade in Coromandel. The Portuguese kings and viceroys also did not try to enforce their monopoly in the Bay of Bengal, although the crown claimed to be the lord of conquest, navigation and commerce of Ethiopia, Arabia, Persia and India. The *Marakayars* played a dominant role in Coromandel shipping and trade. The Sultan of Achin favoured his co-religionists and encouraged the *Marakayars* to trade with Achin where substantial trade was carried on, outside Portuguese control. The Portuguese had no choice but to cooperate with the local *chetti* traders; *Marakayars* stiffly resisted the growth of Portuguese trade in Coromandel. Several instances also show that the *Marakayars* and the private Portuguese traders worked together, the *Marakayars* often having the upper hand in their ownership of ships and merchandise. The Portuguese officials seem to have lacked the resources for undertaking voyages. The seaborne trade from Santhome, Devanampattinam and Nagapattinam were controlled by the Portuguese captains residing there. This disturbed the Muslim networks of free trade to some extent. The Portuguese never had a long chain of factories and fortresses with regular patrol to dominate the trade in this region.

The pattern of Coromandel trade underwent a remarkable change between the early sixteenth century and its closing years, with the introduction of various new maritime routes operated from the Portuguese settlements, and revival of some of the inactive lines between Coromandel and China. Thus the Portuguese trading activities opened the gateway to the Dutch, the English and other Europeans in the expansion of commerce in Coromandel in the seventeenth century.

## NOTES AND REFERENCES

1. J.C. Van Leur, *Indonesian Trade and Society: Essays in Asian Social and Economic History*, The Hague, 1955.
2. Niels Steensgaard, *The Asian Trade Revolution of the Seventeenth Century*, Chicago, 1974; M.A.P. Meilink Roelofsz, *Asian Trade and European Influence in the Indonesian Archipelago Between 1500-1630*, The Hague, 1969.
3. M.N. Pearson, *Merchants and Rulers in Gujarat: The Response to the Portuguese in the Sixteenth Century*, London, 1975; Ashin Das Gupta, *Indian Merchants and the Decline of Surat, 1700-1750*, Wiesbaden, 1979.
4. Sanjay Subrahmanyam, *Merchants, Markets and State in the Early Modern India*, Delhi, 1990.
5. Philip D. Curtin, *Cross-Cultural Trade in World History*, Cambridge, 1984.
6. Sanjay Subrahmanyam, *Improvising Empire: Portuguese Trade and Settlements in the Bay of Bengal*, Delhi, 1990.
7. The fact that the *Vellanvagai* lands existed in the late Chola period and these lands were cultivated by *Vellalars* goes to prove that the *Mudaliars* emerged as a social group. They derived their substantial income from agriculture and later they invested in maritime trade.
8. C.C. Brown, "Sejarah Melayu, Malay Annals", *Journal of the Malaysian Branch of the Royal Asiatic Society*, vol. 25, 1952, pp. 157-59.
9. *A.N.T.T.*, *Gavetas*, XV-8-2; See also *Alguns Documentos*, pp. 460-61.
10. *As Gavetas da Torre do Tombo*, VI, pp. 196-97.
11. *A.N.T.T.*, *C.C.*- I- 37-84 (1527).
12. Roderich Ptak, *Notes on the word Shanhu . . .*, pp. 64-80.
13. *S.I.T.I.*, vol. III, p. 1104 (1537); *A.R.E.*, 69 of 1938-39 (1513) *Nannilam*

*Kalvettugal*, vol. II, Sl. No. 232 of 1978 (1592), 350 of 1953-54 (1558); *T.T.D.E.S.*, vol. III, No. 611 (1506); *A.N.T.T.*, *Nucleo Antigo*, 808, fl. 2v; *S.I.I.*, XVII. 679(1521).

14. Ibid.
15. There is an inscriptional evidence to show that the *Komatis* are Telugu speaking group of *chetti* merchants from Andhra; *S.I.I.*, vol. VI, No. 121. This inscription is from Draksharma dated 1068 A.D.
16. *A.R.E.*, 161 of 1907.
17. *T.T.D.E.S.*, V, No. 474; Barbosa, op. cit., II, pp. 70-3.
18. Barbosa, op. cit., pp. 72-3.
19. Ibid.
20. Castanheda, op. cit., Book II, Chapter II, capitulo III, p. 135; Barros, op. cit., III, II, I, Dec., I. IX, III.
21. *T.T.D.E.S.*, III, No. 338, pp. 72-80, V, p. 106; see also *A.R.E.*, 1936-37, II Para, 61.
22. *A.R.E.*, 260 of 1929-30, 261 of 1929-30 and 293 of 1926-27.
23. *T.T.D.E.S.*, V, Nos. 474 (1545) and 154, pp. 406-408. *Nannilam Kalvettugal*, vol. II, Sl. No. 232 of 1978 (1592), 235 of 1903, line (2) (1599) *Chennaimanagara Kalvettugal*, Sl. No. 81 (e) of 1967. *S.I.I.*, XVII, 679 (1521).
24. *A.N.T.T.*, *C.C.*- Ia - 13-74, fl. 14.
25. *D.I.*, vol. V, p. 671; Castanheda, op. cit., III, p. 135.
26. Castanheda, op. cit., Book II, p. 112.
27. C.R. Boxer, *The Portuguese Seaborne Empire*, 1415-1825, London, 1969.
28. Ibid., *C.C.*- I- 6-82, Raymundo Antonio de Bulhao Patao, ed., *Cartas de Affonso de Albuquerque*, Lisboa, 1903 (hereafter *C.A.A.*), II, pp. 403-19.
29. *A.N.T.T.*, *Nucleo Antigo*, No. 801, fl. 410.
30. A letter written from Goa, 15 Nov. 1527, *A.N.T.T.*, *C.C.*- I-38-1, fl. 4v.
31. Letter of Affonso de Albuquerque to the King of Portugal, 1 April 1512. *Alguns Documentos,* p. 245; *A.N.T.T.*, *C.C.*-Ia-13-74, fl. 14; See also C.R. Boxer, *Further Selections from the Tragic History of the Sea, 1554-65,* Cambridge, 1967, p. 49.
32. *C.S.L.*, III, 436; Sanjay Subrahmanyam, *Improvising,* pp. 241-44.
33. Armando Cortesao & Luis de Albuquerque, op. cit., pp. 89-90.
34. W.H. Moreland, *From Akbar to Aurangazeb: A Study in Indian Economic History*, London, 1923; Surendra Gopal, *Commerce and Crafts in Gujarat in 16th and 17th Centuries: A Study in the Impact of European Expansion on a Pre-Capitalistic Economy*, New Delhi, 1975.
35. Etymology of the word *Marakayar* or *Marakkalarayar* is sometimes said to be derived from the *Tamil Marakkalam* called boat.
36. *C.S.L.*, IV, 340; letter of Antonio Coelho written from Chale, dated 13 August 1546.
37. Thomas Bowrey, *A Geographical Account of the Countries Round the Bay of Bengal 1669 to 1679,* Cambridge, 1905, pp. 257-58; *A.R.E.*, 294 of

1963-64; The Nachikulam inscription from Tiruturaipoondi taluk mentions the existence of *Marakayars* in the sixteenth century. *A.N.T.T., Nucleo Antigo,* 808, fl. 3v. The Diary of Vasco da Gama mentions the ruler of Kunimedu and its flourishing trade with South-East Asia, *Diario de Viagem de Vasco da Gama,* Porto, 1845, vol. I, pp. 291-95.

38. Pires, op. cit., vol. II, pp. 211-72; Correa, op. cit., III, 554, II, 602; Barbosa, op. cit., II, pp. 129-32. The Inscription runs as follows: *"Muhayyudin Vakkosudaya Kappaludaya Mani;"* Barros, op. cit., IV, 12, pp. 412-13; Couto, op. cit., V, 2-4, pp. 164-65.
39. S. Mohammed Husain Nayinar, *Tuhfat-ul-Mujahi-in,* Madras, 1942, p. 81.
40. *A.N.T.T., Gavetas,* 20-4-15; *C.A.A.*, vol. II, p. 301 (1506); *C.C.*-II-15-129 (1508). The two Muslim pilots who assisted were paid five *pardaos* and four *tangas* see *A.N.T.T., C.C.* op. cit., IIa-114-23. Payment made in kind particularly rice *C.C.* IIa-114-46; IIa-115-64.
41. *C.A.A.*, Tomo II, pp. 377-78. The view of Sanjay Subrahmanyam regarding the visit of Portuguese traders purely as an accident in the vicinity of Nagapattinam in 1506 is incorrect. See *Improvising Empire,* op. cit., p. 98. The lengthy text of the letter clearly shows that it was a well planned one and the port is Kunimedu situated far away from Nagapattinam.
42. *A.N.T.T., C.C.*-Ia-5-117, fl. 1-6; letter of Gaspar da India, to King Dom Manuel, is written from Cochin.
43. *A.N.T.T., Gavetas,* 20, Maco 4, Doc. 15; letter of Viceroy to the king of Portugal from Cochin, 27 December 1506.
44. K.M. Panikkar, *Asia and Western Dominance,* London, 1959.
45. *A.N.T.T., C.C.*-IIa-117-156.
46. Ibid.
47. Datu-Zaial-Abidin Bin Abul Wahid, ed., *Glimpses of Malaysian History,* Kuala Lumpur, 1980, p. 23.
48. Ibid.
49. Tome Pires, op. cit., II, p. 273.
50. Letter of Rui de Brito Patalim to the King of Portugal, 6 Jan. 1514, *A.N.T.T., C.C.*-I-14-49; *C.A.A.*, vol. III, p. 94. Tome Pirès, op. cit., II, pp. 273-74.
51. Letter of Albuquerque to the king of Portugal, 1 April 1512, *A.N.T.T., C.C.*-I-22-80.
52. Ibid., Capitulo XXI, Tomo II, Pt. I, p. 162, Capitulo XXVI, Pt. I, p. 216.
53. Artur Basilao de Sa, *Documentacao,* vol. I, pp. 66-74; *L.F.F.R.* Thomaz, "Nina Chatu e o Commercio Portugues em Malaca" in, *Memorias do Centro de Estudos de Mainharia,* vol. V, Lisboa, 1975. See the text of the Royal letter.
54. Simao Botelho, "Tombo do Estado da India" in *Subsidios para a Historia da India Portuguesa,* Lisboa, 1848, pp. 104-108; Couto, op. cit., V, 2, p. 138. Letter of Garcia Chainho, Factor of Malacca to the king of

Portugal, 31 August, 1521, *A.N.T.T., C.C.*-III-7-115.

55. Correa, op. cit., IV, pp. 131-32. *A.N.T.T., C.C.*-I-68-86.
56. *A.N.T.T., C.C.*-I-68-88.
57. Ibid., *C.C.*-I-76-102, fl. 3v, *C.C.*-I-77-18, fl. 2v.
58. Codice Cadaval, MSS 972; Arquivo da casa cadaval, fl. 1v-2, fl. 26v-28v; See also Texeira da Mota, *Um Manuscrito Nautico Seis Cartista re encontrado* Centro do Estudos de Cartografia Antiga, Lisboa, 1975, p. 11.
59. 'Sanjay Subrahmanyam, *Improvising*, pp. 32-4.
60. Elaine Sanceau, *Cartas de D. Joao de Castro*, Lisboa, 1954, p. 235.
61. Antonio Baiao, op. cit., p. 308.
62. Letter of Vedor da Fazenda to the king of Portugal, 17 Feb. 1547 cited in Schurhammer, op. cit., III, p. 360.
63. *A.N.T.T., C.C.* I-76-112; I-82-1; Schurhammer, op. cit, vol. II, p. 81; III, pp. 341 and 604; Silva Rego, Documentacao, IV, No. 38, p. 200, Cartas dos vice-reis da India, No. 154.
64. Rodrigo de Lima Felner, *Subsidios para*, p. 225. See black textiles, *C.C.* I-68-86(1540); Silk cloth, *C.C.* I- 60-17, fl. 8v (1537).
65. *C.S.L.*, II, 493; see also Armando Cortesao and Luis de Albuquerque, op. cit., p. 394.
66. Correa, op. cit., Cap. X, Tomo I, Pt. I, p. 739; Barros, op. cit., Doc. I, Pt. II; Schurhammer, op. cit., vol. III, p. 4.
67. Sanjay subrahmanyam, *Improvising*, p. 40.
68. Ibid., pp. 241-44.
69. Sanjay Subrahmanyam, *Improvising*, op. cit., p .40.
70. Letter of Fr. Lourenco Paes to Leao Henriques, written from Malacca, 3 Dec. 1568, see also 15 Nov. 1567, in *D.I.*, VII, n. 87, p. 355.
71. Sanjay Subrahmanyam, *Improvising*, pp. 341-44.
72. E.P. Mendes da Luz, op. cit., fls. 78, 84 and 84v; L.F.F.R. Thomaz, "Les Portugais dans les mers de l'Archipel au XVI e siecle", *Archipel*, 18, 1979, pp. 105-205.
83. *A.N.T.T., C.C.*-I-77-26; L.F.F.R. Thomaz, "Os Portugueses em Malacca 1511-1580". Baccalaureate Thesis, University of Lisbon, 1964, vol. II, pp. 267-70.
74. *A.H.U., India, Caixa*, 1, Doc. 22 (June 1598).
75. Sanjay Subrahmanyam, *Improvising*, pp. 39 and 74, see Om Prakash, "Long Distance Maritime trade in Asia: Decline and Revival", ed. K.S. Mathew, *Studies in Maritime History*, Pondicherry, 1991, pp. 29-37.
76. *B.N.L., Codice* 1540, fls. 89-91v; three voyages of Malacca given to Simao Teixeira was at the price of 12010 *cruzados* during 1598-99.
77. *A.P.O.-C.R.*, fas. III, Pt. 2a, Doc. 2004, pp. 568-83.
78. Artur Teodoro de Matos, *O Estado da India, Nos anos de 1581-88 Estructura, Administrativa, e Economia, Alguns Elementos, para o seu Estudo*, Ponta Delagada, 1982, p. 37.
79. *A.P.O.-C.R.*, fas. V, Pt. 3a, Doc. 1002, pp. 1364-67.
80. Royal letter of the king to the viceroy dated 25 Jan. 1598, Lisbon,

*A.P.O-C.R.*, I, Doc. 75, p. 122 and the letter of 10 Feb 1598, *A.P.O.-C.R.*, III, Doc. 313, p. 828.

81. *A.H.U. Caixa, India*, XI, Doc. 15 (1592).
82. *A.P.O.-C.R.*, fasc. III, Pt. 1a, Doc. 94, pp. 328-29.
83. Letter of King Filippe I to Mathias de Albuquerque, Lisbon, 1 March 1594, *Boletim de Filmoteca Ultramarina Portuguesa* (hereafter *B.F.U.P.*), vol. 2, Doc. 75, p. 207.
84. *A.H.U., Codice*, 281, fl. 346v; letter of the king to viceroy D. Francisco da Gama, Lisboa, 2 Jan. 1596, *B.F.U.P.*, 3, Doc. 25, pp. 431-35.
85. Order of Viceroy from Goa dated 14 April 1595, in P. Pissurlencer, *Regimentos das Fortalezas da India*, Bastora, Goa, 1951, pp. 245-46.
86. *A.P.O.-C.R.*, III, Pt. 2a, Doc. 325, pp. 801-4.
87. Ibid., III, Pt. 2a, Doc. 351, p. 900.
88. *A.H.U., Codice*, No. 282, fl. 22v.
89. Tome Pires, op. cit., vol. I, pp. 269-72; James Lanchaster, *The Voyage of Sir James Lanschaster to Bengal and the Coast of Indonesia*, London, 1940, p. 107.
90. See the tables given in Vitorino Magahales Godinho, *Mito e Mercadoria, Utopia, e Pratica, de Navegar, Seculos XIII-XVIII* Lisbo a, 1990, p. 338.
91. Schurhammer, op. cit., vol. II, p. 550.
92. *A.H.U., Codice*, No. 281, fl. 281$^{V}$.
93. *A.G.S., Secretarias Provincales*, vol. XV, p. 610.
94. *B.N.L., Codice*, 1976, fls. 7-11; Couto, op. cit., X, Pt. 1a, Liv. 1, Cap. III, pp. 14-16 (1581); H.A.G., *Livros das Moncoes*, Liv. 3B, Cod. 52-55, fl. 2.
95 *A.N.T.T., Fragmentos*, Caixa 3, Maco 3, Doc. 17.
96. Barros, op. cit., III-3-6, p. 139.
97. V.M. Godinho, op. cit., p. 382.
98. *C.C*, II-49-24 (1514)
99. *A.N.T.T., Cartas Orientais*, No. 59, Summary is available in Portuguese.
100. *A.N.T.T., Nucleo Antigo*, 808, fls. 3-3v.
101. *A.N.T.T., C.C.*-59-58; Artur Basilao de Sa, op. cit., II, p. 250 (1537); see also Anthony Reid, "Sixteenth Century Turkish Influence in Western Indonesia", *Journal of South East Asian History*, 10, No. 3, 1969, pp. 400-1.
102. Ibid., *C.C.*-I-22-80 (Sept. 1527).
103. Ibid.
104. Ibid.
105. Letter of the Captain of Ternate Antonio de Brito to the king of Portugal, 11 Feb. 1523, *A.N.T.T., Gavetas*, 18-6-9; Basilao de Sa, op. cit., vol. I, No. 20, p. 132.
106. *A.N.T.T., C.C*,-1a-11-50 (1512). 116. *A.P.O.-C.R.*, Fas. III, Pt. 2a, Doc. 204, pp. 568-83.
107 *A.P.O.-CR*, Fas. III, Pt. 2a, doc. 204, pp. 90-1.
108. Basilio de Sa, op. cit., IV, pp. 90-1 (March 1570).
109. F.P. Mendez da Luz, op. cit., pp. 90-1.

110. Artur Basilio de Sa, op. cit., vol. IV, pp. 90-1.
111. *A.N.T.T., Chancelaria D. Filippe,* Liv. 7, fls. 304v- 305.
112. B.M. *Additional Manuscripts,* No. 28432, fl. 10v.
113. The sultan of Achin asked permission to open a factory at Jeddah for sale of pepper. He also gave an oath in a mosque that he would not be friendly with Christians during 1585, B. Jorge de Lemos, *Historia de cercos de Malaca,* Lisboa, 1982.
113. *B.F.U.P.*, vol. II, p. 230; For details see Bibliotheque Historique de la Marine, Paris, codice MSS 109, No. 7, fls. 182-84.
114. *A.N.T.T., Mss Convento da Graca,* CX 3, VI-L, pp. 205 (18-1-1598).
115. Sebastiâo Gonçalves, *Primeira parte de historia dos religiosos da companhia de Jesus,* Atlantida-Coimbra, 1962.
116. *B.N.L., Fundo Geral,* Codice 8570, fl. 275v.
117. Ibid., Caixa 207, No. 90, fls. 1-2v.
118. *A.N.T.T., Mss Convento da Graca,* CX 6, Tomo II E, pp. 219-20.
119. Barbosa, op. cit., pp. 196 and 207; Pires, op. cit., vol. I, pp. 161 and 227; Barros, op. cit., Decada I, Pt. II, p. 174.
120. Barros, op. cit., Decada III, Pt. I, Ch. I, Cap. IX.
121. Schurhammer, op. cit., vol. II, p. 549.
122. B.P.A.D.E. Evora, *Codice,* CXV/2-1, fl. 155, Livro 18; Manuel Teixeria, *The Portuguese Missons in Malacca and Singapore,* 1511-98, Lisboa, 1967, vol. I, p. 348; see also Enformacao de alguma Coisas de... Reyno da China, Biblioteca Academia Sciencias de Lisboa, see *Cartas do Japao,* vol. I, fls. 249-55.
123. *A.N.T.T., Coleçcão São Vincente,* vol. X, fl. 128.
124. *A.P.O.-C.R.*, fasc. I, Pt. 2a, Doc. 5, pp. 61-74.
125. *A.N.T.T., Coleçcão São Vincente,* X, fl. 128.
126. Letter of Viceroy Dom Duarte de Menezes, 28 Jan. 1588, *A.P.O.-C.R.*, III, Pt. Ia, p. 123, 3 August 1591; *A.P.O.-C.R.*, III, Pt. 1a, pp. 328-29.
127. *A.P.O.-C.R.*, fac. I, Pt. 2a, Doc. 5, pp. 64 and 69.
128. *H.A.G., Livros das Monçoes,* 3A, 1585-1589, Codice 13-15, fl. 1.
129. *A.P.O.-C.R.*, fac. III-I, Doc. 33, p. 116.
130. Ibid., fac. III, 24, X, 140; H.A.G., Livros das Monçoes, No. 3a, 56-8, f. 5.
131. The Chinese mention Mylapore as *Mai-la-pu*. George Philip, "The Seaports of India and Ceylon", *Journal of the China Branch of the Royal Asiatic Society,* 1884, vol. XIX, Pt. I, p. 222.
132. *A.N.T.T., Convento da Graça,* Tomo CX 3, VI-L, pp. 1-4. A.G.S., Secretarias Provinciales, Codice 1479, fl. 258v.
133. Barbosa, op. cit., vol. II, pp. 129-32.
134. L.F.F.R. Thomaz, *De Malaca a Pegu Viagens de um feitor Portugues 1512-1515,* Lisbon, 1966, pp. 187-92.
135. *A.N.T.T., C.C.* I- 77-18, fl. 2v.
137. Manuel Teixeira, op. cit., vol. II, p. 71.
138. L.F.F.R. Thomaz, *De Malacca,* pp. 187-92.

139. Barbosa, op. cit., II, p. 157-58.
140. Barros, op. cit., Dec. III, Pt. I, pp. 164-73.
141. Barbosa, op. cit., II, pp. 217-18.
142. Ibid.
143. Sanjay Subrahmanyam, *Improvising,* p. 12. *C.A.A.*, VII, pp. 5, 20 and 182.
144. *A.N.T.T., C.C.*, Pt. I-76-102, fl. 3v; *C.C.*, Pt. I-77-18, fl. 2v.
145. Silva Rego, *Documentacao*, VI, p. 186.
146. *A.N.T.T., C.C.*, Pt. II-117-123 (1530).
147. Armando Cortesao & Luis de Albuquerque, op. cit., vol. III, Doc. 580, p. 1437.
148. *C.S.L.*, III, p. 456.
149. *A.N.T.T., Coleção São Vincente,* X, fl. 120.
150. *C.S.L.*, III, pp. 79-82.
151. Purchas, op. cit., vol. X, pp. 132-34.
152. Pires, op. cit., vol. I, p. 98; Barbosa, op. cit., II, p. 152.
153. An inscription from East *Rajagopuram* entrance left side from the Thiyaga Perumal temple at Tiruvaiyaru, records sale of pearls and *pavalam*. The text runs as follows, "*Sevappa nayakkar kattalai ittapadi ana-indu purva desathil pala ragu muthu pavalam valayal mani vikkkuradukku*" (line 3).
154. For details see Frederick and Balbi Voyages, in Richard Haklyut, *Voyages*, 8 Vols., London, Dent, Everyman's Library (n.d.).
155. Ibid.
156. Ibid.
157. Ibid.; see also Purchas, op. cit., vol. X, p. 135.
158. S. Jeyaseela Stephen, "Diamond Mining Industry, Vijayanagara state policy and the regional economy of late Medieval South India, A.D. 1509-1642", *Q.J.M.S.*, LXXXVI, No. 2, 1995, pp. 81-112.
159. Mendes da Luz, op.cit., fls. 84-9; letter of Duarte Deigado Varejao written from Panjim, Goa, to the king of Portugal, 1 December 1588 in *B.F.U.P.*, vol. XIV, Doc. 149, p. 575; see also *A.G.S.*, Codice, No. 1551; Boccaro, op. cit., Cap. XXXVI.
160. Letter of D. Filippe to Viceroy Mathias de Albuquerque, Lisbon, 12 Jan. 1591, *A.H.U.* Codice 281, fls. 113$^{V}$-114.
161. Order of Viceroy Francisco da Gama 8 April 1598, in *A.P.O.-C.R.*, fac. III, Pt. 2a, Doc. 349, pp. 897-98.
162. B.N.L., *Fundo Geral* , Codice, 1816, fl. 187.
163. *H.A.G.*, Livros das Monçoes, 1595-1601, Codice 22-3, fl. 400.
164. Castanheda, op. cit., Livro. I and II, p. 156.
165. Pires, op. cit., vol. I, p. 103.
166. Barbosa, op. cit., vol. I, p. 199.
167. Ibid.
168. Basilio de Sa, op. cit., vol. I, p. 104.
169. Pires, op.cit., vol. I, pp. 103-10.
170. *A.N.T.T., Chancelaria D. Filippe,* Liv. 2, fls. 174-174v. A Trader Antonio da Cova was granted voyages to Junk Ceylon see ibid., Liv 24. fl. 72.

171. *A.N.T.T., Manuscritos da Livraria,* MSS., 1104, fls. 97-8.
172. Correa, op. cit., Cap. II, p. 568; G. Schurhammer, "Uma Relação in edita de Padre Manuel Barradas, S.I. Sobre S. Francisco Xavier", *Studia,* II, Lisbon, pp. 60-1.
173. *A.N.T.T., Chancelaria D. Filippe Doaçoes,* Liv. 24, fl. 72; Order issued from Lisbon, dated 18 Feb. 1591.
174. Ibid.
175. B.M. *Additional Manuscripts,* No. 28432, fl. 10, Goa, dated 18 December 1599.
176. *B.N.L.,* Codice 581, fl. 170, these voyages were extinguished during 1607-08.
177. *A.G.S.,* Codice 1551; *B.F.U.P.,* XIV, Doc. 149, p. 575.
178. Silva Rego, *Documentos Remettidos da India ou Livros da Monçoes,* vol. X, Doc. 40, Lisboa, 1982, p. 37.
179. *A.R.E.,* 749 of 1903 (1522), 40 of 1897, 49 of 1900, 50 of 1900 (1539) and 451 of 1905 (1564).
180. K. Devanayagam, *Dharumai Adheena Seppedugal,* Dharmapuram, 1988. Copper plate No. 6, pp. 47-8.
181. Tome Pires, op. cit., vol. II, pp. 271-72.
182. *A.N.T.T., C.C.,* op. cit., II-119-103 (1524). The total rice export order on that day was 220 cottai. It is seen that only 176 *cottai* of rice was exported to Ceylon. The balance was exported to other places.
183. Ibid., *C.C.*-I-25-68, Oct. 1519, letter of João de Silveria to king Dom Manuel, in Genevieve Bouchon, *Mamale de Cananor,* Paris, 1975. Appendix. Document 2, p. 187.
184. Chandra Richard Desilva, "Portuguese Policy towards the Muslims in Ceylon", *The Ceylon Historical and Social Studies,* vol. IX, 1966, p. 114.
185. *C.S.L.,* III, p. 335.
186. J. Wicki, "Duas Relaçoes sobre a Situacao da India Portuguesa nos annos 1568 e 1569", *Studia,* vol. 8, 1961, p. 213.
187. P.E. Picris, *The Kingdom of Jafnapatanam,* Colombo, 1944, p. 7.
188. Tikri Abyesinghe, *A Study of Portuguese Regimentos on Sri Lanka at the Goa Archives,* Colombo (n.d.), p. 8.
189. Barbosa, op. cit., II, p. 113.
190. Ibid., p. 117.
191. Fernão Quyreoz, *The Temporal and Spiritual Conquest of Ceylon,* trs., S.G. Pereira, Colombo, 1930, p. 1194.
192. Adelino de Almeida Caldão, *Livro que,* p. 39; Tikri Abyesinghe, op. cit., p. 9; Pires, op. cit., vol. I, p. 83.
193. Pires, op. cit., vol. I, p. 86. The precious stones of Ceylon were much valued in comparison to those of Pegu with all their sparkle and transparency. The details of prices given by Duarte Barbosa are only common to the perfect rubies and precious stones. Those that were damaged or of a bad colour were sold at a less price. See Barbosa, op. cit., II, p. 219.

194. *A.N.T.T., C.C.*, Pt. 2a-124-7.
195. *B.N.L., Codice Alcobaca*, 475, fl. 170; Correa, op. cit., II, pp. 357 and 409-17.
196. *B.N.L., Fundo Geral*, No. 272, fl. 18-21v.
197. Armando Cortesao and Luis de Albuquerque, op. cit., III, 100; IV, 50.
198. Letter from Antonio Fernandes to Viceroy, 2 August 1546. Letter of Manoel Lobato to Viceroy, dtd. 25 August 1547, *C.S.L.*, II, pp. 335 and 364-72.
199. Purchas, op. cit., vol. II, pp. 227-28.
200. *A.N.T.T., C.C.*, Pt. 2a-117-56.
201. Correa, op. cit., II, 567-68; III, 578; see also Schurhammer, op. cit., vol. II, p. 571.
202. *A.G.S., Secretarias Provinciales,* Codice 1551, fls. 204-15. It mentions 372 quintals of silk and cotton textiles.
203. Steensgaard, "The Return Cargoes of the Carreira da India in the 16th century", in T.R. De Souza, *Indo-Portuguese History: Old Issues and New Questions,* New Delhi, 1984, pp. 13-31.
204. *A.N.T.T., C.C.*, Pt. II-49-24; *C.C.*, Pt. I-6-106.
205. *T.T.D.E.S.*, vol. V, No. 161; *A.R.E.*, 561 of 1919.
206. *S.I.I.*, XXIV, p. XVI.
207. *A.R.E.*, 56 of 1892.
208. Sadhu Subrahmanya Sastry, *Report*, p. 216.
209. Correa, op. cit., Chapter XXXI; See also I.A., October 1912, pp. 238-42.
210. Ibid., pp. 300 and 324-28.
211. Barros, op. cit., Decada II, Liv. VI, Cap. VI, p. 89.
212. *A.N.T.T., Gavetas,* 20-4-15; *C.A.A.*, II, p. 390.
213. The total incoming gold at Malacca was estimated as ten *bahars* in 1510; Pires, op. cit., vol. I, p. 161; C.R. Boxer, *Fidagos in the Far East,* The Hague, 1948, p. 7.
214. Couto, op. cit., Decada VII, Liv. 9, Cap. XVI.
215. For details see gold sales in 1517, *C.C.*, Pt. I-22-62; For sale of gold during 1540, *C.C.*, Pt. I-68-88.
216. *B.N. L., Fundo Geral,* No. 1814, fl. 199.
217. Ibid.
218. S. Rangasvami Sarasvati, op. cit., pp. 61-88.
219. *S.I.I.,* XVI, Pt. II, No. 98.
220. Ibid., XVII, pp. 311-12; see also *S.I.I.,* XVI, No. 671, pp. 311-13.
221. Ibid.
222. Ibid., XVI, Pt. II, No. 98 (1532). The total revenue of these villages had been said to be 1200 *gadayas.* These import-export duties were generally assigned to temples by the rulers.
222. Jose Pereira de Costa, "Gaspar Correia e lenda do Apostolo S. Thome" in *Actas do II Seminario,* p. 861.
224. Wicki, *Duas,* pp. 153-54.
225. Singaravelu, op. cit., pp. 32-3.

226. Wicki, *Duas,* pp. 153-54.
227. Correa, op. cit., I, 74; Fernão Guerreiro, *Relação das Coisas que fizeram os Padres de Companhia de Jesus nas suas Missoes India,* ed., A. Viegas, vol. II, Coimbra, 1930, p. 321; Even Linschoten mentions that the king of Vijayanagar had kept an *atikari* in Mylapore, vol. I, p. 82.
228. H.A.G., *Livros das Monçoes,* Liv. 4, 48-9, 5/2 fl. 754.

6

# Social Environment

Many scholars have attempted to reconstruct the history of Vijayanagara society in light of their study of the various dynasties of Vijayanagara empire from the fourteenth to seventeenth centuries. They generally treat the society in the framework of a fourfold division.[1] Scholars like B.A. Saletore explained the traditional Hindu social order as built around the epigraphical term *varna-shrama-dharma*; this *varna-shrama-dharma* becoming the inspiration in their struggle against the Bahmani rulers.[2] Nilakanta Sastri depicted the Vijayanagara rulers as protectors of Hindu society, defenders of Hindu culture and institutions;[3] they used the epigraphical term *purva mariyadai* to explain the keen attention the rulers gave to building temples and making generous endowments. A. Krishnaswami Pillai continued Nilakanta Sastri's tradition, putting forth the view that the rulers followed the noble tradition of *purva mariyadai bhaddati*—preservation of old culture and tradition.[4] T.V. Mahalingam added that respect for *purva mariyadai* was confined to certain customary rights which certain individuals or groups enjoyed for a long time in Vijayanagara society.[5]

These views of *varna-shrama-dharma* and *purva mariyadai* are, however, not entirely accurate. The kings of Vijayanagara did not only perpetuate the old social order: they encouraged real and fundamental change. The rise of *nayakas* as revenue collectors in Coromandel and the dynamics of Vijayanagara political process did affect Coromandel society. We shall try to highlight the manner in which society reacted to the new milieu.

Burton Stein's study of Vijayanagara state and society challenged the conquest theory suggested by the South Indian historians like Krishnaswami Iyengar, Venkataramanaya, Nilakanta Sastri and A. Krishnaswami Pillai. He hypothesised at first that Vijayanagara expansion into Tamil country resulted in the establishment of segmentary state and society where the

Vijayanagara emperors exercised sovereignty over big and small *nayakattanams*.[6] Later he revised his thought to introduce the patrimonial system where the formal state and all other political forms were brought face to face with a distinct kind of social relations of production, which was neither a feudal nor modern capitalistic system.[7] This view is to some extent acceptable.

The Coromandel society could not have been a static society.[8] Stein himself has described some structural changes that took place in Tamil society in the thirteenth century in the process of change. Some studies on aspects of social life have limited themselves to the social institutions such as marriage, *sati*, women, court life, food and dress, luxuries, games and amusements, religion and education but no one has focused on the structure of society, interrelations between classes and groups and the impact of the process of social change. We shall identify major social parameters and study how the Vijayanagara society was a changing society, with a mixture of classes, groups and economic divisions. The nature of change, its direction and causes which led to this change can be situated in the socio-economic context.

## PEASANTS

In the Coromandel society the position of the peasantry declined, the status of weavers rose vis-a-vis merchants and social mobility increased among particular caste groups. Restructuring of peasant society occurred during the sixteenth century on account of the heavy and unjust tax burden imposed on them by rulers.[9] Taxes prevalent had no relation to the yield of a crop[10] and their living conditions were deplorable. Lands in Devikapuram were uncultivated, the peasants having deserted the place[11] for more hospitable neighbouring areas. In Srimushnam *nayakattanam*, too, the peasants deserted.[12] In Tirukoyilur, some peasants, unable to pay taxes, sold their lands dirt cheap and left.[13] The taxes on peasants using the plough were higher than those on *Kaikolars* and others not using the plough.[14]

The dispirited peasants realised that their problems arose because they were not organised. They began to form voluntary associations to resist extortion[15] and decided to pay only what they thought were just taxes, in proportion to the yield of the crop. Organised peasant activity involved emigration, sale of land, desertion and non-payment of taxes.[16] The vastness of land encouraged them to migrate rather than revolt.

The resulting temporary dislocation in cultivation served very well in settling the peasants' grievances. *Nayakas* promptly undertook remedial measures, resettling the migrant peasants, giving them concessions and revising the tax rates. Thyagara *nayaka* pledged himself to reduce oppressive taxation on the peasants of Magadai *mandalam* and asked them to stop migrating.[17] Seshadhri Ayyan resettled the peasants who had migrated from Polur and Tiruvannamalai region.[18] As late as 1592 we find *nayakas* trying to induce peasants to return to their lands.[19]

But unjust taxation was only one problem of the peasants. Although in the wake of the remedial measures undertaken by *nayakas* general expansion of agriculture took place in Coromandel localities, peasants became poor owing to many other reasons, including probably the frequent droughts and famines. Certain social restrictions imposed on cultivating peasants in Villiyanoor[20] lead us to believe that peasants were reduced to a lower status and led a miserable life.

## WEAVERS AND ARTISANS

Weaving communities comprised *Kaikolar*, *Devangar*, *Saliyar* and *Pattunulkar*. *Kaikolars* were ranked the highest on account of their ritual links with temples. *Kaikola Mudalis* were those appointed to high posts and acted as authorities of various temples.[21] They maintained temple lands[22] and were in some cases paid for their services.[23] They decorated the *mantapam*, fanned the deity with *camaras*, blew the conch and trumphets, lighted lamps with oil supplied by the temple kitchen, supplied plantain leaves from the temple garden for packing *prasadam*, and carried the jewellery box of the deity when it was taken out for sacred bath.[24]

A local ruler bestowed on the weavers of Tribhuvanai, Naduvakkarai and Nemalai the right to go about in palanquins and the right to blow the conch shell on all ritual and other social occasions. These privileges were granted on par with other weavers of the Pennar riverine basin.[25] The weavers of Tiruvennainallur, Tiruttalur and Tirukoyilur were also accorded the same privileges. This indicates that regional inequality of social privileges existed among the weavers in South Arcot district.[26]

In the two flourishing textile production centres of Kanchipuram and Vrinchipuram the weaving community enjoyed certain special privileges and honours, probably on account of their professional skills. A recommendation by these privileged weavers to grant similar social privileges to the weavers of Valudilampattu[27] indicates unity among the weaving community.[28] Similarly, the privileges enjoyed by the *Kaikolars* of Kanchipuram were granted to the *Kaikolars* of Brahamadesam, which included permission to build two storeyed houses, to have double doors, and to bedeck the exterior of their homes with garlands of water *lilies*.[29] Royal charters of special privileges were generally given to the weavers with insignia.[30] Those objecting to the unity of weavers' privileges were punishable and the award of punishment was fixed.[31]

Weavers' unity is demonstrated in the many petitions they made to the local rulers to restore the deprived privileges in many localities.[32] This resulted in consultation among various *nayakas* and rulers like Kongurayar, Karayar and Kachirayar to award equal privileges.[33] Finally the rulers enacted laws to grant social privileges to all weavers on par with those of Kanchipuram.[34] This process of weavers' social transformation was a remarkable feature of the time.

Coromandel economy was supported by artisans who produced various commodities at several villages. The inscriptions generally describe their communal life.[35] Their living quarters were called *cheri*.[36] Some sources club five artisan communities into a single group called *Anjujati Panchalattars*. The artisans of Gingee, Padaividu and Tiruvannamalai, where metal, stone and wood works flourished, enjoyed special social privileges probably due to their professional skill. Some social privileges on important ritual occasions, such as accepting the dress put on the deity and receiving its headgear were at first granted to *Anjujati Panchalattar* of Gingee, Padaividu and Tiruvannamalai alone[37] and were later extended to artisans of other regions,[38] which indicates that there was discrimination of social privileges among *Anjujati Panchalattar*.

The clamour among the artisans of various localities for equality of privileges called *pavadai, parivattam* and *mugam-tudai*[39] was sought to be sorted out in meetings held in temples.[40] Artisans believed that they were descendants of the five sons of *Visvakarma*, son of Siva and his consort, each son representing a craft.[41] The *Anjujati Panchalattar* therefore assembled at the *mukha-*

*mantapa* of the Siva temple or that of his consort for such meetings. Inscriptions at various localities such as Villiyanoor, Tirupati, Kalakhasti and Chandragiri record that these deprived social privileges of artisans were restored to them after the discussion in temples. The unity of the artisan community was an important factor in its success in securing equal social rights among themselves.[42] Anyone who objected to the grant of privileges to artisans was fined twelve *pons.*[43]

The social privileges were, however, not permanent; they could be withdrawn.[44] Thus artisans of Virudhachalam, Nagalapuram and Tirunavalur, who once enjoyed honours like *pavadai* and *parivattam* were deprived of them in 1572 and 1579. The rights had been granted earlier in return for cultivation and service in temples.[45] *Anjujati Panchalattar* was not recognised for their professional skill, but received social rights under the patronage of temples. This state of affairs induced the artisans to canvass the support of traders of the region to regain the privileges.[46] The *Nattavars* of Villiyanoor and Ariyalur consented to restore their privileges.[47] But later on, when restoration of privileges was denied, the artisans emigrated en masse to other villages; faced with this situation, the *Panchalattar* were given assurances of redressal of their grievances.[48] This was a victory of *Anjujati Panchalattar*[49] and indicates that there was social consciousness among artisans at the regional level to fight against exploitation. In this context, it is difficult to estimate the pivotal position of temples and related religious institutions in the social life of Tamil country during Vijayanagara period.[50]

Historians who have studied the social life of artisans of the Vijayanagara period have not highlighted the marked degrees of social inequality in Coromandel society.[51] Many sociologists have advanced theories of social stratification to explain why inequality exists in society. Karl Marx's sociological theory, which is the most popular, sees the determinant of inequality and stratification in all societies through a single approach of economic domination of society by one ruling class. Marxists also explain craft stagnation in production at the secondary sector created by communalistic village bodies. Max Weber's theory differed in many ways from Marx, clearly differentiating between the concepts of class, status and power as distinct axes of inequality which were not reducible into one another or to a more fundamental dimension of inequality. Sociologists of the elitist tradition argue that the existence of elite is necessary and persistent in all human societies. They are much concerned with the circulation of elite and the extent to which new governing individuals or groups replace the older ones. American sociologists of the Functionalist School argue that inequality has not taken root in the attempt by one group to achieve power at the expense of the majority.

All these theoretical discussions on stratification state that inequality embraced a variety of factors within society and may be related to legal, political, social and economic factors. How would they apply to the unique context of Coromandel society? Social scientists declare that the features expounded by them are valid for all societies but Coromandel society did not display such features. The application of these theories of social stratification to Coromandel society would therefore be meaningless.

The Weberian approach, however, offers a particularly valuable framework for examining the Coromandel situation where groups arose in the social and political hierarchy and not directly as part of the bourgeois ruling class. Specialisation in crafts existed in many localities of Coromandel with a wide gap between artisans. While social differentiation of skilled and unskilled artisans led to a continued struggle for the restoration of privileges of the artisans, craftsmen like weavers secured prestige and authority, having closely associated themselves with the functions of the clergy in temples.[52]

## MERCHANTS

M.N. Pearson and Ashin Das Gupta, among others, have studied the place of merchants in society and their relationship with the state and established authority. We shall discuss the role of merchants as partly inside and partly outside the political system.

Merchants had a lower status in society than weavers, who monopolised many titles such as *kandiyadevan, kalingarayan, patta manangkattan* and *ulakalam venran*. The merchants resented this state of affairs. The betel leaf merchants of Villiyanoor, when they saw the privileges of weavers carved in an inscription, bribed the officials concerned to erase them and instead allot some such titles to merchants.[53] The *Kaikolar* and *Devangar* weavers, when they came to know of this, demanded justice from government officials but to no avail. When they migrated in protest, the local ruler Tirumalaideva Maharaya heard of it and deputed an officer, Vijayarayan, to conduct an enquiry. This official ordered the original Kanchipuram copper plate grant to be brought for examination, which was read and compared with a similar copy of privileges inscribed on the walls of the Siva temple at Villiyanoor. He then gave his verdict that the weavers alone were entitled to use the titles.[54] A similar incident occurred in Tiruvamattur in 1567 and the merchants gave an undertaking that they would not claim their lost titles.[55] Apparently, the merchants had to come to terms with the weavers.

In temple affairs, too, the privileges of merchants were less than those of weavers. An inscription notes that the *chetti* merchants of Pattisvaram in Kumbakonam region claimed some privileges in temple offerings in competition with the silk weavers such as receiving betel leaves and arecanut on the occasion of marriage, and making offerings of commodities to the goddess for which the merchants had no precedent. The privilege belonged to *Pattunulkars* alone.[56] Another similar dispute between merchants and weavers of Manampadi was settled in favour of weavers by the officer of Venkatapatidevaraya.[57]

Although merchants participated in the deliberations of the temple assembly, they never enjoyed a privileged status in Coromandel society; the weavers, on the other hand, became a dominant social group through ritual links with temples and specialisation in weaving. A marked feature of the social history of the period was the rise of social consciousness among different communities, aiming at social solidarity among themselves to clamour for privileges and honours. There were no merchants who made political alliances and built up considerable power to redirect the course of political events in the state.

## SLAVES

Slavery as an institution developed because of socio-economic distress, poverty, famine, drought, debt, desertion, and problems of taxes pushing people to sell themselves into slavery. *Kaikolars* owned slaves. The *nayakas* collected *adimaikasu*, that is taxes on the owners of slaves in the Coromandel hinterland.[58] *Mudaliars* and *Padayachi* also owned slaves. Three palm leaf manuscripts in possession of the state Department of Archaeology, Tamil Nadu, describe in detail the condition of slaves during Krishnadevaraya's reign.[59] They record that one Thiyagaraja *Mudaliar* sold a slave named Rayan, son of Santhosi, of *Paraiyar* caste, in the presence of an arbitrator for ten *pons*; Ramachandra Nayinar, a resident of Reddikadalangudi village, sold four of his slaves—Muthan, Vellichan, his wife Parvathy and a male slave—to Subramanya *Mudaliyar* of Manganallur for fourteen *pons*; Subba *Padayachi* sold his slaves—Raman, his wife Mukkatai and their children—to Appachi *Mudaliar* of Ganja village for eighty *pons*. These pieces of evidence show that the family as a whole entered into slavery in the Thanjavur region, where rice cultivation was intensive.

The deeds recording the sale of slaves were called *al-vilai-pirama-isaivu tittu*. The sale was done through an auction and the prices recorded in the presence of an arbitrator. The manuscripts display the signature of slaves, witnesses and that of the writer of the document.[60] A standard clause in the sale deeds was that the slaves were to be the property of the purchaser as long as the mountain, river Cauvery, the earth and grass lasted. The sale of *Paraiyars* had increased in this period. In one instance, a family of seven *Paraiyars* were sold for eight and a half *pagoda* in 1593.[61]

Epigraphical evidence throws light on why an entire family entered into slavery. The main reason appears to have been government taxes charged on families, which led poor families to enter into slavery as a whole. A differential tax was charged on joint families vis-a-vis nuclear families. A joint family paid a quarter *panam* and a nuclear family a half *panam* per month as tax.[62] The ninety-eight castes of *Idangai* and *Valangai* paid one *panam* on each big family, and a half *panam* on small families.[63] On the occasion of marriage the families in the Jambai region had to pay one *panam* as tax.[64] There was also a *talaikattu panam* levied on households;[65] Achyutappa *nayaka* charged two *panams* per head of family and one *panam* per family in 1590 in Thanjavur region.[66]

Possibly also, the expansion of agriculture demanded the employment of slaves for cultivation[67] by individuals and institutions. The social conflicts of this period and the existence of slavery show that there was a wide gap between the privileged and the unprivileged in Coromandel society.

## CASTE

Epigraphs of the period also convey the social ideas relating to the origin of duties and privileges of mixed caste called *Anuloma*.[68] The mythical explanation of caste given in it may be ignored. More to the point are the political and economic circumstances that contributed to changes in the caste system. Members of different *varnas* practised occupations not allowed to them under Hindu Law. Many *Brahmins* had entered into various careers prohibited to them when traditional employment became unavailable. Thus *Brahmins* engaged in wet agriculture in the Thanjavur region[69] and as soldiers in the army of Krishnadevaraya and Vitthaladeva Maharaya,[70] the class of farming and soldierly *Brahmins* emerging unequal in caste rank to the priestly *Brahmins*.[71] It may be construed from the above that the changing society of Coromandel cannot be studied from the angle of caste. The only usefulness of the *varna* system was that it became a readymade instrument for highlighting the ideals set forth in myths and commentaries written by each caste from time to time.

## PORTUGUESE SOCIETY

The history of Coromandel is inextricably interwoven with the Portuguese society of the time. The importance attached to Coromandel trade in Asian trade attracted the Portuguese soldiers residing on the western coast to settle down in Coromandel. Those who wished to discontinue their service for the king began to trade and later settled down in the flourishing Coromandel ports. In the early sixteenth century as many as 300 Portuguese men were trading in Coromandel who had deserted their army and other assigned royal duty.[72] Francisco Rodrigues de Silveira writes that their maltreatment had driven the Portuguese soldiers in Goa to Coromandel. These soldiers-turned-merchants were specially interested in maritime trade of surplus commodities available in Coromandel, particularly rice and textiles; their markets being those areas of Asia which were deficit in these commodities.[73] Pulicat became their asylum port. They sailed in the *naus* of Pulicat and the *junks* of Malacca, which carried textiles and rice.[74]

Gaspar Correa, the Portuguese chronicler, records that preparation for official Portuguese trade commenced only after private Portuguese trade had been established in Coromandel.[75]

Early attempts of the Portuguese viceroy, Francisco de Almeida, who appointed a team of four persons to survey the commercial possibilities and to collect information on the Tomb of St. Thomas at Mylapore, prove that religion and commerce were integrated in the Portuguese policy of overseas expansion.[76]

Exiles and renegades made up another group of Portuguese settlers on Coromandel coast. A piece of evidence laments that there were Portuguese who did not pay any heed to the dictates of their conscience and led a life unbecoming of a Christian. They left Portugal twenty or thirty years earlier, deserting their wives and continued to trade in Coromandel. When hard pressed by the instruments of law or by the missionaries they took asylum in Coromandel engaging in private trade. It is possible to surmise from this that the Portuguese society was a mixture of different elements and they were chiefly commerce-minded. Early sources record that the Portuguese in Coromandel were virtually free from any control and neither the Portuguese governor nor the captain exercised any authority over them.[77]

The Portuguese government did not seriously intend to found colonies on the Coromandel coast. Many *casados* began to trade with Coromandel while residing on the west coast. Some of them began to settle down as early as 1520 and 1530 at San Thome[78] and their number increased to 50 families in 1537. The strength of *casados* increased to 60 in 1538 and 100 in 1544, with the total Portuguese population rising to 500.[79] In the end of 1540s, of the total 6,007 Portuguese in India, 600 lived in Coromandel.[80] Among the Portuguese residents of Coromandel were Diogo Rebello, former factor of the Coromandel and the fishery coast, Miguel Ferreira, another former captain of Coromandel, and Aires de Figureido, the then captain of Coromandel: they were so rich that a letter writer suggested that the king of Portugal could raise a loan from them.[81] Another letter suggested that the king could raise a loan from João Caeyro, Nuno Preto, Christovão Mendes de Vasconcellos and Vincente Nuniz at Santhome since they were the richest *casados* on Coromandel, mainly trading in textiles.[82] Gaspar Correa, who passed through Santhome on two occasions, was surprised to find that the once empty spaces became stately streets and neat roads when the Portuguese settled there.[83]

The *casados* at Pulicat, Santhome, Devanampattinam and Nagapattinam cultivated relations with the local merchants, particularly *Mudaliars, chettis* and *Marakkayars*. They borrowed money from the *chettis*,[84] with which they prospered and became owners of ships and small sea-going vessels.[85]

The Portuguese established the administrative and political centre of their Asian empire initially at Cochin and later at Goa. The *Estado da India* was not a unitary state but a collection of forts, fleets and centres that stretched from East Africa to Japan.[86] Coromandel coast formed a small region of the Portuguese state and the crown's representative was the Portuguese captain appointed in 1522 to look after the administration and trade.[87] He appears to have been preoccupied with the construction of an economic system of the Portuguese empire and also with his personal enrichment. Although the basic objective was to dominate Asian maritime trade in pepper, the Portuguese began to trade in other commodities such as rice and textiles as well. The captain of Coromandel issued the *cartaz*[88] duly signed by the Portuguese factor, a certificate under which ships were permitted to sail in the ocean.[89] Five *pardaos* per *cartaz* were charged from the parties concerned.[90] The factor also maintained some soldiers to assist him in this venture. There were twenty soldiers on roll at the end of 1524, who were paid a total of 14,110 *pardaos* as salary. The amount was disbursed by the *vedor da fazenda* at Cochin.[91]

It is difficult to separately assess the trading interests of the crown from the private interests of the factor of Coromandel; on many occasions they merged. The post of captaincy in Coromandel greatly helped in enhancing the private fortunes of the incumbent, because of which the king of Portugal was faced with a flood of applications for the post. Many incumbents also behaved scandalously,[92] Miguel Ferreira, Cristovão Doria, Braz de Gois and Luis de Mello employing agents to sail illegally to conduct trade with other Asian ports.[93]

The *casados* on Coromandel coast do not seem to have bothered about their king in Portugal, and their trade does not seem to have brought profit to the royal treasury.[94] They began with associating with the native merchants, and in the early seventeenth century they sold cargo to the Dutch to enhance profit.[95] They disapproved of the attempts of the crown to control their activity by appointing captains at various ports in Coromandel, and as early as 1537 the private Portuguese traders wrote to the king to the effect that a permanent captain could be appointed in future from among themselves.[96] The captains of Coromandel were expected to look after the Portuguese traders and advance future prospects of commercial expansion. Santhome, Devanampattinam[97] and Nagapattinam had a captain who controlled the activities of the Portuguese residents.[98]

Various scholars[99] have attempted to classify the Portuguese in India and their politics into various categories according to birth, profession and marriage but it would be fruitless to make water-tight compartments of any general pattern. We may define the Portuguese community as a settled community in terms of their language, culture and, above all, their religion which differentiated them from the native Coromandel society.

Enclaves like Mylapore, Devanampattinam and Nagapattinam were famous in their own right as busy and rich ports; while some settlements such as Porto Novo and Tranquebar became significant only because some Portuguese lived there at the end of the sixteenth century. The missionaries' role in these settlements was important. The Jesuits had established a cordial relationship with the king of Chandragiri and received *manyam* of agricultural lands yielding 300 *pardaos* in the vicinity of Santhome. The Jesuits had also settled at Nagapattinam, where they bought a site for 500 *ducats.*[100] The *nayaka* of Thanjavur desired a church to be built at Tranquebar,[101] which was built by a native Christian, and conversion took place there. The Jesuits also had a residence at Tranquebar.[102] The bishop of Cochin wrote to the king of Portugal that he had sent a vicar to Devanampattinam and a church was built there.[103] The people of Devanampattinam were fond of Fr. Francisco de Oriente. He made conversions but came in conflict with the *Vigario da Terra* of the Franciscans about jurisdiction.[104] When the matter was referred to the king he favoured the Jesuits making conversions at Devanampattinam. This port of Devanampattinam was a major settlement of the Portuguese where two churches existed with 300 Christians.[105] The *nayaka* of Gingee invited Fr. N. Pimenta to build a church at Porto Novo.[106] These pieces of evidence suggest that together with flourishing commerce there was religious toleration. The *Parava* converts began to trade along with the Portuguese and probably settled down at various Coromandel ports.

The *nayakas* encouraged Portuguese trade and permitted their port settlements for the revenue such trade brought them, but exercised control on the activities of the Portuguese. The Vijayanagara rulers raided the Portuguese settlement of Santhome in 1559;[107] in 1577 the *nayaka* of Thanjavur attacked Nagapattinam.[108] And the captains of Santhome, Nagapattinam and

Devanampattinam, though they commanded both the civil and military administration, had no powers to resist the attack of the rulers, their jurisdiction being limited to keep law and order among the Portuguese residents of the settlement.

In this matter, there seems to have been enough to keep the administrators busy. Thus, a *Mestico,* a relative of Francisco de Freitas in Santhome, who had stabbed Symao de Brito, was punished by the captain by being confined in a church; an enquiry was later held when the injured person died. In 1594, Lopo Alvares de Moura, a rich merchant who abducted the wife of another settler, was punished by the captain; earlier, the merchant's house was attacked by the woman's relatives.[109] The Jesuit letters written in 1559 and 1563 note that the Portuguese merchants at Santhome engaged in unlawful trading practices; their chief interest being to make money; they were corrupt and their moral standards were poor.[110] It was these unruly activities of the Portuguese residents that necessitated the appointment of a resident *ouvidor* who lived at Santhome.[111] Their criminal activities could be traced back to their background as criminals and deserters; the missionaries and officials could not control them.[112]

The Portuguese viceroy tried to bring the settlers of Santhome under the official umbrella but failed. An expedition that he sent to Mylapore with orders to destroy the Portuguese settlement and compel the inhabitants to submit to the crown's rule ended disastrously for the crown and the authorities were finally forced to negotiate with the settlers. The settlers' resistance was for fear that they might be transferred from Mylapore and they pleaded with the king to permit them to live quietly there.[113] The Portuguese in Nagapattinam had a comparatively peaceful time throughout the sixteenth century although the captain of Nagapattinam was unable to satisfy the inhabitants who were at war in 1599.[114] While the Portuguese were governed by the captain of the place the natives were ruled by *nayakas* in the ports and governed under local custom and conventions.

## PRICES

Fluctuations in prices and wages are an indicator of people's standard of living. Prices rose and fell when changes in supply and demand were far-reaching. Long-distance trade and country trade flourished in commodities like rice and textiles, when adequate surplus was available. Some scholars[115] affirm that prices could be constructed from European sources and continuous prices are not available before the seventeenth century. This view is wrong since epigraphical evidence gives us enough material to build up a clear picture of prices. These series of statistics are homogeneous, complete and numerous in Coromandel and cover most of the sixteenth century, enough material to calculate averages significant for the study.

This study pertains to twenty-four commodities, namely rice, flattened rice, parched rice, milk, butter, ghee, curd, banana,

PRICE INDEX OF AGRICULTURAL COMMODITIES, 1543-95*

| *Period* | *Sugarcane* | *Betel* | *Arecanuts* | *Coconut* | *Tender Coconut* |
|---|---|---|---|---|---|
| | | *(Unit of 500 numbers' price in Panams)* | | | |
| 1543 | 15 | - | - | 30 | - |
| 1544 | 10 | 1 | 2 | - | - |
| 1545 | 20 | 1.25 | 2.50 | 30 | 20 |
| 1553 | - | - | - | - | 20 |
| 1554 | 10 | - | - | 30 | - |
| 1558 | 10 | 1 | 3.75 | - | - |
| 1561 | - | 1 | 2 | - | - |
| 1564 | 10 | - | 5 | 60 | - |
| 1583 | 15 | 2.75 | 5 | 30 | 15 |
| 1586 | - | 5 | 10 | 30 | - |
| 1588 | - | 3 | - | - | - |
| 1595 | - | - | - | - | 20 |

*Sugarcane, see *T.T.D.E.S.*, vol. V, No. 10, December 1543, Ibid., No. 19, August 1544, Ibid., No. 32, February 1545, Ibid., No. 153, 1554, Ibid., 160, May 1558, Ibid., No. 173, January 1564, Ibid., vol. VI, Pt. I, No. 4, January 1583. Betel, *T.T.D.E.S.*, No.19, August 1544, Ibid., No. 43, July 1545, Ibid., No. 160, May 1558, Ibid., No. 168, December 1561, Ibid., vol. VI, Pt. I, No. 4, January 1583, Ibid., No. 7, 1586. Arecanuts, *T.T.D.E.S.*, vol. V, No. 19, August 1544, Ibid., No. 47, July 1545, Ibid., No. 159, 1555, Ibid., No. 168, December 1561, Ibid., No. 173, January 1564, Ibid., vol. VI, Pt. I, No. 4, January 1583, Ibid., No. 7, 1586. *A.R.E.* 286 of 1951, Srirangam, 1588 Coconuts, *T.T.D.E.S.*, vol. V, No. 10, December 1543, Ibid., No. 32, February 1545, Ibid., No. 153, 1544, Ibid., No. 173, January 1564, Ibid., vol. VI, Pt. I, No. 4, January 1583, Ibid., No. 7, 1586. Tender coconuts, *T.T.D.E.S.*, vol. V, No. 4, March 1545, *A.R.E.* 496 of 1919, Kanchipuram, *T.T.D.E.S.*, vol. VI, Pt. I, No. 4, January 1583.

INDEX OF RICE PRICE, 1543-96*

| *Period* | *Rice (48 Padi Units)* | *Flattened Rice (10 Marakal Units) (Price amount in Panams)* | *Parched Rice (10 Marakal Units)* |
|---|---|---|---|
| 1543 | - | 5 | 3 |
| 1544 | - | 10 | 10 |
| 1545 | 4.50 | 7.50 | 7.50 |
| 1558 | 6 | - | - |
| 1561 | 7.50 | - | - |
| 1564 | 13.50 | - | - |
| 1583 | - | - | 3 |
| 1588 | 1440 | - | - |
| 1592 | - | 6 | 6 |
| 1596 | 6 | - | - |

*Rice, see *T.T.D.E.S.*, vol. V, No. 47, July 1545, Ibid., vol. V, No. 159, 1558, Ibid., No. 168, December 1561, Ibid., No. 173, January 1564, *A.R.E.*, 286 of 1951, Srirangam, *T.T.D.E.S.*, vol. VI, Pt. I, No. 12, August 1596. For flattened rice, see *T.T.D.E.S.*, vol. V, No. 10, December 1543, Ibid., No. 19, August 1544, Ibid., No. 38, March 1545, Ibid., vol. VI, Pt. I, No. 9, July 1592. Parched rice, see *T.T.D.E.S.*, vol. V, No. 8, October 1543, Ibid., No. 19, August 1544, Ibid., No. 34, March 1545, Ibid., vol. VI, Pt. I, No. 4, January 1583, Ibid., No. 9, July 1592.

PRICE INDEX OF SUNDRIES, 1543-90*

| *Period* | *Greengram* | *Bengalgram* | *Pepper* | *Mustard* | *Dhal* | *Cumin* |
|---|---|---|---|---|---|---|
| | | *(Unit of one Marakal in price in Panams)* | | | | |
| 1543 | 0.50 | 0.50 | - | 3 | - | - |
| 1544 | 1 | - | - | 4 | 4 | - |
| 1545 | 1.25 | 1.25 | - | - | - | - |
| 1550 | - | - | 4 | 2 | - | 2 |
| 1553 | - | - | - | 1.25 | 1 | - |
| 1554 | 1 | 1 | - | - | - | - |
| 1558 | 1 | 1 | - | 6 | 1 | 8 |
| 1561 | - | - | - | 2 | - | - |
| 1583 | 2 | - | - | - | - | - |
| 1590 | - | - | 2 | - | - | 4 |

*Greengram, see *T.T.D.E.S.*, vol. V, No. 8, October 1543, Ibid., No. 19, August 1544, Ibid., No. 38, March 1545, Ibid., No. 153, 1554, Ibid., No. 60, May 1558, Ibid., vol. VI, Pt. I, No. 4, January 1583. Bengalgram, *T.T.D.E.S.*, vol. V, No. 8, October 1543, Ibid., No. 38, March 1545, Ibid., No. 25, October 1544, Ibid., No. 160, May 1555. Pepper, *T.T.D.E.S.*, vol. V, No. 125, October 1550, *A.R.E.*, 189 of 1922, Sriperumbudur, 1590. Mustard, *T.T.D.E.S.*, vol. V, No. 8, October 1543, Ibid., No. 19, August 1544, Ibid., No. 125, October 1550, Ibid., No. 141, May 1553, Ibid., No. 160, May 1515, Ibid., No. 168, December 1561. Dhal, *T.T.D.E.S.*, No. 19, August 1544, Ibid., No. 141, May 1553, Ibid., No. 160, May 1560. Cumin, *T.T.D.E.S.*, vol. V, No. 125, October 1550, Ibid., No. 168, December 1561, *A.R.E.*, 189 of 1922, Sriperumbudur.

INDEX OF FRUIT PRICE, 1543-86*

| Period | Banana | Mango | Jackfruit |
|---|---|---|---|
| | (Unit of 1000 Numbers' Price in Panams) | | |
| 1543 | 10 | - | 300 |
| 1544 | 10 | 6 | 250 |
| 1545 | 15 | 20 | 200 |
| 1553 | 10 | - | - |
| 1554 | - | 20 | 500 |
| 1564 | 30 | - | - |
| 1583 | 20 | - | - |
| 1586 | 20 | - | 2500 |

*For bananas, see *T.T.D.E.S.*, vol. V, No. 8, October 1543, Ibid., No. 25, October 1544, Ibid., No. 34, March 1544, *A.R.E.*, 146 of 1919, Kanchipuram, *T.T.D.E.S.*, vol.V, No. 160, May 1558, Ibid., No. 173, January 1564, Ibid., vol. VI, Pt. I, No. 4, January 1583, Ibid., No. 7, 1586. Mangoes, see *T.T.D.E.S.*, vol.V, No. 25, October 1544, Ibid., No. 32, February 1545, Ibid., No. 153, 1554, Ibid., No. 160, May 1558. Jackfruits, *T.T.D.E.S.*, No. 8, October 1544, Ibid., No. 25, October 1544, Ibid., No. 32, February 1545, Ibid., No. 153, 1554, Ibid., No. 160, May 1558, *T.T.D.E.S.*, vol. VI, Pt. I, No. 7, 1586.

mango, jackfruit, tender coconut, sugarcane, coconut, betel, arecanut, cumin, dhal, mustard, Bengal gram, green gram, pepper, jaggery, refined sugar and gingelly oil. Tirupati abounds in relevant inscriptional evidence. The price lists drawn up for that region are compared with the prices at other places such as Kanchipuram, Sriperumbudur and Srirangam. The price details of the period up to 1530 for these regions are found in epigraphs cumulatively, which makes our exercise difficult. Here, the Portuguese sources containing price details may be used.[116] The rest of the period poses no problem.

Judging from inscriptional evidence, prices for any commodity rose when demand was high and supplies were short. Thus prices increased when agricultural production declined and harvests fluctuated frequently and sharply from year to year. Price increase in one sharp burst had to do with demand and supply. There were famines and drought in Coromandel between 1531 and 1532,[117] 1535 and 1540,[118] 1583 and 1586.[119] In these years, the prices swelled. Rice always formed a part of exports, so prices rose high. Another reason may be the increasing population with the migration of Kannada and Telugu-speaking people under the patronage of Vijayanagara rulers.[120]

Dairy products saw a range of variations. Butter probably owed

PRICE OF DAIRY PRODUCTS, 1544-95*

| *Period* | *Milk* (6 Nali Units in Panams) | *Curds* | *Butter* (1 Nali Unit in Panams) | *Ghee* |
|---|---|---|---|---|
| 1544 | 1 | 0.50 | 1 | - |
| 1545 | - | - | 1 | - |
| 1558 | - | - | - | 2 |
| 1561 | 1.50 | 0.75 | - | 1 |
| 1564 | 3 | - | - | - |
| 1583 | - | - | 1 | - |
| 1590 | - | - | - | 0.50 |
| 1595 | - | - | - | 1 |

*For milk see, *T.T.D.E.S.*, vol. V, No. 25, October 1544, Ibid., No. 168, December 1561, Ibid., No. 173, January 1565. Curds see, *T.T.D.E.S.*, No. 25, October 1544, Ibid., No. 168, December 1561. Butter see, *T.T.D.E.S.*, vol. V, No. 25, October 1544, Ibid., No. 47, July 1545, *T.T.D.E.S.*, vol. VI, Pt. I, No. 4, January 1583. Ghee, *T.T.D.E.S.*, vol. V, No. 159, 1558, Ibid., No. 168, December 1561, *A.R.E.*, 189 of 1922, Sriperumbudur, *A.R.E.*, 382 of 1919, Kanchipuram.

its stable price to its ranking as semi-luxury food, for which the demand was highly elastic: a relatively small fall in its price could bring about a considerable change in the consumption of butter and vice versa. The price of ghee decreased throughout the period, perhaps because it was an item used in temple offerings. The prices of milk and curd continuously increased perhaps on account of the numerous taxes levied on cattle. Revenue terms such as *nall erudu, nar pasu, nall erumai, nar kida* and *idaitturai* imply collection of cattle revenue in Coromandel.[121] The *nayaka* of Srimushnam collected one-fourth *panam* per cow, a half *panam* per buffalo, and a quarter *panam* on eight sheep.[122] *Sulavari* tax was levied on cattle belonging to the temples, these being branded with trident marks. *Sadam* tax was payable by the *Manradis* or shepherd community.[123] Achyutappa *nayaka* of Thanjavur collected twenty *panam* per annum from the shepherds of Tiruvannamalai.[124] The multiple levy of cattle taxes and also on owners of milch animal probably preceded the increase of prices in milk and curd.

Prices of manufactured goods such as oil, jaggery and refined sugar rose less steeply than the price of basic foodstuff, the difference being on account of the different elasticities of demand. During the drought in 1540 ten large chickens were sold for a *panam*; in 1560 four chickens alone fetched a *panam*.[125]

PRICE OF MANUFACTURED GOODS, 1543-96*

| Period | Refined Sugar (5 Visai) | Gingelly Oil (4 Alakku) | Jaggery (9 Visai) |
|---|---|---|---|
| | | (Price in Panams) | |
| 1543 | - | 0.50 | 9 |
| 1544 | 10 | 0.50 | 9 |
| 1550 | - | - | 9 |
| 1553 | 15 | - | 6 |
| 1558 | 10 | 0.50 | 6 |
| 1561 | 10 | - | - |
| 1583 | - | - | 4.50 |
| 1586 | - | - | 4.50 |
| 1592 | - | 0.50 | 9 |
| 1596 | - | - | 9 |

*For refined sugar see, *T.T.D.E.S.*, vol. V, No. 25, October 1544, Ibid., No. 141, May 1552, Ibid., No. 160, May 1558, Ibid., No. 168, December 1561. Gingelly oil, *T.T.D.E.S.*, vol. V, No. 9, October 1543, Ibid., No. 10, August 1544, Ibid., No. 160, May 1558, *T.T.D.E.S.*, vol. VI, Pt. I, No. 9, July 1592. For jaggery see, *T.T.D.E.S.*, vol. V, No. 8, October 1543, Ibid., No. 19, August 1544, Ibid., No. 125, October 1550, Ibid., No. 141, May 1553, Ibid., No. 160, May 1558, *T.T.D.E.S.*, vol. VI, Pt. I, No. 4, January 1583, Ibid., No. 7, 1586, Ibid., No. 9, January 1592, Ibid., No. 12, August 1596.

Thus the price movement for different commodities had monetary and non-monetary causes.

In the context of the period under discussion, the rise in prices was a price revolution indeed, though this term might be sound inappropriate by the standards of twentieth century. It would be useful to study the economic and social context in which inflation occurred.

Currency and the supply of bullion have frequently been adduced by historians and economists to account for price trends of the medieval period. The most traditional economic theory of price changes is one which relates price changes to the supply of the circulating medium. It says that prices probably rose in response to the higher output of bullion, mostly from South-East Asia and Pegu; the tendency of prices to decline has been put down to decline in the output of silver.

But facts appear otherwise. At most times Coromandel seems to have suffered from dearth of silver. Even if bullion came into Coromandel it did not necessarily or always add to the amount of coinage in circulation, since silver was also hoarded in temples and royal treasuries and never used as a medium of exchange. Historians of South India generally associate control over coinage closely with state power. That the import of precious metals circulating in coins in Coromandel fuelled inflation is in line with the monetary theory; and since we see a rise in prices equally for all products we may agree with the hypothesis of Irfan Habib that movements in prices can be directly related to the currency in circulation. The turning point in the history of Coromandel prices was that the prices of all commodities began to decline slightly at the end of the sixteenth century, but the price was never less than the earlier level from which the jump had taken place. There was no general stability of prices except oil and butter. The fact that the rise in prices was very gentle indicates that the quantity of money in the hands of people did not multiply. It may therefore be construed that the price revolution had affected the peasants and artisans who were already burdended with heavy taxation.

## WAGES AND SALARIES

Many historians assume that wages in the medieval period were determined more by customary valuation than prices. Many epigraphs provide statements regarding wages and salaries for work done for the temples. Some details of expenses so incurred are recorded in the inscriptional evidence. When the draft was prepared and the epigraph was carved, the details were probably not known and the spaces for them were left blank. After the work was completed these blanks were not filled.[126] This poses some difficulty in collecting details for the second half of the sixteenth century.

Temples generated considerable amount of employment. *Nayakas* drew up inscriptions recording the assignment of servants in the temples.[127] The temple of Srimushnam had as many as 360 permanent labourers.[128] Cooks, called *swayampoki,* were employed in preparing *prasadam.*[129] *Viniyogam seyyum parupatakarar* was in-charge of distribution of *prasadam.*[130] A share of the *prasadam* was generally allotted to all permanent servants.[131] Female dancers in temples, called *devaradiyars,* received wet and dry lands as *padi jivitam*, besides salary.[132] The temple servants received extra remuneration of periodical cash payments if they performed

MONTHLY SALARY OF SEMI-SKILLED TEMPLE SERVANTS, 1506-50*

| *Period* | *Gardener* | *Watchman* | *Water Supplier* | *Cooks* |
|---|---|---|---|---|
| | | *(Salaries in Panams)* | | |
| 1506 | 12 | 1 | - | - |
| 1515 | - | - | - | 3 |
| 1518 | 5 | - | - | - |
| 1524 | - | - | 6 | - |
| 1535 | 5 | - | - | - |
| 1538 | 4 | - | - | - |
| 1544 | - | - | - | 2 |
| 1547 | - | - | - | 1 |
| 1550 | - | 0.50 | 5 | - |

*For gardeners see, *T.T.D.E.S.*, vol. III, No. 6, pp. 16-18, Ibid., No. 105, 139, pp. 272-74, *A.R.E.* 2 of 1938-39 Srirangam, *T.T.D.E.S.*, vol. VI, pp. 194-95. Watchman, *T.T.D.E.S.*, vol. III, No. 7, Ibid., vol. V, No. 125. Water-supplier, *T.T.D.E.S.*, vol. III, No. 161, Ibid., vol. V, No. 125. Cooks, *T.T.D.E.S.*, vol. III, No. 105, Ibid., vol. V, No. 90.

MONTHLY SALARY OF PROFESSIONALS IN TEMPLES, 1506-53*

| *Period* | *Kaikolar* | *Sculptor* | *Dancer* | *Kankanippar* |
|---|---|---|---|---|
| | | *(Salaries in Panams)* | | |
| 1506 | 1 | 0.50 | 1 | 1 |
| 1512 | - | 0.50 | - | - |
| 1513 | 1 | - | - | - |
| 1515 | 2 | 1 | 3 | 2 |
| 1520 | 2 | - | - | - |
| 1531 | 2 | - | - | - |
| 1539 | - | 1 | - | - |
| 1544 | 2 | - | - | - |
| 1545 | - | 1 | - | - |
| 1553 | - | - | - | 3 |

**Kaikolars* see *T.T.D.E.S.*, vol. III, Nos. 7, 31, 105 and 139, vol. IV, No. 135, vol. V, No. 25. For sculptor see, *T.T.D.E.S.*, vol. III, Nos. 7, 29, 105, vol. IV, No. 135, vol. V, No. 29. Dancers, *T.T.D.E.S.*, vol. III, Nos. 7 and 105. *Kankanippar*, *T.T.D.E.S.*, vol. III, Nos. 13 and 105, *A.R.E.*, 496 of 1919 Kanchipuram.

additional functions besides regular duty in the temples.[133] Musicians, carpenters, watchmen and storekeepers were also given salaries and included in the permanent establishment.[134]

The monthly salary of Kaikolar, sculptors, dancers, etc. had increased in the first half of the sixteenth century. The reason may be the increased demand for their professional skill. Semi-skilled labourers and professionals also received a major share of daily *prasadam*, besides land and money grants. Semi-skilled labourers like watchman, water supplier, gardener and cook were paid monthly salary, which fluctuated in the first half of the sixteenth century, first increasing and then decreasing, perhaps for reasons of fluctuation in supply. Evidence also shows that Tirupati and Srirangam temples paid uniform salary to gardeners.

Cash wages paid daily are found in the temple records. It would seem that daily wages were paid only to temporary hands. Among such employees were: *tiruvidi pandam piditharam*, who was paid *tivatti-sumak-kuli* for torch bearing;[135] *muntandupintandu-pidikkaravar*, for carrying the deity mounted on the big *vahanams* in the streets during a procession;[136] *pandal* makers, who erected *pandals* with dried coconut leaves and bamboo poles to provide shade around the temple and decorated it with festoons and pendants, and who were paid *pandal-singarikka-al-kuli*;[137] *ther-niminda-al*, who pulled the car and were paid *vadam-piditha-kuli*[138] (*vadam-piditha* standing for the thick ropes by which the car was drawn); *vanam-sudikkum-al*, incharge of setting off the fire crackers;[139] and *kodi-kudai-al*, who carried the banner and umbrella of the deity during the procession.[140]

Tirupati and Kanchipuram temples paid uniform daily wages

DAILY WAGES OF UNSKILLED WORKERS IN TEMPLES, 1506-53*

| *Period* | *Bell-ringer* | *Umbrella Bearer* | *Vahanam Bearer* | *Vinnappam Seyvar* |
|---|---|---|---|---|
| | | *(Wages in Panams)* | | |
| 1506 | - | - | - | 1 |
| 1508 | 1 | - | - | - |
| 1515 | - | - | - | 1 |
| 1520 | 1 | - | - | - |
| 1530 | - | 2 | - | - |
| 1538 | - | 2 | - | - |
| 1543 | - | - | 1 | - |
| 1544 | - | - | 1 | - |
| 1553 | - | - | - | 1 |

*For bell-ringer, see, *T.T.D.E.S.*, vol. III, No. 16, Ibid., No. 139. For flag and umbrella bearer, see *T.T.D.E.S.*, vol. III, No. 187, vol. IV, No. 118. Vahanam bearer, see *T.T.D.E.S.*, vol. V, Nos. 8 and 25. Vinappam Seyyvar, see *T.T.D.E.S.*, vol. III, Nos. 7, 13 and 105, *A.R.E.* 496 of 1919 Kanchipuram.

to *vinappam seyvar* during the first half of the sixteenth century. Semi-skilled labourers like flag and umbrella bearers, bell-ringer and *vahanam* bearers were paid fixed daily wages throughout the first half of the sixteenth century. The wages never increased because these labourers were hired only on festival days.

Salaries moved both upward and downward, the rise in salary being, to some extent, on account of the expanding labour-intensive economy; and the reason for fall in salary in certain employments may be that the demand for their services did not increase. High mortality owing to famines[141] may also have contributed to salary fluctuations. Although prices generally increased throughout the sixteenth century, the wages of ordinary people increased in the second half of the century, witness the wage levels of rice-pounders and cooks.[142]

An analysis of prices, wages and occupation and their inter-relationships shows that Coromandel society was changing in its socio-economic context and there existed marked differences between groups and classes in society. The belief of some scholars[143] that peasants and artisans of Tamil country made no protest after A.D. 1450 may be summarily rejected; we have seen that several tensions exploded in the form of uprisings and revolts to secure social privileges and tax reduction. There were also social changes in the occupation and status of people. The study of price revolution noticed here and the inflow of bullion and imports of precious metals lead us to conclude that monetisation of the economy was initiated in this period. The wages earned by peasants, artisans and temple servants were no longer sufficient for the minimum subsistence of their family. Merchants were able to participate in the growth of the economy and strengthen their position. They also made attempts to narrow the social distance with other status groups. The economic development of Coromandel was thus accompanied by social changes which sharpened the differentials in income and property.

## NOTES AND REFERENCES

1. B.A. Saletore, *Social and Political Life in the Vijayanagara Empire*, vol. I, Madras, 1934, pp. 27 and 34.
2. Ibid.
3. K.A. Nilakanta Sastri, *A History of South India*, Madras, 1976, p. 309.
4. A. Krishaswami Pillai, *The Tamil Country under Vijayanagara*, Annamalai

Nagar, 1964, p. 102.

5. T.V. Mahalingam, *Administration and Social Life under Vijayanagar,* Madras, 1940, p. 101.
6. Burton Stein, *Peasant State and Society in Medieval South India,* Delhi, 1980, pp. 439-51.
7. Burton Stein, "Vijayanagar and the Transition into Patrimonial Systems", Anna Libera Dallapicola, ed., *Vijayanagar City and Empire,* Stuttgart, 1985, p. 75; Karashima opines that social formation of Vijayanagara rule in the Sixteenth Century seems to have displayed some resemblance to Feudalism which characterised Medieval Western Europe and Japan; N. Karashima, "Nayak's rule in North and South Arcot districts in South India during the Sixteenth Century", *Acta Asiatica,* 48, Tokyo, 1985.
8. The Sanskrit composite expression *Varna Shrama Dharma* included three fundamental proposition of Indian Society. Varna represented the structural code within which only the *Brahmans* enjoyed an exclusively defined status through performance of rituals. Shrama signified whether an individual inherited at birth by the code of varna should choose to remain within the structural limits. The term *Dharma* finally turned the other two propositions into an overarching idea of capacity. K.N. Chaudhuri, *Asia before Europe: Economy and Civilization of the Indian Ocean from the Rise of Islam to 1750,* Cambridge, 1990, p. 55.
9. *A.R.E.*, 353 of 1912, 355 of 1912, 395 of 1912 and 396 of 1912.
10. Ibid., 216 of 1917 (1429).
11. Ibid., 199 of 1940-41 and 190 of 1940-41 (1512).
12. Ibid., 246 of 1916 (1513) and 247 of 1916 (1504). Transcript line six of the text runs as follows: *"Rekhai erina idinalle kudikku nerukkam aki kudiyum kulaindadu".*
13. Ibid., 33 of 1921-22 (1505-1506).
14. Ibid., 140 of 1915-16 (1522).
15. Ibid., 92 of 1918.
16. Ibid., 50 of 1916.
17. Ibid., 442 of 1913.
18. Ibid., 161 of 1941-42.
19. Ibid., 190 of 1938-39.
20. Ibid., 198 of 1936-37 (1575).
21. Ibid., 482 of 1919-20 (1573).
22. Ibid., 356 of 1912 (1533).
23. Ibid., 482 of 1919-20 (1573).
24. *T.T.D.E.S.*, vol. V, No. 2, vol. II, Nos. 35, 135 and 140 and vol. IV, Nos. 3 and 39.
25. *A.R.E.*, 368 of 1917; 1918, part II, para 70 (1503).
26. Ibid., 422 of 1925-26, 221 of 1928-29 and 162 of 1918-19.
27. Ibid., 291 of 1928-29.
28. Ibid., 368 of 1917.
29. Ibid., 136 of 1905, 151 of 1905 and 454 of 1916.
30. Ibid., 422 of 1925 and 473 of 1921.
31. Ibid., 368 of 1917.
32. Ibid., 162 of 1918.
33. Ibid., 291 of 1928-29.

34. Ibid., 41 of 1922.
35. Ibid., 372 of 1912, 59 of 1914-15, (1429) 201 of 1936- 37) and 257 of 1926-27.
36. *S.I.T.I.*, vol. II, p. 637. Epigraphs mention *Kollancheri* and *Kammalacheri* in many places.
37. *S.I.I.*, vol. II, No. 25; *A.R.E.*, 493 of 1937-38.
38. Ibid.
39. *A.R.E.*, 273 of 1939-40 and 293 of 1928-29; *S.I.I.*, vol. III, p. 47.
40. Ibid., 198 of 1937 (1575). They assembled before Tirukamiyyappar temple of Villiyanoor.
41. The five sons are named as *manu, mayasilipi, thurastra, visvagna* and *daivagna*.
42. N. Karashima, "The Kammalars of Sixteenth Century in South Arcot District in South India", K.V. Ramesh, S.P. Tewari and M.J. Sharma, *Dr. G.S. Gai Feliciation Volume*, Delhi, 1990, pp. 205-8.
43. *A.R.E.*, 65 of 1922 (C) and 378 of 1922 (B).
44. *S.I.I.*, vol. III, p. 47; *A.R.E.*, 293 of 1928-29 (1574).
45. *A.R.E.*, 293 of 1928-29, 620 of 1904 and 273 of 1939-40; *S.I.I.*, vol. XVII, p. 388.
46. Ibid., 103 of 1906, 198 of 1937 and 493 of 1938.
47. Ibid., 198 of 1937 (1575) and 493 of 1938 (1573).
48. Ibid., 80 of 1938-39 (1582).
49. Ibid., 340 of 1925-26 (1533).
50. Peter Granda, op. cit., p. 133.
51. Vijaya Ramaswamy, "Artisans in Vijayanagar Society", *Indian Economic and Social History Review* XXIII(4), 1985; N. Karashima, op. cit., pp. 205-8.
52. *A.R.E.*, 356 of 1912-13 (1533) and 482 of 1919-20 (1573).
53. Ibid., 201 of 1936-37 (Achyutadevaraya period).
54. Ibid.
55. *A.R.E.*, 41 of 1922 (1546).
56. Ibid., 257 of 1926-27.
57. Ibid., 218 of 1930-31 (1601). See also *ARE* 1912-13 c.p. 13. (1576) Kanchipuram.
58. Ibid., 445 of 1913 (1502)
59. The original texts of the Manuscripts have been published in the Journal *Kalvettu*, No. 17, pp. 1-3, see for texts pp. 3-6.
60. Ibid.
61. *A.R.E.*, 296 of 1911.
62. Ibid., 47 of 1888 (Achyutadevaraya period) 246 of 1916.
63. Ibid., 103 of 1906 (1532).
64. Ibid.
65. *A.R.E.*, 149 of 1942 and 426 of 1929.
66. Ibid., 426 of 1929.
67. Ibid., 334 of 1954-55 (1568).
68. P.V. Jagadisa Aiyar, *South Indian Shrines*, Madras, 1920, p. 375.
69. *E.I.*, vol. XII, pp. 340-48.
70. *A.R.E.*, 47 of 1906, for details see also *A.R.E.* 47 of 1904; 52 of 1905, where we find *Brahmanas* occupation as soldiers.

71. K.N. Chaudhuri, op. cit., p. 56.
72. *A.N.T.T.,C.C.*, III-9-94. *C.C.*-I-107-86. This manuscript date 12 December 1565 mentions that two other Portuguese had left the Crown service for not having paid the salary and food allowances.
73. Cunha Rivara, *A.P.O.*, Fasc. 6.113, Silva Rego, op. cit., III, 252.
74. *A.N.T.T., C.C.*, I-9-92; *C.C.*-I-16-106.
75. Correa, op. cit., II, pp. 721-22.
76. Ibid., I. p. 739, II, 722-87, III, 419-24.
77. Silva Rego, op. cit., II, p. 147(f) *A.N.T.T., Gavetas*, XV-12-2 (1533-35).
78. Correa, op. cit., III, p. 424.
79. Silva Rego, op. cit., II, 252-54 and III, 165. See for statistics of Portuguese residents in Coromandel, *C.C.*, III-9-94 (1521); Elaine Sanceau, CLS, op. cit., III, pp. 64-5.
80 *A.N.T.T., Casa Forte*, No. 48, *CSL*, vol. V, fl. 101-101v.
81. *A.N.T.T., Gavetas*, XV-12-2 (1533-35).
82. Ibid., (1533-35 and 1538). The list contains the name of forty-eight individuals who were wealthy in this period.
83. Silva Rego, Historia das missoes op. cit., I, p. 453.
84. *A.N.T.T., C.C.*, Pt. I - 68-88. The document records that the *chettis* demanded against reason of Justice when Diogo Nunez had no money to return and when his business was at loss.
85. Miguel Fereira owned four navios, Elaine Sanceau, Cartas de D. Joao de Castro, op. cit., p. 293.
86. L.F. F.R Thomaz. Les Portugais dans les mers de l'Archipel au XVI e Siecle, *Archipel* 18, 1979, pp. 105-25.
87. Correa, op. cit., vol. II, Pt. II, chap. IX, p. 721.
88. Cunha Rivara, *A.P.O.*, op. cit., Fasc. V, Pt. I, pp. 30-31.
89. Correa, op. cit., 1922, Tomo I, p. 298.
90. K.S. Mathew, *Portuguese Trade with India in the Sixteenth Century*, New Delhi, 1983, pp. 80-1.
91. *A.N.T.T., C.C.*, IIa-122-129 (1524).
92. Elaine Sanceau, *Carta*, op. cit., p. 293.
93. Ibid.
94. *A.N.T.T., C.C.*, I 9-92; *C.C.*, II - 49-24.
95. *A.N.T.T.*, MSS. D.R.I., Liv. 30, fl. 39v (1635).
96. *A.N.T.T., C.C.*, I - 59-58 (1 Sept. 1537). Silva Rego, op. cit., vol. II, pp. 249-55.
97. King Filippe I appointed Damiao Pacheco as captain of Devanampattinam. See *Chancellaria de D. Filippe I*, liv. 17 fl. 295v.
98. *A.N.T.T., Nucleo Antigo*, No. 808; *Chancelaria D. Joao III*, Livro 21, fl. 159.
99. M.N. Pearson, "The People and Politics of Portuguese India During Sixteenth Century" in Daniel Alder and Waren Dean, (eds), *Essays Concerning the Socio economic history of Brazil and Portuguese India*, Gaineville: University Press of Florida, 1977, pp. 2-4.
100. *D.I.*, vol. XV, pp. 334-44, 756-59; Purchas, His pilgrims, op. cit., vol. X, p. 207.
101. Ibid.

102. Ibid.
103. Cunha Rivara, *A.P.O.*, op. cit, II, p. 213. (22 Feb.1589)
104. *B.F.U.P.*, V, 559, 597 (16 Jan. 1585 and 23 Nov. 1589).
105. Ibid, vol. I, p. 299; *A.R.S.I.*, Goa, 32, 654v.
106. C.S. Srinivasacharai, *A History of Gingee and Its Rulers*, Annamalainagar, 1943, pp. 100-1; Manuel Fernandes a Parava merchant was trading with Devanampattinam. Schurhammer, op. cit., vol. II, p. 556.
107. Diogo de Couto, *Decada*, op. cit., XVII, pp. 55-6.
108. Paulo da Trinidade, Conquista espiritual do oriente, Lisboa, 1967; see also *Sahitya Ratnakahara* canto X, sloka 68, III, 68, 972.
109. Letter of Miguel Ferreira to D. Joao de Castro, 26 June 1546, Santhome. in Sanjay Surahmanyam, *Improvising*, pp. 245-46. Annual letter from Francisco Caral at Goa, 17 December 1594 in *D.I.*, XVI, pp. 750-51.
110. *D.I.*, vol. VI, pp. 89-93.
111. F.P. Mendes da Luz, *Livro das Cidades*, op. cit., pp. 1-144.
112. BNL Codice 1976, fl. 136-140v.
113. Correa, op. cit., IV, p. 112(1539-40) *A.N.T.T.*, *Gavetas*, 11-8-18-fl. 2. (1538).
114. B.M. *Additional Manuscripts*, No. 28432, fl. 10 (18 December 1599).
115. Sanjay Subrahmanyan, "Precious Metal flows and prices in Western and Southern Asia, 1500-1750: some comparative and conjunctual aspects", *Studies in History*, 7, 1.n.s.1991 (pp. 79-105) (p. 94).
116. One *marakkal* of rice, one *alakku* of ghee, one *uri* of green gram, pepper and vegetables cost 1500 *panams* in 1518 vide *T.T.D.E.S.*, vol. III, Nos. 124, 125 and 126. Similarly for the years of 1519 and 1521 see *T.T.D.E.S.*, vol. III, Nos. 131 and 149. Portuguse Source *A.N.T.T.*, Nucleo Antigo 808 fl. 2-3v contains price details for the commodities of pepper, rice, horse-gram, saffron, etc. for the year 1526. One *Faracola* of pepper 13 *panams*; one *Faracola* of saffron 2.50 *panams*; one *Kottai* of rice ten *panams;* one *Kottai* of *Aval* six *panams*; one *Kottai* of horsegram seven *panams*; one *Marco* of arecanuts thirty *panams*.
117. *A.R.E.*, 179 of 1924, p. 115. The year mentioned as Khara and Nandana in inscriptions relate to the years 1531 and 1532.
118. Ibid., 655 of 1919 and 179 of 1924 B; *S.I.T.I.*, vol. I, pp. 372-73.
119. *D.I.*, vol. XIII, p. 502 and vol. XIV, p. 491.
120. *A.R.E.*, No. 10 of 1912-13 (A).
121. *A.R.E.*, 352 of 1916 and 118 of 1967 (Mylapore) *Chennaimanagara Kalvettugal* 358 of 1912 (1518).
122. Ibid., 247 of 1906 (1504).
123. Ibid, 127 of 1906. Karashima, "Nayak's rule", *Acta Asiatica*, pp. 23-6.
124. *A.R.E.*, 426 of 1919 (1590).
125. Gaspar Correa, op. cit., tomo IV, pp. 131-32; tomo II, p. 722.
126. *S.I.I.*, XVI, P. V; *A.R.E.* 478 of 1919 (1515) (Kanchipuram). The reason for leaving blank spaces in the inscription without carving the details of wages can be explained since we find in an inscription that only a portion of money has been paid while engraving the edict was in progress and the balance being paid in 1574, *T.T.D.E.S.*, IV, p. 71.
127. *A.R.E.*, 223 of 1912 (Tirupatiyur temple, Sadasivaraya period).

128. Ibid., 1916, p. 147.
129. Ibid., 421 of 1919 (1591).
130. *S.I.T.I.*, vol. I, No. 372, p. 355 (1521).
131. *A.R.E.* 32 of 1938-39, 69 of 1938-39 (Srirangam); *T.T.D.E.S.*, IV, No. 11, p. 24 (Tirupati), 535 of 1919 (1558) Kanchipuram.
132. *I.P.S.*, No. 718; *S.I.T.I.*, vol. II, p. 839. No. 20 (1530), IV, p. 14, No. 5 (1530), V, p. 85, 1530, 535 of 1919 (1558) Kanchipuram; *S.I.T.I.*, vol. I, pp. 42-5. The Kugaiyur temple had fourteen *Devaradiyars* who received plot of wet lands. They enjoyed the lands during their work and service in temple. *A.R.E.* 117 of 1918 (1524). The detail regarding *Devaradiyar* is incomplete in another inscription of Valikondapuram. See *A.R.E.* 288 of 1944.
133. *T.T.D.E.S.*, III, pp. 278-79.
134. *S.I.T.I.*, vol. I, pp. 42-5 (Sittamur 1582) and p. 534 (Sriperumbudur 1590); *T.T.D.E.S.*, V, p. 111 (Tirupati, Sadasivaraya period), 535 of 1919 (Kanchipuram 1558).
135. *A.R.E.* 373 of 1919 and 535 of 1919 (Kanchipuram 1540); *T.T.D.E.S.*, V, No. 92 (Tirupati 1547).
136. Ibid., 373 of 1919 (Kanchipuram 1540).
137. *S.I.T.I.*, vol. I, No. 405, p. 392 (Kanchipuram 1553).
138. *A.R.E.* 535 of 1919 and 380 of 1919 (Kanchipuram 1558, 1572).
139. Ibid., 380 of 1919 and 535 of 1919 (1572, 1558).
140. Ibid., 373 of 1919 (Kanchipuram 1540). See also K.V. Raman, *Sri Varadarajaswamy Temple—Kanchi: A Study of Its History, Art and Architecture*, New Delhi, 1975.
141. Letter of Dom Joao de Castro to D. Luis dated 30 Oct. 1540, *investigador Portuguez*, Lisboa, vol. XVI, p. 279.
142. For rice-pounder see, *S.I.T.I.*, vol. I, pp. 393 and 351, *A.R.E.* 382 of 1919. For temple cooks see, *A.R.E.* 374 of 1953-54, 382 of 1919, *T.T.D.E.S.*, vol. V, No. 125.
143. Ravi Arvind Palat, "Popular Revolts and the State in Medieval South India: A Study of the Vijayanagara empire 1360-1565". *Bijdragen tot de Taal -land -en Volkenkunde , Deel,* 142, 1986, p. 128.

# Conclusion

Under the medieval Cholas, Coromandel in the tenth century took off from subsistence economy and made significant progress in agriculture, non-agriculture, trade and exchange. Warfare and agriculture were not the only two noble professions known to Tamils then, as is sometimes believed. Maritime trade gradually increased with the Arabs and the Chinese, and merchants from Coromandel traded with various ports of the Indian Ocean.

The Vijayanagara kings governed Coromandel with considerable care, fully aware of its revenue yielding capacity. Under them, Coromandel became an important production centre of rice and textiles for Asian trade.

The nature of sixteenth-century Coromandel economy and society is a matter of debate among scholars. Immanuel Wallerstein's world-systems perspective embraces the idea of both 'world empires' as well as of the 'world-economies'. A world system whether it is a world-economy or a world empire need not include the whole world and there can be many world empires as well as world economies. In the past many world economies came into being and one such was the Coromandel world system that existed since antiquity. In the sixteenth century the core of the south Indian economy was located at the capital of Vijayanagara city with which the economy of Coromandel as a periphery was linked to south Indian world empire. Flow of bullion from Malacca and China besides precious stones from Ceylon and Pegu played a vital role for prospering Vijayanagara economy in the first half of the sixteenth century. This did not last long and with the battle of Talikota in 1565 Coromandel that remained as a link changed its course and emerged as a world empire with the emergence of two Nayaka kingdoms of Gingee and Thanjavur. It was at this later date Coromandel economy got incorporated into the European world economy after the expansion which contained in the seventeenth century. Wallerstein, who viewed the pre-colonial world economy as one based upon the capitalistic mode of production, with Europe at its core and the rest of the world as contributing to the core, observed that pre-colonial Coromandel was not a world system. It would not, however, be quite correct to say that the Coromandel economy was peripheral to its European counterpart. Coromandel commerce of the time was not merely a trade in luxuries and non-essentials. The region had many independent, distinctive and special characteristics which had hardly anything to do with contemporary European world economy.

Was Coromandel at least an *economie monde* as Fernand Braudel conceives it? Perhaps not, given that the situation in the Bay of Bengal differed considerably from that in the Mediterranean.

Andre Gunder Frank, in his study of underdevelopment in the periphery vis-a-vis its relationship with the core, opined that underdevelopment arose not from poverty but from the wealth which ended up with the metropolis. In an exploitative relationship, the centre extracted the surplus from the satellites. This problem of international capitalism, which did not change fundamentally from the sixteenth century onwards, caused underdevelopment.

To some extent, Gunder Frank's theory applies to sixteenth-century Coromandel. Parallel features do exist between the Vijayanagara centre and the Coromandel localities as between the core and the periphery, but this parallel is not exact. Frank's theory appears largely static whereas we find general expansion and development in the Coromandel localities in agriculture, crafts and exchange.

Geographically, going by the evidence of inscriptions and Portuguese sources, the Coromandel region was restricted to the area from Adirampattinam to Durgarajapattinam on the east coast. The term Coromandel as extending to the Godavari delta possibly gained wider currency later.

Among territorial divisions of the Vijayanagara empire, *rajya* was the largest. *Simai* or *nayakattanasimai* emerged as the most common division granted to *nayakas*. Some *kottam* were converted into *simai*. A new division called *parru* emerged on the riverine basin with expanding cultivated area. *Nadu* units and their boundaries changed from time to time and some of them were converted into *parru*. With the growth in the power of *nayaka, uchavadi* declined as administrative division.

To consider *nayakas* as warrior chieftains would mean over-emphasising the military aspect. Extended kinship was a criterion followed by Vijayanagara rulers in granting *nayakattanam*. Phrases used in inscriptions, such as "for the merit of", are not explanatory of the feudal character: they do not fit in with the inscriptional text and context; in fact they show the widespread belief of gathering merit for heaven, as explained in the *Dharma sastras*.

Although initially *nayakas* were appointed in the fourteenth century to protect temple property and conduct worship, the picture changed significantly in the sixteenth century, when they became rulers of the locality. This change came about on account of the system of revenue farming introduced by Vijayanagara rulers in various Coromandel localities. *Nayakas* appointed various revenue officers. For collecting revenue, treasuries of various kinds existed at different places. The *nayakas* paid revenue to the Vijayanagara rulers during the month of *Asvina* (September/October).

The adoption of this system of polity became necessary because of the large area covered by the Vijayanagara empire. For effective rule, indirect taxation alone was possible. Revenue was raised by farming out to *nayakas* the right to rule the territory, with the responsibility of collecting the revenue. Revenue farming was the most important facet of Coromandel political economy. In forest zones given on revenue farming, *kirtas* ruled.

Under the rule of *nayakas*, the nature of land ownership changed and agricultural production expanded. Not all lands were owned by the king. Temples, which appear to have been major landowners, began to sell. Uncultivated temple lands were taken away from temples and distributed to peasants to settle. Peasants were not displaced since the temples insisted that they should not be evicted when lands were given for cultivation.

Among the emerging new landowners, caste-based communities like *Mudaliar, Chetti, Reddiar* and *Kaikolar* predominated. *Kaikolars* shared their land use rights among their own community. Gifting of land to its purchaser emerged as a practice, the intention being to establish clear title over the property. The sale price of land was at some places fixed by the cultivating peasants.

Temples also directly cultivated the land, supervised by a temple employee, in this period. The agricultural labourers were serfs of the temples, having been dedicated to the deity of the temple and owned by the temple for life. Temple lands were also given out for sharecropping, with the owner's share being a minimum of one-third and going up to three-fourths.

Agricultural lands were of five types, namely *nanjey, punjey, thottam, nattam* and *padugai*, based on the type of land, range of cropping pattern, season and irrigation. The shift from the traditional riverine basin to dry area of cultivation was an important feature in expanding agriculture. Both wet and dry lands were leased out, the lease payment being in cash plus kind in the ratio of 1:1 and 1:2. Paddy, of four varieties, was the most commonly grown crop under wet cultivation. Cotton of three types was cultivated in *karisal* and alluvial soil. Sugarcane was cultivated on the riverine basin of Pennar, Vellar and Palar. Oil seeds were grown in the interior dryland. Reclaimed forest lands were converted into new peasant settlements called *palayam*. On reclaimed wastelands cultivation of plantain, turmeric, ginger, arecanut and coconuts was encouraged.

Minor irrigation systems such as wells, channels and canals were dug at various places. Investment in irrigation was considered a spiritual act. Materially, it was not very paying to the enterprising individual, since a major share of the produce thus enhanced always went to the landowner. Irrigational sources were maintained generally from the fish lease money of tanks. An incentive to investment in temple irrigational works was a share of *prasadam* (sacred food). The Cauvery dam catered to the needs of delta regions; a tax called *kallanai* was collected for its maintenance and repairs. The levy of water cess by *nayakas* demonstrates the amount of control they exercised. Collective management of the irrigation system, though beneficial economically to the participants, led to disputes between temple authorities and people of the place, between two localities and between two temple authorities. The *nayakas* appointed arbitrators to settle the matter and took care of water management.

Control over land, or more accurately control over the produce of land, was vested with *nayakas*. They introduced various land measurements and units of revenue calculated solely to enhance their revenue. Wet cultivation was taxed differently from dry cultivation. Lands newly brought under cultivation were taxed according to the type of cultivator's residence and mobility. There was also graded assessment. The preference was for cash payment although revenue collection in kind did exist. Migration tended to be a major form of peasant protest against unbearable tax burden. Various land disputes of the period and land boundary stones attest that land hunger existed. Merchants invested in land in large numbers.

The growth of *pattadai,* which appears to have engaged in mass production of goods, activated craft production. Textile production, both cotton and silk, for local consumption and export particularly to South and South-East Asia, was an important feature of craft economy. Kanchipuram and Virinchipuram emerged as the two leading textile centres. Various weaving villages sprang up in the hinterland of the ports of Pulicat, Kunimedu and Nagapattinam. *Nayakas* and temples encouraged the producers, providing them facilities like a place of work; creating weavers' settlements; granting tax free lands for a period ranging from one to six years; granting vacant plots for construction of houses in the streets around the temples; buying from them the textiles required by the temples; and giving them social privileges.

The production of textiles which was thus encouraged led to an increase in *nayakas*' revenue. They directly collected, on annual basis, a minimum loom tax of one and a quarter *panam* and a maximum of six *panam.* Taxes were levied on textile dyeing centres also. Among the manufacturing innovations were: the emergence of master weavers; improved machinery and implements; technological change from patterned loom to draw loom; and organisation of weaving in some form of putting-out system. Some Portuguese merchants controlled twelve weaving families in Pulicat region.

Essential consumer products such as sugar and oil were manufactured depending upon the environmental conditions and patronage given by *nayakas* for its growth. Littoral craft of salt manufacture flourished at Tiruvottiyur, Taiyur and Marakkanam on the Coromandel coast. Availability of iron in the hinterland of Coromandel was a contributing factor towards manufacture of cannons and cannon balls which were purchased by the Portuguese. Some iron had also been exported by the Portuguese from the port of Kunimedu. Smithy had flourished and the *nayakas* collected taxes called *ulaipattam* for the furnace used by blacksmiths. Jewellery work flourished and the goldsmiths paid a tax called *thattavabattam.* Sculpture and carpentry flourished under the patronage of temples. Guilds of producers functioned as self regulated unit. The craft economy had moved from the traditional pattern, and it suffered from development to some extent owing to the rules and regulations. Taxes were imposed by *nayakas* with widespread revolts of producers. Production could have suffered by the desertion of the worker groups who protested claiming certain social privileges. Move from petty artisanal villages to specialised craft producing centres was a notable feature. This is not to describe that sixteenth century was the period of prosperity but resulted in the way that unequal distribution of wealth took place in this region. Craft production of Coromandel shows clear indications that it was separated from agriculture. Constant struggle for supremacy between the textile producers and trading merchants was common in this period. Pre-industrial Coromandel witnessed advanced system of technology in the manufacture of cannons and cannon balls. This shows the manufacture of artillery was not hampered by the *nayaka* rulers in the sixteenth century Coromandel.

Trade and urbanisation also progressed. With the arrival of the Portuguese, the *varna* ideology changed and permitted non-Vaisyas to practise trade. Brahmins entered into occupations such as military and agriculture, which were considered of lower status, and which created caste ranks unequal to the priestly Brahmins in society. Many *Parava* converts joined hands with the Portuguese traders who sailed to various ports conducting trade. *Nagarams* became important urban wholesale markets, with a guild composed of *Nagarattars*, the resident mercantile community. *Nagarattars* administered the market and levied market taxes. *Nayakas*, who emerged as protectors of markets, ordered the creation of *pettai* for rural wholesale trade, giving certain market concessions to attract merchants to settle there. Protection fees were collected from such markets. Some temples also contributed to the establishment of *pettai*, probably in anticipation of donations from merchants.

Weekly markets for sale of rural products were held at Tindivanam, Thazhamdhondi, Gingee, Tenmahadevimangalam and Tiruvannamalai on a particular day of the week, which brought merchants and consumers in close touch with the manufacturers. The periodical fairs and festivals created a wider economic system of inter-regional commerce and also helped in the growth of religious centres like Tirupati. Commodities for sale were stamped and charged a duty called *mudrayam*. Godowns were provided for commercial storage. Certain commodities like yarn, oil, betel leaf and textiles were monopolised by certain merchant groups. Similarly, specialised marketing centres came up for agricultural and non-agricultural products, demonstrating a certain amount of market sophistication. Bazaars specialised in bullion trade.

Bullocks were the chief means of transport to markets, besides head loads, pack asses and horses. Thirteen major land routes connected various ports and towns of South India. The surrounding villages were also connected with the towns through vertical and horizontal linkages to support the trade economy. The fact that various transit taxes, secondary duties and market levies were collected by *nayakas* shows that the king had no direct control in Coromandel local markets. In course of time trade guilds appear to have declined and individual merchants became dominant.

New colonies emerged in the suburbs of Coromandel towns, which were either open or fortified. Open towns were those with religious importance and fortified towns with political significance. Flourishing trade was always a catalyst in the process of urbanisation. Various fort towns like Gingee, Vellore, Vallam and Chandragiri emerged, enclosing immediate neighbouring regions where trade and crafts combined to some extent with administration.

Rice formed an important commodity of coastal trade with Malabar. Thirumalairayanpattinam was the chief port of country trade, which was replaced by Nagapattinam with the advent of the Portuguese.

Coromandel society broadly comprised of two groups based on their occupation, namely cultivators (*ulukudi*) and artisans of manufacturing class (*pattadaikudi*). The peasant society began to change in consequence of the rise of Tamil peasant groups, called *vanniyar*, who were affiliated with *idangai* and who controlled the lands as early as the fourteenth century. In the sixteenth century, when the burden of heavy taxation drove them to wretchedness, peasants migrated to more agreeable neighbouring places. *Nayakas* rehabilitated the migrant peasants through tax revision and concession. The social restrictions to which certain peasants in Coromandel were subject show that the peasant's was a sorry lot.

The production of commercial textiles and the volume of external trade led to the appearance of weavers as a dominant and privileged labour group. Privileges were bestowed both by *nayakas* and temples. *Kaikola* weavers, because of their ritual links with temples, enjoyed high social status and occupied key posts. There was solidarity among them, and weavers of one place, if they enjoyed privileges at one place, strove to attain these for fellow weavers in other localities.

A similar solidarity existed also among artisans, and artisans at Padaividu, Gingee and Tiruvannamalai helped fellow artisans at other places to secure the same social privileges as they enjoyed. *Nayakas* consulted each other about awarding these privileges, in order to halt the migration of artisans. Social and religious privileges were given to weavers and *kammalars* because *nayakas* and temples benefited by the growth of these crafts people. The merchants' status in society was lower than that of weavers, a state of affairs they failed to change.

Slaves were found in houses and temples, slavery having developed on account of the high rate of family taxes introduced by *nayakas*.

Portuguese traders who settled down at various ports adopted their own way of life, trading with various ports in country trade and international commerce. They established contacts with native merchants, borrowing loans and exchanging commodities. The prices of commodities generally increased—in a sort of price revolution—on account of the import of bullion and precious stones into Coromandel, since the expansion of Coromandel economy largely depended on the inflow of bullion from South and South-East Asia. Salaries of semi-skilled workers and professionals employed by temples, who were paid in terms of temple food in addition to monthly payment, fluctuated.

Some uniformity existed in Coromandel maritime trade in the nature of commodities, ports of destination and community of merchants, which supports Sinnapah Arasaratnam's view that a unitary system of trade exchange existed in the pre-modern history of maritime Asia. The commercial fortunes of the hinterland greatly influenced those of the Coromandel ports.

Indigenous merchants formed three groups such as *Mudaliars, Chettis* and *Marakayyars*. The Portuguese expansion in Coromandel was marked by their relentless hostility to *Marakayyars*, whom they could not supplant. With the arrival of the Portuguese, the ports of Pulicat and Nagore, which had been flourishing in the early sixteenth century, declined, and their trade and commerce were diverted to Santhome and Nagapattinam, where the Portuguese settled. The port of Kunimedu, where *Marakayyars* were the leading merchants, however, continued to be a dominant port throughout the sixteenth century, thwarting Portuguese attempts to divert its trade to Devanampattinam, close to Kunimedu, where they settled. South-East Asian rulers like the sultan of Malacca and port officials like the *shahbandar* of Pasai, who conducted trade with Coromandel in the early sixteenth century, gradually withdrew from direct trade, both on account of the risk involved and the control and domination exercised by the Portuguese in overseas trade, but the *Marakayyars* could not be subdued. A substantial share of their trade was carried on with South-East Asia, encouraged by the Muslim sultanate of Achin. While in the rest of the globe Lisbon became the source of epochal change, the Portuguese could not dislodge the *Marakayyars* either in coastal trade or overseas trade of Coromandel. Private Portuguese traders in Coromandel had no inhibitions about joining hands with the *Marakayyars* to strengthen their trade. Thus *Marakayyars* continued in strength and carried on trade with the Dutch in Coromandel in the seventeenth century. The Portuguese presence, however, changed the course of Coromandel trade in certain specific directions, particularly to Goa and Macao.

Metals and luxuries generally formed part of the commodities exchanged for the goods of Coromandel. This composition of imports contributed to the economic growth of the region. The prosperity of the region may have been a reason why even after the battle of Talikota Coromandel kept up its pace of economic development. This also might have prompted the Vijayanagara rulers to shift their capital from Penukonda to Chandragiri and further towards Vellore in the Coromandel region.

There appears to have been an independent commercial world system of Coromandel at least in the sixteenth century, which was caught between the world systems of China and Europe. If at all Coromandel became the periphery of the European world system, it did so in the later centuries when the commercial enterprise by the Dutch and the English increased.

It would be difficult to apply the Wallersteinian world system to Coromandel, since Wallerstein does not provide for local systems in his analysis. Coromandel had its diversity. It had a typical inventory of trading goods such as rice and textiles. It had a monetised non-subsistence sector, marked by the accumulation of capital and specialisation of economic functions. Growth of ports, forts, temple towns and administrative towns was a feature of urban development and these towns clearly had a more important role in the commercial economy of the region.

The trend was towards the growth of money economy. Villages received most of their requirements from outside, which fostered the growth of money economy. The growth of a market in land, attested by the sale and purchase of lands noticed in the epigraphs, also proves an unmistakable trend towards the growth of money economy. Economic growth was not uniform all through the sixteenth century: it was cyclical, depending on various factors such as failure of agricultural production, famines and droughts alternating with periods of slow growth, recession and sometimes depression. It was a system that was for the first time actively participating in the economy of Asia and Europe.

# APPENDIX A

## ALPHABETICAL LIST OF TERRITORIAL DIVISIONS, 1500-1600

*Name / Modern identification / Reference / Year*

### 1. SIMAI

Adinadu / Chittoor dt. / *TTDES* IV, (167) / 1540
Ammaiyappanvattu / Chidambaram / *JOR* , XII, 169-78 / 1530
Apparpillai / Kumbakonam tk. / *ARE* 318-1955-56 / 1507
Arakonam / North Arcot dt. / *TTDES* VI, pt. I, pp. 43-5 / 1584
Arni / North Arcot dt. / *TTDES* III, pp. 81-86 / 1511
Ayilur / Musiri tk. / *SITI* II, p. 748 / 1532
Ayyappadi / Thanjavur dt. / *ARE* 60-1937 / 1562
Bhuvanagiri / South Arcot dt. / *ARE* 125-1904 / 1510
Chandragiri / Chandragiri tk. / *ARE* 60-1941-42 / 1500
Chingleput / Chingleput tk. / *EI* XIV, pp. 170 / 1528
Cholamandala / Tiruvarur tk. / *ARE* 298-1950-51 / 1570
Darasuram / Kumbakonam tk. / *ARE* 288-1903 / 1517
Devamandala / Chidambaram tk. / *SITI* I, p. 179 / 1514
Devanur / Gingee tk / *ARE* 240-1904 / 1550
Erumigu / North Arcot dt. / *TTDES* IV, pp. 47-8 / 1553
Gandikota / North Arcot dt. / *TTDES* V, pp. 435-8 / 1558
Gangaikonda / Villupuram tk. / *SITI* II, p. 924 / 1592
Gokula gunta / Nagari tk. / *TTDES* IV, p. 281 / 1540
Gingee / Gingcc tk. / *ARE* 240 1904 / 1550
Idaivasal / Chingleput dt. / *SITI* I, 405 / 1582
Irakutanallur / South Arcot dt. / *ARE* 465-1937-38 / 1532
Jagdavacheri/ Tiruttani tk. / *TTDES* V, pp. 355-7 / 1551
Kachipattu / Chittoor dt. / *SITI* I, 532 / 1590
Kalaipakkam / Chingleput tk. / *ARE* 1-1935 / 1532
Kalakhasti / Kalakhasti tk. / *NDI* I, G.82 / 1500
Kalathur / Chingleput tk. / *ARE* 87-1933 / 1542
Karivachi / Vilupuram tk. / *SII* XVI, p. 80 / 1519
Kayapakkam / Gingee tk. / *ARE* 240-1904 / 1550
Kondavali / North Arcot dt. / *TTDES* VII, p. 194 / 1514
Kottur / North Arcot dt. /*TTDES* V, pp. 442-3 / 1560
Kulittalai / Trichy dt. / *SITI* II, p. 693 / 1552

Kunrattur / Saidapet tk. / *SII* XVII, p. 104 / 1550
Kuppa / Tirukoyilur tk. / *ARE* 273-1939-40 / 1572
Madainallur / Sulurpet tk. / *NDI* III, pp. 1316-17 / 1513
Madanallur / North Arcot dt. / *TTDES* III(99) / 1514
Mappedu / Tiruvallur tk. / *ARE* 61-1947-48 / 1530
Mudiyarai / South Arcot dt. / *ARE* 240-1904 / 1550
Munnuruva / Tindivanam tk. / *ARE* 241-1904 / 1532
Nagamangalam / Chittoor dt. / EC XII Mi. 64, p. 110 / 1509
Nagari / Nagari tk. / *TTDES*, p. 302 / 1547
Nagariyil / Polur tk. / *SITI* III, p. 1210 / 1582
Nallur / Trichy tk. / *ARE* 321-1951 / 1577
Nandivala / N.I. / *ARE* 8-1933 / 1537
Nandivaram / Chingleput tk. / *ARE* 34-1935 / 1550
Nangur vattam / Nagore / *JOR* XII, p. 169 / 1530
Narayanavanam / Chittoor dt. / *ARE* 112-1942-43 / 1578
Ninraiyurnadu / North Arcot dt. / *TTDES* V, pp. 123-7 / 1545
Padainadu / Sulurpet tk. / *NDI*, p. 448 / 1524
Padaividu / Polur tk. / *ARE* 358-1912 / 1518
Palaya / Saidapet tk. / *TTDES* V, pt. I, pp. 55-62 / 1592
Palaiayam / North Arcot dt / *TTDES* V, p. 75 / 1545
Palaiyur / Polur tk. / *ARE* 1933-34, p. 38 / 1505
Palavettu / Satyavedu tk. / *TTDES* VI, pp. 33-40 / 1583
Pallikonda Pattana / SA dt./ *ARE* 269-1929 / 1546
Pampundi / North Arcot dt. / *ARE* 507-1919 / 1548
Pandanallur / N.I. / *ARE* 1-1933 / 1572
Paravattur / North Arcot / *ARE* 288-1953-54 / 1595
Perambakkam / Tiruvallur tk. / *ARE* 111-1932-33 / 1579
Perambakula / Chingleput dt. / *ARE* 117-1932-33 / 1518
Perumbedu / Madurantakam tk. / Further I, p. 321 / 1586
Perumber / North Arcot dt. / *TTDES* IV, pp. 284-5 / 1541
Perumpalai / N.I. / *TTDES* V, pp. 363-6 / 1552
Perunkanchi / Gingee tk. / *ARE* 240-1904 / 1550
Perum kudai / N.I. / *TTDES* A.I., p. 248 / 1533
Perunagari / Saidapet tk. / *TTDES* V, p. 273 / 1547
Perur / Chittoor tk. / *TTDES* V, pp. 442-4 / 1560
Polur / North Arcot dt. / 352-1940-41 / 1517
Poonamallee / Saidapet tk. / 300-1938-39 / 1509
Puliyur / Kallakurichi tk. / *TVMTI* no. 440 / 1591
Pulal / Saidapet tk. / 487-1920 / 1529
Rajarajapura / South Arcot dt. / 125-1904 / 1597

Salaipakkam / Chingleput tk. / *ARE* 575-1919 / 1539
Saluvanayakana / Kumbakonam tk. / *ARE* 318-1955-56 / 1507
Sengattu / Kotta N.I. / *TTDES* V, p. 359 / 1572
Silakonda / N.I. / *TTDES* V, p. 359 / 1551
Siruvangur / South Arcot dt. / *ARE* 104-1906 / 1549
Srikumtanaruhur / Thanjavur dt. / *JOR* XII, p. 169 / 1530
Sriperumbudur / Chingleput dt. / *ARE* 189-1922(c) / 1590
Tatavadicheri / Saidapet tk. / *TTDES* III, pp. 33-40 / 1521
Tenkarai / Kallakurichi tk. / *ARE* 106-1918 / 1562
Thanjavur / Thanjavur tk. / *ARE* 1919, p. 104 / 1509
Tindivanam / Tindivanam tk. / *ARE* 1939-40 / 1519
Tiruchirapalli / Trichy tk. / 105-1936-36 / 1500
Tirukkadigai / North Arcot dt. / *ARE* 288-1953-54 / 1500
Tirukkalumalam/ Shiyali tk./ Dharmuai CP no. 6 / 1513
Tirukoyilur / South Arcot dt. / *ARE* 262-1934-35 / 1588
Tirunavalur / South Arcot dt. / *ARE* 273-1939-40 / 1572
Tiruttani / Chingleput dt. / *ARE* 112-1942-43 / 1578
Tiruvadigai / South Arcot / *SITI* I, pp. 76-7 / 1552
Tiruvali / Shiyali tk. / *TTDES* V, pp. 207-8 / 1530
Tiruvannamalai / North Arcot dt. / *SII* VIII, 158 / 1567
Tiruvarur / Tiruvarur dt. / C.P. no. 10-1936-37 / 1528
Tulaiparivayil / North Arcot dt. / *TTDES* VI, pp. 33-40 / 1583
Uthagamandala / Tiruvannamalai tk. / *TVMTI* no. 430 / 1570
Valaivathur / Arcot tk. / *ARE* 30-1933-34 / 1519
Vayalaikavur / Chingleput dt. / *SITI* I, p. 392 / 1532
Vayalur / Chingleput dt. / *ARE* 97-1933 / 1600
Vendavadi / Polur tk. / *TTDES* V, pp. 207-8 / 1547
Vidatoni / North Arcot dt. / *TTDES* V, 207-8 / 1546
Villupuram / South Arcot dt. / *TTDES* IV, p. 63 / 1534
Virabharayar / North Arcot dt. / *SITI* I, p. 126, 466-1921 / 1519
Viranarayana / Chidambaram tk. / *SITI* I, pp. 37-8 / 1530
Virapandyanallur / Tirukoyilur tk. / 55-1936, 60-1936 / 1534
Viravanallur / Gingee tk. / *SITI* I, pp. 37-8 / 1550
Vandavasi / North Arcot dt. / *ARE* 460-1920 / 1519

## 2. KOTTAM

Amur / Chingleput tk./ *SITI* I, p. 485 / 1536
Damal / Arakonam tk. / *SITI* I, p. 333 / 1540
Eyir / Kanchipuram tk. / *SITI* I, p. 376 / 1517
Ikkattu / Tiruvallur tk. / *ARE* 624-1904 / 1520

Kalathur / Chingleput tk. / *ARE* 525-1915 / 1588
Kalaiyar / Cheyyar tk. / *ARE* 195-1943-44(B) / 1510
Kunravadhana / Gummidipoondi tk. / 628-1904 / 1514
Manavir / Tiruttani tk. / *ARE* 624-1904 / 1520
Paduvur / Walajah tk. / *TTDES* V, pp. 51-2 / 1544
Paiyur / Ponneri tk. / *ARE* 624-1904 / 1520
Palkunra / Tiruvannamalai tk. / *ARE* 515-1938 / 1510
Pulal / Saidapet tk. / *ARE* 487-1920 / 1520
Puliyur / Saidapet tk. / *ARE* 90-1945-46 / 1510
Sengadu / Tiruvallur tk. / *ARE* 321-1954-55 / 1542
Tirukkanjeri / Tiruttani tk. / *ARE* 288-1953-54 / 1595
Tiruvengada / Chittoor tk. / *TTDES* V, pp. 51-2 / 1537
Uttukadu / Kanchipuram tk. / *SITI* I, p. 350 / 1509

### 3. PARRU

Adikamangalam / Trichy tk. / *ARE* 139-1948 / 1546
Alampadi / Panruti tk. / *ARE* 263-1913 / 1583
Alishukattu / Chidambaram tk. / *SITI* I, p. 21 / 1582
Andakalur / Chidambaram tk. / *ARE* 334-1913 / 1585
Annamangalam / Gingee tk. / *ARE* 515-1938 / 1510
Arasur kil / Chidambaram tk. / *SITI* I, p. 21 / 1582
Arayiraveli / Chingleput tk. / *SITI* I, p. 485 / 1536
Brahmadesam / Cheyyar tk. / 240-1906 / 1510
Cholakulavali / Panruti tk. / 378-1921 / 1572
Erumbur / Panruti tk. / *ARE* 348-1913/ 1582
Gandagopalan / Cheyyar tk. / *TTDES* I, p. 273 /1552
Gingee / Gingee tk. / *TVMTI* no. 382, 391 / 1509
Idaiyar / Panruti tk. / 293-1928-29./ 1572
Irandayiraveli / Chingleput tk. / 322-1954-55 / 1536
Irungolapadi / Gangaikondacholapuram / 263-1916 / 1583
Iruvara / Tiruttani tk. / 70-1958-59 / 1529
Kalavai / Polur tk. / 179-1963-64 / 1593
Karumavur / Chidambaram tk. / 250-1940 / 1502
Kavanur / Chidambaram tk. / *SITI* I, p. 21 / 1582
Kenurkondan / Chidambaram tk. / 348-1913 / 1582
Kilā / Chidambaram tk. / *SITI* I, p. 21 / 1582
Koviyur / Chidambaram tk. / *SITI* I, p. 21 / 1582
Kurichi / Srimushnam tk. / 265-1916 / 1582
Malai / N.I. / 183-1941-42 / 1514

Mel / Tiruvannamalai tk. / *TVMTI* no. 42 / 1556
Mudiyanur / Tindivanam tk. / 66-1906 / 1557
Mugandur / Polur tk. / 117-1933 / 1518
Muka / Chittoor tk. / *TTDES* III no. 167 / 1527
Murugamangalam / Polur tk. / *ARE* 359-1912 / 1511
Naduvakkarai / Villupuram tk. / 368-1912 / 1503
Narayanavanam / Chittoor dt. / 628-1905 /1524
Nenmeli / South Arcot dt. / 368-1912 / 1503
Olugarai / Pondicherry U.T. / 368-1912 / 1533
Pakkam / Wardiwash tk. / 421-1929 / 1570
Palai / North Arcot dt. / 624-1904 / 1520
Palangur / Iraivasanallur tk. / 175-1906 / 1531
Pannirandu / South Arcot dt. / 493-1937-38 / 1572
Perumugai / North Arcot dt. / 235-1904 / 1562
Pidagai / South Arcot dt. / 493-1937-38 / 1572
Pirambil / Nannilam tk. / 260-1930 / 1537
Pullur / Nannilam tk./ Kalvettugal II, no. 233 / 1526
Rajagambira / Malaikadaikatta, Polur tk. / 104-1943 / 1527
Sengundram / Chidambaram tk. / *SITI* I, p. 21 / 1582
Sholiyapuram / North Arcot dt. / 341-1954-55 / 1544
Siruvelur / North Arcot dt. / *TVMTI* no. 405 / 1538
Singamulam / North Arcot dt. / *TVMTI* no. 417/ 1581
Sriramamangalam / North Arcot dt. / 708-1904 / 1527
Srirangam / Trichy tk. / *ARE* 261-1936-37 / 1563
Sriringur / Panruti tk. / 293-1928-29 / 1573
Tellar / North Arcot dt. / 75-1935 / 1507
Tenkaraikoyilur / Chidambaram tk. / 348-1913 / 1582
Tholuvur / Chidambaram tk. / *SITI* I, p. 19 / 1582
Tirubhuvanaimadevi / South Arcot dt. / 368-1917 / 1503
Tirukalukunram / Chingleput dt. / 117-1932-33 / 1518
Tirukalumalam / Shiyali tk. / Dharumai CP. no. 6 / 1513
Tirunaraiyur/ Nannilam tk. / Kalvettugal III / 1519
Tiruvalli / Nannilam tk. / 423-1918 / 1583
Ukkal / N.I. / 344-1955 / 1528
Uttara Tiruvarangam / South Arcot dt. / 66-1906 / 1557
Uttiramerur / Kanchipuram tk. / *SITI* III, p. 1116 / 1521
Vadakkidaindu / South Arcot dt. / 65-1922 / 1573
Vagaur / Pondicherry U.T. / 378-1921 / 1572
Vilandai / South Arcot dt. / 249-1916 / 1500
Yerumbur / Chidambaram tk. / *SITI* I, p. 21 / 1582

## 4. NADU

Adaiyar / Tiruvannamalai tk. / *TVMTI* no. 481 / 1526
Adi / North Arcot dt. / *TTDES*, pp. 47-8 / 1520
Agudi / Chingleput dt. / *SII* XVII, 680, 624-1904 / 1541
Ambattur / Saidapet tk. / *ARE* 127-1922 / 1520
Anjur / Gummidipoondi tk / *TTDES* V, pp. 330-1 / 1520
Anna / Tiruvannamalai tk / *TVMTI* no. 375 / 1506
Attur / Kalakhasti tk. / *ARE* 177-1924 / 1517
Egmore / Madras dt. / *SII* XVII, 680 / 1520
Idaiyarru / Lalgudi tk. / *ARE* 666-1962-63 / 1506
Illathur / Tiruttani tk. / 624-1904 / 1520
Innambar / Kumbakonam tk. / *SII* XXIII, p. 379 / 1573
Kachchiyur / Chingleput dt. / 624-1904 / 1520
Kalathur / Chingleput tk. / 87-1933 / 1542
Kalavai / North Arcot dt. / 16-1935 / 1550
Kalimalai / Cheyyar tk. / *TTDES* V, p. 371 / 1521
Kamalai / Sulurpet tk / *NDI* III, p. 1316 / 1513
Karamba / Thanjavur tk. / 260-1930 / 1534
Karapperu / Saidapet tk. / *SII* XVII, 680 / 1520
Kilaipaderi / Satyavedu tk. / *TTDES* II, 4 / 1502
Kilangu / Trichy / *ARE* 2-1939 / 1535
Kilipayirrur / Musiri tk. / IPS no. 730, 741 / 1510
Konadi / Sriperumbudur tk. / 8-1933 / 1537
Koneri / Kanchipuram tk. / *SITI* I, p. 432 / 1595
Kundavur / Tirupati tk. / *SII* XVIII, p. 286 / 1544
Kulaipallur / Cheyyar tk. / 704-1904 / 1544
Kumili / Chingleput dt. / 118-1934 / 1533
Kunrattur / Thanjavur dt. / *SITI* III, p. 1263 / 1511
Kunrattur / Saidapet tk. / 240-1910 / 1524
Kunrur / Tiruttani tk. / 240-1910 / 1535
Kunrusa / Kulittalai tk. / IPS no. 741 / 1527
Kurumbirai / Chingleput tk. / *SITI* I, p. 336 / 1588
Mahendravadi / North Arcot dt. / 341-1954-55 / 1544
Mala / Musiri tk. / 105-1936-37 / 1544
Manappidai / Trichy tk. / 105-1936-37 / 1551
Mandakolathur / Polur tk / Filliozat, p. 121 / 1585
Mangadu / Saidapet tk. / 90-1945-46 / 1500
Mathur / Villupuram tk. / *SII* XVII 207, 212, 214 / 1537
Mavalur / Sriperumbudur tk. / 18-1955 / 1542

Melkunra / North Arcot dt. / *ARE* 708-1904 / 1527
Melmala / Musiri tk. / *SITI* II, p. 748 / 1530
Melsingili / Trichy tk. / *ARE* 93-1938 / 1553
Meyyur / Polur tk. / *TTDES* V, pp. 355-7 / 1551
Mugandur / Chingleput dt. / *SII* XXVI, pp. 171-2 / 1518
Naipalli / Chengam tk. / 34-1934-35 / 1548
Nedungaram / North Arcot dt. / 26-1935 / 1530
Ninraiyur / Chittoor dt. / *SII* XVII 680 / 1514
Niravellur / Sriperumbudur tk / *SITI* I, p. 350 / 1595
Oyma / Tindivanam tk. / 241-1904 / 1532
Palaiyur / Sriperumbudur tk. / *TVMTI* no. 381 / 1509
Panaiyur / Gingee tk. / 240-1904 / 1551
Pangala / Tiruvannamalai tk. / 71-1945-46 / 1526
Pangu / N.I. / *TTDES* I, p. 275 / 1546
Paranthaka / Trichy tk. / *SII* XXIII, p. 379 / 1573
Pathur / Kanchipuram tk. / *ARE* 344-1955 / 1528
Perumur / Chandragiri tk. / 183-1941-42 / 1514
Perundiama / Walajah tk. / *TTDES* V, pp. 51-2 / 1544
Poliyur / North Arcot dt. / *ARE* 624-1904 / 1520
Ponagai / Sulurpet tk. / *NDI* III, pp. 1316-17 / 1513
Puluguru / North Arcot dt. / *TTDES* V, p. 363-6 / 1552
Rajagambira / Polur tk. / *TTDES* V, p. 371 / 1552
Sela / North Arcot dt. / *ARE* 266-1930 / 1573
So / North Arcot dt. / *SII* XVII 680 / 1520
Settakadu / Trichy tk. / *ARE* 93-1938 / 1553
Tachchur / Polur tk. / 149-1941-42 / 1552
Tesapatti / Chengam tk. / *TVMTI* no. 397 / 1534
Thanigai / Tiruttani tk. / 624-1904 / 1506
Tiraimur / Kumbakonam tk. / *ARE* 211-1907 / 1544
Tirukkadavur / Thanjavur dt. / Further I, p. 171 / 1504
Tirukkadigai / North Arcot dt. / 288-1953-54 / 1595
Tirumunaipadi / South Arcot dt. / Jaina no. 417 / 1581
Tiruvelundur / Mayavaram tk. / 493-1907 / 1518
Tuyya / Chittoor dt. / 1-1981-82 / 1527
Udaikadu /Gingee tk. / Jaina No.417 / 1581
Vadalundan / North Arcot dt. / *SII* XVII, 680 / 1520
Valla / South Arcot dt. / 127-1906 / 1532
Vangoppadi / Tirukoyilur tk. / 127-1906 / 1532
Vattiyur / N.I. / 92-1903 / 1547
Vavalur / Kanchipuram tk. / 116-1897 / 1509

Velur / North Arcot dt. / *SITI* I, p. 318 / 1521
Vengal / Saidapet tk. / *SII* XVII, 688 / 1520
Vennaiyur / Chidambaram tk. / *SITI* I, p. 15 / 1530
Vilimalai / Kanchipuram tk. / *EI* XIV, p. 770 / 1528
Virpedu / Cheyyar tk. / 48-1900 / 1540
Viruddachalam / South Arcot dt. / 11A (CP)-1934-35 / 1597

*Abbreviations:* tk = taluk; dt = district; N.I. = not identifiable
C.P. = copper plate; U.T. = Union territory; *JOR* = Journal of Oriental Research; Further = Further Sources of Vijayanagara History; Jaina = Jaina inscriptions in Tamilnadu

## APPENDIX B

# CHRONOLOGICAL LIST OF RULERS (1500-1600)

---

*Regnal year/ Nayakattanam (place) / Nayaka (name) / Rajya / Reference*

---

### 1. RULERS WITH NAYAKA TITLE

1500 / Sriperumbudur / Narasa Nayaka / P.R. / 90-1946
1500 / Vandalur / Dalavay Bommu Nayaka / P.R. / 35-1935
1500 / Poonamallee / Vasal Mallappa Nayaka / P.R. / 90-1945-46
1500 / Marakkanam / Echappa Nayaka / P.R. / 39-1919
1501 / Sembakkam / Uyyala Ammana Nayaka / P.R. / 78-1934
1501 / Kanchipuram / Annama Nayaka / P.R. / 445-1913
1502 / Tiruvur / Kesvaraya Nayaka / P.R. / 339-1939-40
1502 / Tirukkadavur / Rama Nayaka / TJR / *TTDES* III, pp. 1-3
1502 / Cholamandalam / Narasa Nayaka / CMR / 195-1924
1504 / Devikapuram / Tirumalai Nayaka / P.R. / 395-192
1504 / Kugaiyur / Tulukkana Nayaka / TVR / 98-1918
1505 / Palaiyur / Erama Nayaka / P.R. / *ARE* / 1933-34, p. 38
1506 / Uraiyur / N.L. / TRR / 699-1962-63
1507 / Kodangi / Lingamaya Nayaka / P.R. / 54-1934-35
1508 / Tellar / Tirumalai Nayaka / P.R. / *ARE* 1934-35, p. 72
1509 / Nandivaram / Nagama Nayaka / P.R. / 50-1935
1509 / Gangapuram / Kattaiya Nayaka / TVR / 575-1938
1510 / Cheyyar / Ramappa Nayaka / P.R. / 144-1940
1510 / Padainadusimai / N.L. / C.R. / *NDI* I CP 15
1510 / Taiyur / Vira Narasimha Nayaka / P.R. / 390-1912
1510 / Tiruvannamalai / Chinnappa Nayaka / P.R. / *TVMTI* p. 100
1512 / Tindivanam / Tirumalai Nayaka / P.R. / 35-1905
1514 / Kugaiyur / Akki Timmappa Nayaka / TVR / 409-1913
1514 / Tirukoyilur / Chinnappa Nayaka / TVR / 219-1935
1514 / Devamandalasimai / Munnappa Nayaka / TVR / *SITI* I, p. 35
1514 / Villupuram / Aryadeva Nayaka / TVR / 13-1922
1514 / Thanjavur / Chinnappa Nayaka / TJR / 413-1921
1517 / Tiruvadigai / Saluva Nayaka / TVR / *SII* VI, no. 72
1517 / Trichy / Mallappa Nayaka / TJR / 230-1912

1518 / Padaividu / Harihara Nayaka / P.R. / 358-1912
1519 / Devikapuram / Ettappa Nayaka / P.R. / *ARE* 1911-14, p. 122
1519 / Palangurparru / Timmappa Nayaka / TVR / 110-1933-34
1519 / Valavathursimai / Vaiyappa Nayaka / TVR / 30-1933-34
1520 / Bhuvanagiri / Timmappa Nayaka / TVR / 494-1938
1520 / Sembiyamangalam / Timmappa Nayaka / TVR / 494-1938
1521 / Gingee / Krishnappa Nayaka / TVR / 860-1917
1521 / Brahamadesam / Tirumalai Nayaka / P.R. / 352-1912
1521 / Tiruvur / Sadasiva Nayaka / P.R. / 403-1913
1522 / Ulavur / Saluvaraja Nayaka / P.R. / 22-1933
1522 / Gingee / Timmappa Nayaka / TVR / 319-1921
1522 / Ponneri / Perumukkil Nayaka / P.R. / 168-1930
1523 / Poonamallee / Tirumalai Nayaka / P.R. / 341-1939-40
1525 / Poonamallee / Balayya Nayaka / P.R. / 300-1939-40
1527 / Devikapuram / Tirumalai Nayaka / P.R. / 357-1912
1527 / Nedungunram / Namasivayya Nayaka / P.R. / 708-1904
1527 / Tiruvur / Sadasiva Nayaka / P.R. / 332-1939-40
1527 / Tiruvur / Isvara Nayaka / P.R. / 341-1939-40
1527 / Chandragiri / Vaiyappa Nayaka / C.R / 131-1943-44
1529 / Puzhal simai / N.L. / P.R. / 487-1920
1530 / Kanchipuram / Saluva Nayaka / P.R. / 110-1940-41
1530 / Vellore / Bommu Nayaka / P.R. / 127-1906
1530 / Gingee / Vaiyappa Nayaka / P.R. / 860-1917
1530 / Jambai / Venkatadri Nayaka / TVR / 106-1906
1531 / Kanchipuram / Narasimharaya Nayaka / P.R. / *EI* XXIII, p. 200
1531 / Chellathur / Akkalappa Nayaka / P.R. / 127-1944
1532 / Vellore / Bommu Nayaka / P.R. / *SII* I, p. 847
1532 / Thanjavur / Sevappa Nayaka / TJR / V. Vriddhagirisan, p. 237
1532 / Jambai / Bommu Nayaka / TVR / 127-1906
1532 / Padaividu / Kalatissura Nayaka / P.R. / 374-1912
1534 / Virapandyanallur / Kondama Nayaka / TRR / 60-1935-36
1534 / Cheyyar / Ekambara Nayaka / P.R. / 404-1912
1538 / Padaividu / Srirangappa Nayaka / P.R. / 91-1939-40
1542 / Mappedu simai / Srirama Nayaka / P.R. / 61-1947-48
1542 / Tiruvadigai / Chinna Timma Nayaka / TVR / S.K. Aiyenger, p. 205

1545 / Narasingapuram / Linga Nayaka / P.R. / S.K. Aiyenger, p. 210
1547 / Gingee / Vaiyappa Nayaka / TVR / 418-1937-38
1547 / Perunkanchi simai / Vaiyappa Nayaka / TVR / 1-1919
1547 / Pulipurambur / Surappa Nayaka / TVR / 48-1948-49
1548 / Tiruvadigai / Surappa Nayaka / TVR / 482-1919
1548 / Pampundi simai / N.L. / P.R. / 507-1919
1549 / Vellore / Bommu Nayaka / P.R. / *SII* I, p. 84
1552 / Irakutanallur / Surappa Nayaka / TVR / 391-1912
1553 / Pangalanadu / Erama Nayaka / P.R. / 579-1926
1560 / Sembakkam / Virupaksha Nayaka / P.R. / 112-1934
1560 / Thanjavur / Sevappa Nayaka / TJR / 206-1939
1561 / Bhuvanagiri / Timmappa Nayaka / TVR / 538-1962
1563 / Marudur / Krishnappa Nayaka / TVR / 222-1934-35
1564 / Virapandyanallur / Kondama Nayaka / TVR / 60-1935-36
1567 / Sriperumbudur / Chinna Nayaka / P.R. / 186-1922
1567 / Gingee / Krishnappa Nayaka I / TVR / 273-1940
1570 / Sivaram / Narasappa Nayaka / TVR / 338-1939-40
1577 / Devikapuram / Agastayappa Nayaka / P.R. / 399-1913-14
1577 / Thanjavur / Achyutappa Nayaka / TJR / 22-1897
1578 / Perambakkam / Tirumalai Nayaka / P.R. / 111-1932
1578 / Narayanavanam / Krishnappa Nayaka / C.R. / 112-1942-43
1578 / Tiruttani / Bangaru Nayaka / C.R. / 112-1942-43
1579 / Nagalapuram / Krishnama Nayaka / C.R. / 620-1904
1580 / Gingee / Kondama Nayaka / TVR / 280-1931
1582 / Sriperumbudur / Tirumalai Nayaka / P.R. / 194-1922
1582 / Tiruvadigai / Venkatappa Nayaka / TVR / 254-1937
1582 / Trichy / Timmappa Nayaka / TJR / *SITI* I, p. 42
1583 / Vellore / Lingama Nayaka / P.R. / 395-1911
1584 / Bhuvanagiri / Kondama Nayaka / TVR / 266-1916
1589 / Gingee / Krishnappa Nayaka / TVR / 339-1913
1590 / Tiruvur / Narasappa Nayaka / P.R. / 338-1939-40
1593 / Madurantakam / Lingama Nayaka / P.R. / Further, I, p. 321

## 2. RULERS WITH RAJA, RAYA AND OTHER TITLES

1500 / Mannivakkam / Goppayaraja / P.R. / 169-1930
1500 / Pennadam / Timmarajayan / TJR / 269-1928-29
1502 / Tiruvur / Kasavaraja / P.R. / 339-1940

1504 / Srimushnam / Kachchiraya / TJR / 247-1916
1506 / Trichy / Kondamarasaya / TRR / 148-1943-44
1507 / Uraiyur / Ramayachola Maharaja / TJR / 94-1906
1517 / Polur / Bukkaraju / P.R. / 352-1940-41
1518 / Vithalapuram / Kulasekara ayyan / P.R. / 117-193 3
1519 / Karivachi simai / Peddaraju / P.R. / *SII* XVI p. 80
1520 / Iraivasanallur / Ramaiya / TVR / 495-1937-38
1521 / Tirukkadavur / Apatsahayan / TJR / *SII* XII, p. 45
1521 / Vittalapuram / Kulasekharayyan / P.R. / 117-1973
1521 / Anniyur / Allasani Peddana / P.R. / *ARE* 1916, p. 143
1522 / Tandalam / Ramadasar / P.R. / *TTDES* III, p. 308.
1525 / Valangaiman / Vinaitirarpillai / TJR / 622-1962-63
1530 / Thanjavur / Chinnaraja / TJR / MAR 1917, p. 55
1531 / Trichy / Bhogayyadevamaharaja / TRR / 253-1916
1532 / Kalaipakkam / Poruttar pillai / P.R. /1-1935
1532 / Kunimedu / Virabhadhra Mudaliar / P.R. / 241-1904
1532 / Siddhalingamadam / Sarivappayan / TVR / 182-1936-37
1532 / Sriperumbudur / Kalathinatha Mudaliar / P.R. / 90-1947-48
1533 / Kunimedu / Mummidi Reddiyar / P.R. / 246-1925
1535 / Uraiyur / Tipparajar / TJR / 268-1939-40
1536 / Tellar / Tirthara Pillai / P.R. / *SITI* I, p. 4885
1537 / Tirukoyilur / Bhogayadevamaharaja / TVR / 356-1921
1538 / Kalavakkam / Pillaiporuttar / P.R. / 1-1935
1538 / Senalur / Kempadeva annagal / P.R. / 194-1921
1539 / Valudilampattu / Tandava Perumal / TVR / *ARE* 1937-38, p. 106
1544 / Kanchipuram / Vallabharaya / P.R. / 341-1955
1544 / Marudur / Vittaladevamaharaja / TRR / 8-1937
1548/ Maladu / Obaladevamaharaja / TVR / 261-1931
1549 / Tiruvottiyur / Timmayya / P.R. / 122 1939-40
1549 / Chandragiri / Tirumalaraja / C.R. / 131-1943-44
1550 / Nandivaram / Venkatadri ayyan / P.R. / 45-1881
1552 / Kulitalai / Anantalvar Pillai / TJR / *SITI* II, p. 693
1555 / Chandragiri/ Chinna Timma / C.R. / *TTDES* I, p. 26
1556 / Narumpundipettai / Irampattevamaharaja / P.R. / *TVMTI* no. 422
1557 / Magadimandalam / Obaladevamaharaja / TVR / 66-1906
1558 / Tiruvaiyaru / Venkatdri / TJR / 179-1911-12
1567 / Chitrakudi / Arasukarar / TJR / 102-1946-47

1570 / Tiruvannamalai / Venkatarasayyan / P.R. / *TVMTI* no. 429
1571 / N.L. / Chinna Nallanayinar / TVR / 67-1945
1572 / Tiruvennainallur / Tirumalaiayyar / TVR / 273-1939-40
1572 / Tiruvadigai / Maddu Venkatappa / TVR / 254-1937
1573 / Ariyalur / Malavaraya / TVR / 493 -1937-38
1578 / Sriperumbudur / Ramaraja / P.R. / 185-1922
1581 / Arasur / Amnaya / TJR / 259-1916
1586 / Kalakhasti / Ankhabhupala / C.R. / S.K. Aiyengar, p. 308
1588 / Tirukoyilur / Virupparasar / TVR / 265-1934-35
1592 / Uttiramerur / Nagan / P.R. / A. Krishnawami, p. 286
1596 / Vriddhachalam / Kandiyadevar / TVR / R. Sewell, List C.P. no. 75
1597 / Kodikarai / Solaga Salavacha / TVR / Heras, Aravidu, p. 407

*Abbreviations:* P.R. = Padaividu Rajya; C.R. = Chandragiri Rajya; TVR = Tiruvadigai Rajya; TRR =Tiruchirapalli Uchavadi; TJR = Thanjavur Uchavadi; N.L. = name lost; MAR = Mysore Archaeological Reports

## APPENDIX C

## LAND HOLDERS OF CASTE BOUND COMMUNITIES (1500-1600)

*Community / Region / Reference*

Panta Reddis / Takkolam / *ARE* 269 of 1921
Pangala Reddis / Udaiyar Palayam / *SITI* II. p. 640
Reddiyars / Tiruvannamalai / *TVMTI* nos. 375, 376
Reddis / Putalapattu / *ARE* 1 of 1981-82
Kaikolars / Kanchipuram / *ARE* 346 of 1923-24
Kaikolars / South Arcot / *ARE* 285 of 1928-29
Kaikolars / Coromandel / *ARE* 99 of 1936
Chettiyars / Chandragiri / *TTDES* I, p. 248
Chettiyars / Tirupati / *TTDES* IV, no. 281
Chettiyars / Coromandel / *ARE* 31 of 1933-34
Manradis / Tiruvennainallur /*ARE* 194 of 1935
Manradis / Kanchipuram / *ARE* 219 of 1935
Manradis / Coromandel / 386 of 1916
Brahamanas / Nannilam / *EI* XII, pp. 340-8
Brahamanas / Tindivanam / *ARE* 306 of 1910
Brahamanas / Tirupati / *TTDES* III, no. 91
Mudaliars /Kanchipuram / R. Sewell, Anti, p. 201
Mudaliars / Coromandel / R. Sewell List, p. 20
Kammalars / South Arcot / *ARE* 247 of 1916
Panchalattars / Nagalapuram / *ARE* 620 of 1904
Pallis / Coromandel / *TTDES* II, no. 24

## APPENDIX D

## STATISTICAL DETAILS OF TAXES LEVIED ON WEAVERS (1500-1600)

*Weaving Centre / Year / panam per loom per annum / Name of tax / Reference*

Srimushnam / 1504 / 3 / Tarikadamai / *ARE* 247 of 1916
Tiruppanangadu / 1510 / lost / Nulayam / *SII* XXII, p. 190
Tiruchengodu / 1511 / 3 / Tarikadamai / *ARE* 140 of 1915-16
Aragal / 1513 / 3 / Tarikadamai / *ARE* 409 of 1913
Devikapuram / 1532 / 1 1/2 / Pattunulayam / *ARE* 364 of 1912
Vrinchipuram / 1532 / 6 / Tarikadamai / *ARE* 52(a) of 1888
Anniyur / 1560 / 3 / Tarikadamai / *ARE* 622 of 1915
Pillaipalayam / 1561 / 5 1/2 / Tarikadamai / *ARE* 2 of 1913
Kanchipuram / 1562 / 5 1/2 Tarikadamai / *ARE* 88 of 1921
Tiruvannamalai / 1574 / N.A. / Tarikadamai / *ARE* 423 of 1919
Tiruvottiyur / 1600 / lost / Tarikadamai / *ARE* 208 of 1912

## APPENDIX E

## MULTIPLE TYPES OF MARKET LEVIES OF COROMANDEL (1500-1600)

*Marketplace / Year / Name of tax /*

Putalapattu / 1516/ Magamai[1]
Tirukoyilur / 1531 / Kudiraikankikkai[2]
Kunimedu / 1532 / Nattuayam / Udiri tirvai / Tundappidarai[3]
Tirupati / 1533 / Ullayam / Perayam / Anuppu / Mulaivisam / Taragu[4]
Teniyapalli / 1540 /Magamai[5]
Tirupati / 1554 / Teppattu sarakku / Navarasa vargam[6]
Tiruvannamalai /1569/ Tirvai / Ayam / Anuppu /Allu[7]
Chidambaram/ 1581 / Milagu taragu[8]
Tindivanam / 1583/ Magamai[9]
Tiruppundurutti / 1588 /Magamai[10]
Tiruvannamalai / 1590 / Magamai[11]

1. *ARE* 53 of 1907
2. *SII,* XXII, p. 144
3. *ARE* 241 of 1904
4. Sadhu op. cit., pp. 251-52
5. *ARE* 64 of 1907
6. *TTDES* V, p. 407
7. *ARE* 427 of 1929
8. *ARE* 348 of 1913
9. *ARE* 30 of 1905
10. *ARE* 119 of 1931
11. *TVMTI,* No. 438

# APPENDIX F

## COROMANDEL: TERRITORIAL UNITS, 1500-1600

(See Map on page 26)

SIMAI

1. Arakonam
2. Arani
3. Ayilur
4. Bhuvanagiri
5. Chandragiri
6. Chingleput
7. Darasuram
8. Devanur
9. Gangaikonda
10. Gokulagunda
11. Gingee
12. Jagdavacheri
13. Kalaipakkam
14. Kalakhasti
15. Kanchipuram
16. Kalathur
17. Karivachi
18. Kayapakkam
19. Kulitalai
20. Kunrattur
21. Kuppa
22. Madainallur
23. Mappedu
24. Munnuruva
25. Nagari
26. Nallur
27. Nandivaram
28. Nangurvattatu
29. Narayanavanam
30. Padainadu
31. Padaividu
32. Palavettu
33. Paravattur
34. Perumbakkam
35. Perambukula
36. Perumbedu
37. Perummber
38. Perumkanchi
39. Perunagari
40. Polur
41. Poonamalle
42. Puliyur
43. Pulal
44. Saluvanayakana
45. Srikuntamaruhur
46. Sriperumbudur
47. Thanjavur
48. Tindivanam
49. Tiruchirapalli
50. Tirukkadigai
51. Tirukkoyilur
52. Tiruttani
53. Tiruvadigai
54. Tiruvali
55. Tiruvannamalai
56. Tiruvarur
57. Vayalur
58. Villupuram
59. Viranarayana
60. Wandiwash

PARRU

61. Alishukattu
62. Arasurkil
63. Erumbur
64. Olugarai
65. Tellar
66. Tirubhuvanai
67. Uttiramerur
68. Srimushnam
69. Elavanasur

NADU

70. Ambattur
71. Anjur
72. Attur
73. Egmore
74. Idaiyarru
75. Ilathur
76. Innambar
77. Kachchiyar
78. Kalavai
79. Kamalai
80. Kilangu
81. Koneri
82. Kudavur
83. Kulaipallur
84. Mangadu
85. Mathur
86. Melkunra
87. Mugandur
88. Naripalli
89. Nedungunram
90. Ninraiyur
91. Oyma
92. Panaiyur
93. Pangala
94. Perumur
95. Ponagai
96. Rajagambiram
97. Tachchur
98. Tesapatti
99. Tiraimur
100. Tirukkadaiyur
101. Tirumunaippadi
102. Tiruvelundur
103. Tuyya
104. Vangoppadi
105. Velur
106. Vengalnadu
107. Vennaiyur
108. Vriddhachala

KOTTAM

109. Damal
110. Amur
111. Eyir
112. Ikkadu
113. Kalathur
114. Kaliyur
115. Manavir
116. Paduvur
117. Paiyur

## COROMANDEL: CRAFT PRODUCTION CENTRES, 1500-1600

(See Map on page 71)

❑ *Coton Weaving Centres*

1. Cuddalore
2. Tellar
3. Srimushnam
4. Asthamangudi
5. Villiyanoor
6. Tirubhuvanai
7. Anniyur
8. Perunagar
9. Nemali
10. Tiruchanur
11. Valangaiman
12. Tirupullanam
13. Kunrattur
14. Naduvakkarai
15. Tiruvannamalai
16. Manampadi
17. Narayanavanam
18. Yalamari
19. Tindivanam
20. Tiruchengat-tankudi
21. Tillaisthanam
22. Konerirajapuram
23. Tiruvidaimarudur
24. Vrinchipuram
25. Arcot
26. Koyilanur
27. Kilapalayam
28. Kulattur
29. Tiruvakkarai
30. Vriddhachalam
31. Tirukachchur
32. Tirukoyilur
33. Mangadu
34. Pennadam
35. Marakkanam
36. Nerkunram
37. Devanur
38. Puliparakoyil
39. Tiruvottiyur
40. Sriperumbudur
41. Attur
42. Tiruvennainallur
43. Kunimedu
44. Gangaikondachola-puram
45. Tiruvaigaur
46. Brahamadesam
47. Tiruvalanjuli
48. Tiruvenkadu
49. Nenmalai
50. Selinganallur

● *Jewel and Metal work Centres*

1. Tirumala
2. Tiruvannamalai
3. Elavanasur
4. Villiyanoor
5. Tirupati
6. Kalakhasti
7. Chandragiri
8. Tiruvadigai
9. Nagalapuram
10. Tindivanam
11. Ariyalur
12. Padaividu
13. Gingee
14. Villupuram
15. Thanjavur
16. Santhome
17. Pulicat

▲ *Oil Press*

1. Tirumayam
2. Kanchipuram
3. Tirukkalambur
4. Ponnarrur

○ *Salt Pans*

1. Manali
2. Taiyur
3. Marakkanam

■ *Wood Craft Centres*

1. Tiruvaiyaru
2. Tiruvalangadu
3. Tirunavalur
4. Idaiyur
5. Tirupati
6. Tiruvamattur

✱ *Stone Carving Centres*

1. Kalakhasti
2. Nagalapuram
3. Tirumala

⊙ *Textile Dyeing Centres*

1. Devikapuram
2. Manimangalam
3. Kalathur
4. Tirupangadu

\+ *Silk Weaving Centres*

1. Pillaipalayam
2. Pattiswaram

## COROMANDEL: MARKETS AND URBAN CENTRES, 1500-1600

(See Map on page 92)

● *Periodical Markets*

1. Sadurangapattinam
2. Manalur
3. Kugaiyur
4. Chidambaram
5. Putalapattu
6. Tiruppunduriti
7. Teniyapalli
8. Vellore
9. Marakkanam
10. Kalakhasti
11. Nagapattinam
12. Nagore
13. Kunimedu
14. Pattiswaram
15. Villiyanoor
16. Tiruvamattur
17. Vrinchipuram
18. Tiruvadigai

○ *Weekly Markets*

1. Gidangil
2. Gingee
3. Tiruvannamalai

■ *Nagarams*

1. Arani
2. Puttur
3. Kanchipuram
4. Chandragiri
5. Padaividu
6. Uttiramerur
7. Sriperumbudur
8. Tirumylapore
9. Tirichengattankudi

✱ *Jewel Trading Centres*

1. Pulicat
2. Tiruvarur
3. Thanjavur
4. Devikapuram
5. Agaram
6. Tirupati
7. Santhome

▲ *Horse Trading Centres*

1. Tirukoyilur
2. Rishivandiyam

❑ *Urban Centres*

1. Poonamallee
2. Kanchipuram
3. Devikapuram
4. Tiruvannamalai
5. Tindivanam
6. Tirukkoyilur
7. Thanjavur
8. Tiruvadigai
9. Tiruchirapalli
10. Padaividu
11. Bhuvanagiri
12. Gingee
13. Chandragiri
14. Vellore
15. Tiruttani
16. Sriperumbudur
17. Polur
18. Kunimedu
19. Tiruvaiyaru
20. Kalakhasti
21. Uttiramerur
22. Chingleput

## OVERLAND TRADE ROUTES OF COROMANDEL, 1500-1600

(See Map on page 96)

1. Goa
2. Bankapur
3. Vijayanagara
4. Bellary
5. Rayadurga
6. Penugonda
7. Udayagiri
8. Chandragiri
9. Tirupati
10. Sri Kalakhasti
11. Tiruvallur
12. Pulicat
13. Santhome
14. Kanchipuram
15. Vellore
16. Arcot
17. Arani
18. Polur
19. Tiruvannamalai
20. Gingee
21. Tindivanam
22. Marakkanam
23. Kunimedu
24. Villiyanoor
25. Attur
26. Salem
27. Kaveripuram
28. Mysore
29. Beluru
30. Namakkal
31. Srirangam
32. Chidambaram
33. Bhuvanagiri
34. Kumbakonam
35. Tiruvidaimarudur
36. Nagapattinam
37. Tanjore
38. Madurai
39. Rameswaram
40. Tuticorin
41. Punnaikayal
42. Cape Comorin
43. Aryankavu
44. Quilon
45. Cochin
46. Palghat
47. Calicut

# Glossary

| | |
|---|---|
| *alfândega* | Customs house |
| *alvará* | Decree of the Portuguese king or viceroy, valid for a limited period |
| *arrátel* | Portuguese weight equivalent to a pound |
| *arroba* | Portuguese weight of 32 *arrateis,* equivalent to a quarter of a heavy quintal |
| *atikan* | Officer |
| *bahar* | A measure of weight commonly used in South Asia and South-East Asia, which varied according to commodity and region |
| *beatilha* | Derived from Portuguese; linen cloth, sometimes dyed, sometimes stripped or embroidered |
| *brahmadeya* | Grant of incomes to *Brahmans,* usually a village or land granted to *Brahmans* |
| *candy, candil* | A measure of weight, equivalent to 480 *arrateis* |
| *cartaz* | Pass issued by the Portuguese to a merchant ship |
| *casado* | Married Portuguese settler |
| *chetti* | South Indian merchant caste |
| *chintz* | Derived from Malay; a cotton or silk worked in colours |
| *cruzado* | Portuguese coin, usually silver, with a fixed value of 360 reis in Coromandel |
| *devadana* | Usually grant to temples |
| *devanga* | Telugu weaving caste |
| *estado da India* | State of India, the Portuguese empire east of the Cape of Good Hope to the region of Japan |
| *factor* | Originally a commercial agent, the executive head of a factory |

| | |
|---|---|
| *fidalgo* | Petty nobleman or a Portuguese gentleman, literally "son of a somebody" |
| *fusta* | Single-masted oared boat with about forty oarsmen and of about forty tons; same as the foist in English |
| *gantas* | Unit of weight called Khandi. One Khandi was equal to 211.14 kg. at Pulicat and Nagapattinam to measure rice. |
| *kaikolar* | A group of weavers |
| *kalam* | A unit, generally used for measuring rice and paddy in Coromandel |
| *kaniyatchi* | Hereditary right to land or property |
| *kuttagai* | Lease |
| *mahamandalesvara* | Governor of a *mandalam* (large territory) |
| *manradis* | Shepherd community |
| *marakkal* | A unit of measurement |
| *mathapura* | Lands owned by Mutts |
| *mestico* | Of mixed blood, Eurasian |
| *moplah* | Malabar Muslim descended from immigrant Arab merchants and local women |
| *muri* | Plain cloth |
| *nagarattar* | Members of a Nagaram, particularly merchants |
| *nakhoda* | Captain of an Indian vessel |
| *nau* | derived from Portuguese, large ship, Carrack |
| *nayaka* | Chief or leader; in Vijayanagara period it usually meant a chief of a territory |
| *nayakattanam* | Territory assigned by the Vijayanagara king to a nayaka |
| *ola* | Lit.: a palmyra leaf; hence the leaf on which a deed or document is written |
| *ovuidor* | Judge |
| *panam* | A gold coin used in Coromandel. One *panam* was equal to 28.8 to 29.4 *reis* at Pulicat and Nagapattinam. |
| *pardao, pardau* | An Indo-Portuguese coin with 360 *reis* |

| | |
|---|---|
| *pon* | Gold coin equal to ten *panam* |
| *povãcao* | Village |
| *prasadam* | Sacred food offered to the deity |
| *quintal* | Hundredweight (59 kg); 4 *arrobas* |
| *reddis* | Telugu speaking community |
| *regimento* | A sort of *Alvaras;* it denoted an act of law |
| *reis, real* | smallest Portuguese monetary unit |
| *relacão* | High court, the tribunal of justice at second instance |
| *shahbhandar* | Head of a group of foreign merchants at a port, generally a port official |
| *simai* | Territorial unit applicable to any extent of territory |
| *sridhanam* | Dowry |
| *sthanattar* | Temple official |
| *tanga* | Silver coin valued at 60 *reis* |
| *ulavukaniyatchi* | Cultivating land rights |
| *varahan* | Gold coin synonymous with *pagoda* |
| *vedor da Fazenda* | Comptroller of revenue |
| *xerafim* | Standard silver coin of Portuguese India valued at 300 *reis* |

# Select Bibliography

References to archival sources appear in a form designed for ready reference: by name of the archives, series, volume, page and location. This convention is necessary because a given document may appear with different volume and page numbers at more than one place.

## PRIMARY SOURCES:

### I. Manuscript Sources: (Portuguese)

### PORTUGAL

A. ARQUIVO NACIONAL DA TORRE DO TOMBO, Lisboa

*Corpo Cronologico*
Followed by Maço and Document Numbers

*Part I*

6-82; 7-62; 9-92; 13-113; 14-49; 16-106; 22-80; 25-68; 30-36; 37-84; 38-01; 59-58; 68-86; 68-88; 76-102; 77-18; 77-26;107-86; 112-51.

*Part IA*
11-50; 13-74.

*Part II*
41-144; 49-24; 114-21; 117-22; 117-123; 118-38; 118-40; 118-41; 119-103; 120-17.

*Part IIA*
20-35; 30-196; 117-156; 117-170; 117-489; 120-25; 122-129; 124-07; 129-208; 129-749.

*Part III*
07-115; 09-115.

*Carta Orientais:*
no. 59

*Casa Forte:*
MSS. No. 48.

*Chancelarias Reais:*
D. Filipe Liv. 02; 07 and Liv. 24;
D. Sebastião & Henrique, Liv. 22.

*Fragmentos:*
Caixa 3, maço 3, doc. 17.

*Colleção Sao Lourenco:*
vol. *V*

*Colleção Sao Vicente:*
vol. X

*Manuscritos do Convento da Graça:*
CX 3, VI-L; CX 6, II E;

*Manuscritos da Livraria:*
no. 1104

*Nucleo Antigo:*
nos. 801; 808.

B. ARQUIVO HISTORICO ULTRAMARINO, Lisboa

*Caixas da India:*
Caixa 01. doc. 22. Caixa 11. doc. 15.
Codice 281 and 282.

C. BIBLIOTECA DA AJUDA, Lisboa

Codices 51-8-45; 51-8-46; 52-7-63.
MSS Cod. no. 46-XII-30

D. BIBLIOTECA NACIONAL DE LISBOA, Lisboa

*Fundo Geral:*
nos. 90; 207; 272; 465; 475; 581; 1540; 1814; 1816; 1976; 2702; 8570.

E. BIBLIOTECA PUBLICA E ARQUIVO DISTRITAL, Evora

Codice CXV/2-1; C III/2-17
Reservados.752

SPAIN

F. ARCHIVO GENERAL DE SIMANCAS, Valladolid

Secretarias Provinciales Codice, 1479, 1551.

UNITED KINGDOM

G. BRITISH MUSEUM, London

Additional Manuscripts No. 28432.

INDIA

H. HISTORICAL ARCHIVES, Panjim, Goa

Monçoes do Reino: 2B, 3A; 3B; and 4.
Mss Codex no. 3027, pt. I.
Privilegos, Alvares e Regimentos, Liv. 2.

## II. Printed Documents and Contemporary Chronicles (PORTUGUESE)

*As Fazendas Armadas* Portugueses, 1496-1650, Rio di Janeiro, 1937.

Baiao, Antonio, *Historia quninhista in edito do segundo cerco do Dio, Ilustado com a correspondencia original Tambem, in edita de D. João de Castro, D. João de Mascarenhas e outras,* Coimbra, 1925.

Biker, J.F.J., *Colecção de Tratado e Concertos do pazes que o Estado da India Portuguesa fez com os reis e Senhores em que teve relações nas partes da Asia e Africa oriental desde o principio da conquista ate ao fim do seculo XVIII,* vols. 1-14, Lisboa, 1881-87.

Bocarro, Antonio, *Decada 13, da Historia da India,* Lisboa, 2 vols., 1876.

Bragança Pereira, *Arquivo Portugues Oriental,* 11 vols., Bastora, Goa, 1936-40.

Bulhao Pato, Raymundo Antonio de (ed.) *Cartas de Affonso de Albuquerque,* 1-7, Lisboa, 1888-1935.

Coelho Ramos, *Alguns documentos da Torre do tombo a cerca das navegações e Conquistas Portuguesa,* Lisboa, 1892.

Correa, Gaspar, *Lendas da India,* reprint, Porto, 1975, 4 vols.

Cortesao, Armando and Luis de Albuquerque (eds.), *Obras Completas de D. João de Castro,* vol. III, Coimbra, 1976 da Cunha Rivara, J.H. Archivo Portuguez Oriental. 6 Fasciculos in 9 vols, 1857-76.

da Luz, F.P. Mendes, "Livro da Cidiades e fortalazas que o Coroa de Portugal tem nas partes da India, e das capitanias e mais Cargos que nelas ha, e da importancia deles", *Studia,* no. 6, July 1960.

de Albuquerue, Affonso, *Cartas de Affonso de Albuquerque,* 7 Vols., Lisboa, 1884-1935.

de Almeida Calado, Adelino, "Livro que trata das Coisas da India e do Japão" in *Boletim Bibilioteca da Universidade Coimbra,* vol. XXIV, 1960, pp. 1-138.

de Barros, Joao, *Decada da Asia,* I to IV, 8 vols. (1777- 78), Lisboa, 1973.

de Castanheda, Fernão Lopes, *Historia do descobrimento e Conquista da India pelos Portugueses,* 9 books in 2 vols., reprint, Porto, 1975.

de Fernao, Queyroz, *The Temporal and Spiritual Conquests of Ceylon* S.G. Pereira (tr.), Colombo, 1930.

de Lemos, Jorge, *Hystoria dos cercos que os Achens e Laos pu serao a fortaleza de Malaca,* Lisboa, 1982.

de Lima Felner, Rodrigo Jose (ed.) *Subsidios para a Historia da India Portugueza,* Lisboa, 1868.

de Sa' Artur Basilio, *Documentaçã para a historia das missões do padroado portugues do oriente* Insul India, 5 vols., Lisboa, 1954-58.

Diario da Viagem de Vasco da Gama,2 Vols, Porto, 1945.

do Couto, Diogo *Decada da Asia,* IV to XII, Lisboa, 1973-74 (1777-78).

Gonçalves, Sebastião P. *Primeiras parte da Historia dos religiosos da companhia de Jesus,* Atlantida-Coimbra, 1962.

Guerreiro, Fernao, Relação *Anual das Coisas que fizeram os padres da companhia de Jesus nas suas Missões India,* 3 vols., Coimbra, 1930.

Pissurlencar, Panduranga S.S., *Regimentos das Fortalezas da India,* Bastora, Goa, 1951.

Ribeiro, Luciano, *Registo da Casa da India,* 2 vols., Lisboa, 1954-55.

Sanceau, Elaine, *Colecção de Sao Lourenco,* 3 vols., Lisboa, 1973-83 (Documentacao Ultramarina Portuguesa, vols. VI-VIII).

———, *Cartas de D. João de Castro,* Lisboa, 1954.

Schurhammer, Georg. "Uma Relação in Edita de Padre Manuel Barradas, S.I. Sobre S. Francisco Xavier", *Studia,* II Lisboa, 1958, pp. 43-90.

Silva Rego, Antonio, *Documentação para a Historia das Missões do Padroado Portugues do Oriente,* vol. 1-12, Lisboa, 1947-58.

——— (ed.), *As Gavetas da Torre do Tombo,* vols. 1-12, Lisboa, 1960-75.

———, *Documentos remetidos da India ou Livros das Monções* vol. X, Lisboa, 1982.

Trinidade, Frei Paulo da, *Conquista Espiritual do Oriente,* Lisboa, 1964.

Wicki, Jose and J. Gomes, *Documenta Indica,* vols. 1-18, Roma, 1948-88.

———, "Duas relações sobre a situação da India Portuguesa nos annos 1568 e 1569", *Studia,* vol. 8, 1961, pp. 133-220.

## III. Epigraphical Sources

Aiyar, K.R. Srinivasa, *Inscriptions in the Pudukottai State,* Pudukkottai, 1929.

Annual Report on Epigraphy (Including Indian, and South Indian epigraphy from 1881 to 1922, 1923 to 1945) For the years 1887-1981, (Govt. Published 1890 to 1990) (Except for the years 1925-26, 1950-51, 1957-58, 1959-60, 1966-67, 1969-70, 1970-71, 1972-73, 1973-74, 1974-75 and 1975-76).

———, (Unpublished 1981-82, Mysore).

Balasubramanian, S.R., "The Chidambaram inscription of Achyutadevaraya" *Journal of Oriental Research,* vol. XII, pt. II, April-June 1938, pp. 169-78.

Butterworth, Alan and Venugopal Chetty, *A Collection of the Inscriptions on Copper Plates and Stones in the Nellore District.* 3 vols., Madras, 1905.

Deivanayagam, K. *Dharumai Adheena Seppedugal,* Dharamapuram, 1988.

Ekambaranathan, A. and C.K. Sivaparakasam, *Jaina Inscriptions in Tamilnadu,* Madras, 1987.

*Epigraphia Carnatica,* vols III, V and X, Mysore, 1974.

*Epigraphia Indica* (Govt. Pub.) Calcutta/New Delhi, vols., VI (1900); IX (1907); XII(1913); XXII, (1978).

Filliozat, Jean and Vasundhara Filliozat, *A Copper Plate Inscription of Srirangaraya,* Pondicherry, 1986.

Nagaswamy, R., *Chennaimanagar Kalvettugal* (Inscriptions of Madras), Madras, 1972.

———, *Tiruturaippundi Kalvettugal,* Madras, 1978.

Padmavati, A. *Nannilam Kalvettugal,* 3 vols, Madras, 1979-80.

Ragangachari, V., *A Topographical List of the Inscriptions of the Madras Presidency* (collected till 1915) with notes and references, 3 vols., Madras. 1919.

Rao, T.A. Gopinatha, *Copper Plate Inscriptions Belonging to the Sri Sankaracharya of the Kamakoti Peeth,* Madras, 1916.

Rao, Rama M., *Telugu Inscriptions of Andhradesa,* Tirupati, 1969.

Sastry, Sadhu Subrahmanya, *Tirumalai-Tirupati Devathanam Epigraphical Series,* 6 vols., Madras, 1931-38.

South Indian Inscriptions (Publication of the Archaeological Survey of

India), Texts of Vols. I, III, IV, V, VI, VII, VIII, IX, X, XVI, XVII, XXI, XXII, XXIII, XXIV, XXVI, Madras, New Delhi, 1890-1990.

Srinivasan, P.R. and Marie Louise Reiniche. *Tiruvannamalai, A Saiva Sacred Complex of South India,* Inscriptions vol. 1.1 and 1.2, Pondicherry, 1990.

Subramaniam, T.N., *South Indian Temple Inscriptions* (Madras Govt. Oriental Series), Madras, vol. I, (1953); vol. II (1954); vol. III; Pt. I (1955), Pt. II (1957).

## IV. Travelogues

Balbi, Gaspero, "The voyage of Gasparo Balbi", in Samuel Purchas, *His Pilgrims,* vol. X, Glasgow, 1905.

Barbosa, Duarte, *The Book of Duarte Barbosa,* 2 vols., New Delhi, 1989.

de Federici, Caesar, "The travels of Caesar de Federici" in Purchas, *His Pilgrims,* vol. X, Glasgow, 1905.

di Varthema, Ludovico, *The Itinerary of Ludovico di Varthema of Bologna from 1502 to 1508,* London, 1928.

Fitch, Robert, "The voyage of Robert Fitch", in Purchas, *His Pilgrims,* vol. X, Glasgow, 1905.

Lanchaster, James, *The Voyage of Sir James Lanchaster to Bengal and the Coast of Indonesia,* London, 1940.

Nuniz, Fernao, "Chronicle of Fernao Nuniz", in Vasundhara Filliozat (ed.), *Vijayanagar Empire,* New Delhi, 1980.

Paes, Domingos, "Narrartive of Domingos paes", in Vasundhara Filliozat (ed.), *Vijayanagar Empire,* New Delhi, 1980.

Pires, Tome, *The Suma Oriental of Tome Pires and the Book of Rodrigues,* 2 vols., New Delhi, 1990.

Van Linschoten, John, *The Voyages of John Van Linschoten to the East Indies,* 2 vols., London, 1885.

## V. Secondary Works and Recent Studies

Aaleshir, Dinsha, "The Legend of Vellore Talayarkan", *Indian Antiquary,* II (172), p. 154.

Abraham, Meera, *Two Medieval Merchant Guilds of South India,* New Delhi, 1988.

Abyesinghe, Tikiri, *A Study of the Portuguese Regimentos on Srilanka at the Goa Archives,* Colombo, n.d.

Appadurai, Arjun, "Right and Left Castes in South India", *Indian Economic and Social Histroy Review,* Vol.XI. (2-3), 1974. pp. 216-60.

Ayyar, Jagadisa, "Construction of forts", *Quarterly Journal of the Mythic Society,* vol XII, 1921-22, p. 368.

Ayyengar, S. Krishnaswamy, *Sources of Vijayanagar History,* Madras, 1924.

Banga, Indu, *Ports and their Hinterlands in India 1700-1950,* New Delhi, 1992.

Bouchon, Genevieve, *Mamale de Cananor,* Paris, 1975.

Boxer, C.R., *Further Selections from the Tragic History of the Sea, 1554-1565,* Cambridge, 1967.

———, *Fidalgos in the Far East,* The Hague, 1948.

Braudel, Fernand, *The Mediterranean and the Mediterranean World in the Age of Philip II* , Sian Reynolds (tr.), 2nd ed., London, 1981.

———, *Capitalism and Civilization, 15th-18th Century,* Sian Reynolds (tr.), 3 vols., London, 1981-84.

Brown, C.C. (tr.), "Sejarah Melayu, Malay annals", *Journal of the Malayasian Branch of the Royal Asiatic Society,* vol. 25, 1952, pp. 157-59.

Champakalakshmi, R., "Peasant State and Society in Medieval South India, Review Article", *Indian Economic and Social History Review,* XVIII (3-4) July-Dec. 1981, pp. 411-26.

Chaudhuri, K.N., *Asia before Europe: Economy and Civilization of the Indian Ocean from the Rise of Islam to 1750,* Cambridge, 1990.

Chicherov, A.I., *India: Economic Development in the 16th-18th Centuries* (Outline history of crafts and trade), Don Danemanis (tr.), Moscow, 1971.

Chitnis, K.N., *Socio-Economic Aspects of Medieval India,* Poona, 1979.

Correa Affonso, John, *Jesuit Letters and Indian History,* Bombay, 1969.

Dallapicola, Anna Libera, *Vijayanagara City and Empire,* Stuttgart, 1985.

Danvers, Frederick Charles, *The Portuguese in India,* 2 vols., London, 1894.

Datuk-zainal-Adidin-Bin Abdul Wahid, *Glimpses of Malaysian History,* Kuala Lumpur, 1980.

Davey, Ranganatha, "The historical geography of the Cauvery delta with special reference to the Tanjore District", *Journal of Madras Geographical Association,* 12 (2), July 1937.

de Albuquereue, Luis and Inacio Guerreiro, (eds.), *Actas do II Seminario Internacional de Historia Indo-Portuguesa,* Estudos de Historia e Cartografia Antiga Memorias: 25, Lisbon, 1985.

de Matos, Artur Teodoro, *O Estado da India nos Anos de 1581-1588: Estructura Administrativa e Economica Alguns Elementos Para o Seu Estudo,* Ponta Delgada, 1982.

de Silva, Chandra Richard, "Portuguese Policy towards the Muslims in Ceylon", *Journal of Historical and Social Studies,* IX, 1966, p. 114.

———, "The Cartaz system and monopoly trading in the Bay of Bengal: a study of the Portuguese in Asian Trading in the second half of the sixteenth century", *International Conference on Indian Ocean Studies,* II, (G) Collection of Papers, 1984.

Dikshitar, Somasundara, *Tamil Pulavarkal Varalaru, Pathinaram nuttrandu* (History of the Tamil poets of the Sixteenth century), Madras, 1939.

Durby, H.C., "The problem of geographical description", *Transactions of the Institute of British Geographers,* no. 30, 1962, pp. 22-31.

Faria, Manoel Severim da, *Vida de João de Barros,* Lisboa, 1778.

Frank, Andre Gunder, *Capitalism and Underdevelopment in Latin America,* New York, 1969.

Godinho, Vitorino Magalhaes, *Mito e Mercadoria, Utopia e pratica de navegar seculos XIII-XVIII,* Lisboa, 1990.

Gopal, Surendra, *Commerce and Crafts in Gujarat in 16th and 17th Centuries: A Study in the Impact of European Expansion on a Pre-capitalistic Economy,* New Delhi, 1975.

Granda, Peter August, "Gift after purchase in Vijayanagara period", *Journal of the Epigraphical Society of India,* no. 6, 1976, pp. 25-37.

Habib, Irfan M., *The Agrarian System of Mughal India,* 1565-1707, Bombay, 1963.

———, "Potentialities of capitalistic development in the Economy of Mughal India", *Journal of Economic History,* XXIX (1), March 1969, pp. 32-78.

Hall, Kenneth R., *Trade and Statecraft in the Age of the Colas,* New Delhi, 1980.

Heras, Henry, *The Aravidu Dynasty of Vijayanagara,* Madras, 1927.

Jayasree, K., *Agrarian Economy in Andhra under Vijayanagar,* New Delhi, 1991.

Karashima, Noboru, *South Indian History and Society: Studies from the Inscriptions, A.D. 850-1800,* New Delhi, 1984.

———, "Nayaka rule in North and South Arcot Districts in South India during the Sixteenth century", *Acta Asiatica,* vol. XLVIII, 1985, pp. 1-26.

———, *Towards a New Formation: South Indian Society under Vijayanagar rule,* Delhi, 1992.

Karashima, Noboru, and Y. Subbarayulu and P. Shanmugam, *Vijayanagara Rule in Tamil Country as Revealed through a Statistical Study of Revenue Terms in Inscriptions,* Tokyo, 1988.

———, *Studies in the Socio-Cultural Changes in Rural Villages in Tiruchirapalli District*, Tokyo, 1980.

———, "Kammalars of the Sixteenth Century in South Arcot District in South India", in K.V. Ramesh, S.P.Tewari and M.J. Sharma (eds.), *Dr. G.S. Gai Felicitation Volume*, Delhi, 1990.

Krishnaswami, A., *The Tamil Country under Vijayanagara*, Annamalai Nagar, 1964.

Kumar, Dharma, "Private property in Asia: the case of medieval South India", *Comparative Studies in Society and History*, XXVII(2), 1985, pp. 340-66.

Ludden, David, "Ecological zones and the cultural economy of irrigation in southern Tamilnadu", *South Asia*, New Series, I (1), 1978, pp. 1-13.

Mahalingam. T.V., *Administration and Social Life under Vijayanagara*, Madras, 1940.

———, "Inscriptions in Tamil Nadu" in J.P. de Souza, and C.M. Kulkarni (eds.), *Historiography in Indian Languages, Delhi*, 1977, p. 84.

———, *South Indian Polity*, Madras, 1940.

———, *Economic Life in Vijayanagar Empire*, Madras, 1951.

———, *Mackenzie Manuscripts, Summaries of the Historical Manuscripts of the Mackenzie Collection* vol. I (Tamil and Malayalam), Madras, 1972.

Mangalam, S.J., *The Historical Geography and Toponomy of Andhra Pradesh*, New Delhi, 1986.

Marx, Karl, *Capital*, Moscow, 1971.

Mathew, K.S., *Portuguese Trade with India in the Sixteenth Century*, New Delhi, 1983.

———, "Medieval Deccan and the maritime trade of India", *Andhra Pradesh History Congress*, vol. XVI, Karim Nagar, 1992, pp. 39-53.

———, "Socio-Economic History of Medieval India and Portuguese Historians", *Purabhilekh-Puratatva*, 7(1), Jan-June 1989, pp. 1-17.

———, "Trade in the Indian Ocean and the Portuguese System of Cartazes", in Malyn Newitt (ed.), *The First Portuguese Colonial Empire*, Exeter, 1986, pp. 69-84.

Meersman, Achilles, *The Franciscans in Tamilnadu*, Schoneck-Beckenried, 1962.

Mitchell, George, and Vasundhara Filliozat, *Splendour of the Vijayanagar Empire: Hampi*, Bombay, 1981.

Mumford, Lewis, *The City in History, its Origin, its Transformants and its Prospects*, London, 1961.

Murton, Brian J., "Some propositions on the spread of village settlement in interior Tamilnadu before 1750 AD", *Indian Geographical Journal,* XLVIII, 1973, pp. 56-72.

Om Prakash, "Long distance maritime trade in Asia: decline and revival" in K.S. Mathew (ed.), *Studies in Maritime History, Pondicherry,* 1991, pp. 29-37.

Palat, Ravi Arvind, *The Agrarian System of the Jayankonda Cholamandalam,* M. Phil. Dissertation, Jawaharlal Nehru University, New Delhi, 1981.

———, "Popular Revolts and the state in medieval South India: a study of Vijayanagara empire 1360-1565", *Bijdragen Tot de Taal-Land-in Volkenkunde,* Deel 142, 1986, pp. 128-44..

Panchamuki, R.S., "The Coinage of the Vijayanagara dynasties", in *Vijayanagara Sexcentenary Commemoration Volume,* Dharwar, 1936, pp. 101-17.

Parthasarathy, T.S., *Koyil olugu,* Tirupati, 1954.

Pearson, Michael Naylor, *The Portuguese in India,* The New Cambridge History of India, reprint, Hyderabad, 1987.

———, "The people and politics of Portuguese India, during the sixteenth century", in Daniel Alder and Waren Dean (eds.), *Essays Concerning the Socio-Economic History of Brazil and Portuguese India,* Gainesville, 1977.

———, *Merchants and Rulers in Gujarat: The Response to the Portuguese in the Sixteenth Century,* London, 1975.

Perlin, Frank, "Proto-industrialization and pre-colonial South Asia", *Past and Present,* XCVIII, 1983, pp. 30-95.

Pieris, P.E., *The Kingdom of Jafnapatnam,* Colombo, 1944.

Pirenne, Henri, *Medieval Cities, their Origins and the Revival of Trade,* Princeton, 1949.

Polyani, Karl, *Traders and Trade,* New York, 1975.

Pouchepadass, J. (ed.), *Colection Purursartha (13) De la royaute a l'etat dans le mondie Indien,* Paris, 1991.

Ptak, Roderich & Dietmar Rothermund, *Emporia, Commodities and Entreprenueurs in Asian Maritime Trade,* Stuttgart, 1991.

———, "Notes on the word Shanhu and Chinese coral imports from maritime Asia 1250-1600", *Archipel* no. 39, 1990, pp. 64-80.

Raghotham, Venkata, *Temples, Kings, Warriors: Role of Warrior Chieftains in the Political Structure of Late Medieval South India AD 1350-1565,* Ph.D. Dissertation, University of Hawaii, 1987.

Ramaswamy, Vijaya, *Textiles and Weavers in Medieval South India,* Delhi, 1985.

———, "Artisans in Vijayanagara society", *The Indian Economic and Social History Review,* XXIII (4), 1985, pp. 417-43.

———, "Master Weavers in South Indian Textile Production", *Journal of the Economic and Social History of the Orient,* XXVIII, 1985, p. 300.

———, "Weaver folk traditions as a source of history", *Indian Economic and Social History Review,* XIX, (1), p. 55.

Rao, Hari, *History of Srirangam Temple,* Tirupati, 1976.

———, *Koyil Olugu: The Chronicle of the Srirangam Temple with Historical Notes,* Madras, 1961.

Rao, Velacheru Narayana, *et al., Symbols of Substance: Court and State in Nayaka Period Tamilnadu,* Delhi, 1992.

Reid, Anthony, "Sixteenth Century Turkish Influence in Western Indonesia", *Journal of South East Asian History,* 10(3), 1969, pp. 400-1.

Roelofsz, Meilink A.P., *Asian trade and European Influence in the Indonesian Archipelago between 1500-1630,* The Hague, 1969.

Sampath, M.D., *Chittoor through the Ages,* Delhi, 1979.

Sarasvati, A. Rangasvami, "Political maxims of the Emperor Poet Krishnadevraya", *Journal of Indian History,* VI, 1925, pp. 61-88.

Sarkar, H.B., *Trade and Commercial Activities of Southern India in the Malayo-Indonesian World,* (Upto A.D. 1511), vol. I, Calcutta, 1986.

Saletore, B.A., *Social and Political Life in the Vijayanagara Empire,* (A.D. 1346-1646), 2 vols., Madras, 1934.

Sastri, Kuppuswami, *A Short History of the Tanjore Nayak Princes,* Tanjore, 1903.

Sastri, K.A. Nilakanta, *A History of South India from Pre-Historic Times to the Fall of Vijayanagara,* Oxford, 1955.

———, *Sources of South Indian History with Special Reference to South India,* Madras, 1964.

Sastri, K.A. Nilakanta and N. Venkataramayya, *Further Sources of Vijayanagar History,* Madras, 1946.

Schurhammer, George, *St. Francis Xavier: His life, His Times,* vol. I and III, Roma, 1977.

Schutle, Josef Franz, *Valignano's Mission Principles for Japan,* 2 vols., John J. Coyne (tr.), The Institute of Jesuit Sources, St. Louis, Missouri, 1985.

Sewell, Robert, *A Forgotten Empire,* New Delhi, 1962.

———, *List of Inscriptions and Sketch of the Dynasties of Southern India,* Madras, 1884.

Shanmugam, P., "Pattadai and industries in the Tamil country under the Vijayanagara Rule", *Journal of Asian and African Studies,* no. 37, 1989, pp. 31-49.

Singaravelu, S., "The ambassadorial mission of Lakshmana Hang Tuah from the Kingdom of Malacca to the Kingdom of Vijayanagara in South India", *Tamil Studies,* II(1), 1982, pp. 32-3.

Sircar, D.C., *Indian Epigraphy,* Delhi, 1965.

———, *Indian Epigraphical Glossary,* Delhi, 1966.

Srinivasachari, C.S., *A History of Gingee and its Rulers,* Annamalai Nagar, 1943.

Steensgard, Niels, Carracks, *Caravans, and Companies: The Structural Crisis in the European and Asian trade in the Early Seventeenth Century,* Copenhegan, 1973.

———, "The return cargoes of the Carreira da India in the sixteenth century" in T.R de Souza (ed.), *Indo-Portuguese History: Old Issues and New Questions,* New Delhi, 1984, pp. 13-31.

Stein, Burton, *Peasant State and Society in Medieval South India,* Delhi, 1980.

———, "Circulation and the Historical Geography of Tamil Country" in *Journal of Asian Studies,* XXVII(1)1978.

———, *All the Kings Mana: Papers on Medieval South Indian History,* Madras, 1985.

———, *Vijayanagara,* The New Cambridge History of India, vol. 1.2, Cambridge, 1990.

———, *Essays on South India,* Delhi, 1976.

Stephen, S. Jeyaseela, "Pulicat based shipping and trade, A.D. 1500-1530", *Purabhilekh-Puratatva,* vol. IX, Pt. 2, July-December, 1991, pp. 1-11.

———, *Pre-Industrial Coromandel: A Study of Polity, Economy and Society, (A.D. 1500-1600),* Ph.D. Dissertation, Pondicherry University, 1992.

———, "The state, decentralization and revenue farming: some aspects of Vijayanagara rule in the Coromandel region during the sixteenth century", *Journal of the Institute of Asian Studies,* vol. XI, No. 1, September, 1993, pp. 1-15.

———, "Entrepot of Malacca in the trading world of South East Asia and Portuguese netwroks of overseas commerce with the ports of Tamil country in South India, 1511-1598", *Journal of the Institute of Asian Studies,* vol. XII, No. 2, March 1995, pp. 16-28.

———, "Diamond mining industry: Vijayanagara state policy and the regional economy of late medeiveal South India, A.D. 1509-1642, *Quarterly Journal of the Mythic Society,* vol. LXXXVI, No. 2, April-June 1995, pp. 81-112.

———, "External trade from coastal Tamilnadu to Malay peninsula: An examination of Portuguese archival records relating to the export of textiles", *Proceedings of the Tamilnadu History Congress, Madras,* vol. 1, 1995, pp. 141-46.

———, "The role of the Tamil muslim mercantile community of the Marakkayars in the late medieval maritime trade on the Coromandel coast: A study chiefly based on Portuguese sources, 1506-1537, *Islamic Culture,* vol. LXIX, No. 4, October 1995, pp. 59-71.

Subbarayalu, Y., *Political Geography of the Chola Country,* Madras, 1973.

———, "Chavadi: an administrative division of the Vijayanagar Empire", *Proceedings of the South Indian History Congress,* 1987, pp. 84-7.

———, *Vallam Excavations,* Tanjore, 1984.

Subrahmanyam, Sanjay, *Improvising Empire: Portuguese Trade and Settlement in the Bay of Bengal, 1500-1700,* Delhi, 1990.

———, *The Political Economy of Commerce: Southern India 1500-1650,* Cambridge, 1990.

———, *Merchants, Markets and State in the Early Modern India,* Delhi, 1990.

———, "Precious Metal flows and prices in Western and Southern Asia 1500-1750: Some comparative and conjectural aspects", *Studies in History,* 7,1. n.s. 1991, pp. 79-105.

———, *The Portuguese Empire in Asia, 1500-1700: A Political and Economic History,* London, 1993.

Teixeira, Manuel, *The Portuguese Missions in Malacca and Singapore, 1511-1598,* Lisboa, 1967.

Teixeira de Mota, *Um Manuscrito Nautico Seis Cartista Reencontrado Centro do Estudos de Cartografia Antiga,* Lisboa, 1975.

Thomaz, L.F.F.R., *De Malaca a Pegu: Viagens de um Feitor Portugues* (1512-1515), Lisboa, 1966.

———, "Nina Chatu, e o comercio Portugues em Malaca", *Memorias do centro de Estudos de Marinha,* vol. V, 1976, pp. 3-27.

———, *Os Portugueses em Malacca 1511-1580,* Baccalaurate Thesis, Universidade de Lisboa, 1964.

Venkataram, K.S., *The Andhra Case for Madras Re-examined,* Madras, 1949.

Venkataramanayya, N., *Studies in the History of the Third Dynasty of Vijayanagara,* Madras, 1939.

Viraragavacharya, T.K.T., *History of Tirupati,* 2 vols., Tirupati, 1953.

Vriddhagesan, *The Nayaks of Tanjore,* Annamalainagar, 1942.

Whiteway, R.S., *The Rise of Portuguese Power in India,* London, 1899.

Wicki, Jose, "Jesuit Residence of St. John in Santhome Mylapore 1549-1598", in Anand Amaladas (ed.), *Jesuit Presence in Indian History*, Anand, 1988, pp. 54-61.

Wilson, H.H., *Glossary of Judicial and Revenue Terms*, London, 1855.

Winius, George, "The Shadow Empire of Goa in the Bay of Bengal", *Itinerario*, VII(2), 1983, pp. 83-101.

Wink, Andre, *Land and Sovereignty in India: Agrarian Society and Politics under the 18th Century Maratha Svarajaya*, Cambridge, 1986.

———, "Maratha revenue farming", *Modern Asian Studies*, XVII(4), 1983, pp. 591-628.

# Index